AF553972

INDIAN RENAISSANCE IN MODERN INDIA

Encyclopaedic History of India Series

INDIAN RENAISSANCE IN MODERN INDIA

Dr. Mahesh Vikram Singh
Professor, Deptt. of History
Mahatma Gandhi Kashi Vidyapeeth
Varanasi (UP)

Dr. Brij Bhushan Shrivastava
Head of Deptt., Ancient History, Archeology & Culture
SMMTPG College, Ballia (UP)

CENTRUM PRESS
NEW DELHI-110002 (INDIA)

CENTRUM PRESS
H.O.: 4360/4, Ansari Road, Daryaganj,
New Delhi-110002 (India)
Tel: 23278000, 23261597, 23255577, 23286875
B.O.: No. 1015, Ist Main Road, BSK IIIrd Stage,
IIIrd Phase, IIIrd Block, Bangalore-560085 (INDIA)
Tel: 080-41723429
Email: centrumpress@gmail.com
Visit us at: www.centrumpress.com

Indian Renaissance in Modern India

First Edition, 2011
ISBN 978-93-80836-88-1

PRINTED IN INDIA

Printed at Mehra Offset Press, Delhi

प्रो. विपिन चंद्रा
अध्यक्ष
Prof. Bipan Chandra
Chairman

नेशनल बुक ट्रस्ट, इंडिया
नेहरू भवन
5 इंस्टीट्यूशनल एरिया, फेज़-II, वसंत कुंज, नई दिल्ली-110 070
फोन/ Phone: 011-26121880 फैक्स/ Fax: 011-26121883
NATIONAL BOOK TRUST, INDIA
Nehru Bhawan
5 Institutional Area, Phase II, Vasant Kunj, New Delhi-110 070
ई-मेल / E-mail: chairman@nbtindia.org.in
वेबसाइट / Website: www.nbtindia.org.in

FOREWORD

The term 'history' is derived from the Greek word 'historia' that means knowledge acquired through investigation. Obviously, this knowledge can be correct if the method of investigation is objective and not vitiated by any kind of bias. In other words, if the study of human past is comprehensive and obtained through scientific inquiry, it can provide perspective on the present day problems and help one plan for the future.

A true historian has to identify the sources that can be most useful in a given context. Documents, coins, archaeology, anthropology, geography, travel accounts, oral traditions, mythology and so on can be useful but they can be used only after their veracity is tested and they are critically examined. They should be checked and counter-checked.

Over the centuries, one finds the study and writing of history vitiated by biases. There are numerous instances in which historical data have been distorted to support or oppose certain preconceived ideas and purposes. Strictly speaking such history is just like fiction to accord with preconceived notions and serve some ulterior purposes.

The study of the past has never been static. Conclusions go on changing because of the discovery of new materials and tools of investigation. To give a concrete example, the carbon 14 or radiocarbon dating test has revolutionized the study of civilizations and settlements, especially of prehistoric times, for which written documents, coins, etc. are seldom available. This method has enabled historians to determine more accurately than before the time period of a particular civilization or settlement. This method was discovered only 70 years ago by American scientists.

In our country, excavations brought to light the Indus Valley Civilization and its various features, hitherto unknown. Similarly, no complete text of Kautilya's Arthashastra was available before it was discovered by Shamasastry, the chief of the Mysore Government Oriental Library in the first decade of the last century. Likewise, people's knowledge of the history of the Buddhist period got extended after excavations at Sarnath and the ruins of the Asokan period at Patna. In the future, if the Harappan inscriptions are deciphered, our knowledge of the Indus Valley Civilization will increase enormously. All these instances underline the fact that our knowledge of history is never static and its frontiers go on extending.

In the light of what has been said above the encyclopedic history is going to be of great help to students interested in Indian history. It is comprehensive and as far as possible free from biases. It includes the latest materials, and objective conclusions.

Prof . Bipan Chandra
Professor Emeritus, JNU
Chairman, National Book Trust, India

Contents

Preface

The people of India have had a continuous civilization since 2500 B.C., when the inhabitants of the Indus River valley developed an urban culture based on commerce and sustained by agricultural trade. This civilization declined around 1500 B.C., probably due to ecological changes. During the second millennium B.C., pastoral, Aryan-speaking tribes migrated from the northwest into the subcontinent. As they settled in the middle Ganges River valley, they adapted to antecedent cultures.

The political map of ancient and medieval India was made up of myriad kingdoms with fluctuating boundaries. In the 4th and 5th centuries A.D., northern India was unified under the Gupta Dynasty. During this period, known as India's Golden Age, Hindu culture and political administration reached new heights. Islam spread across the Indian subcontinent over a period of 500 years. In the 10th and 11th centuries, Turks and Afghans invaded India and established sultanates in Delhi. In the early 16th century, descendants of Genghis Khan swept across the Khyber Pass and established the Mughal (Mogul) Dynasty, which lasted for 200 years. From the 11th to the 15th centuries, southern India was dominated by Hindu Chola and Vijayanagar Dynasties. During this time, the two systems—the prevailing Hindu and Muslim—mingled, leaving lasting cultural influences on each other.

The first British outpost in South Asia was established in 1619 at Surat on the northwestern coast. Later in the century, the East India Company opened permanent trading stations at Madras, Bombay, and Calcutta, each under the protection of native rulers. The British expanded their influence from these footholds until, by the 1850s, they controlled most of present-day India, Pakistan, and Bangladesh. In 1857, a rebellion in north India led by mutinous Indian soldiers caused the British Parliament to transfer all political power from the East India Company to the Crown. Great Britain began administering most of India directly while controlling the rest through treaties with local rulers.

In the late 1800s, the first steps were taken toward self-government in British India with the appointment of Indian councillors to advise the British viceroy and the establishment of provincial councils with Indian members; the British subsequently widened participation in legislative councils. Beginning in 1920, Indian leader Mohandas K. Gandhi transformed the Indian National Congress political party into a mass movement to campaign against British colonial rule.

—Authors

1

Bengal Renaissance

The Bengal Renaissance refers to a social reform movement during the nineteenth and early twentieth centuries in the region of Bengal during the period of British rule. The Bengal renaissance can be said to have started with Raja Ram Mohan Roy (1775-1833) and ended with Rabindranath Tagore (1861-1941), although there have been many stalwarts thereafter embodying particular aspects of the unique intellectual and creative output. Nineteenth century Bengal was a unique blend of religious and social reformers, scholars, literary giants, journalists, patriotic orators and scientists, all merging to form the image of a renaissance, and marked the transition from the 'medieval' to the 'modern'.

Background

During this period, Bengal witnessed an intellectual awakening that is in some way similar to the Renaissance in Europe during the 16th century, although Europeans of that age were not confronted with the challenge and influence of alien colonialism. This movement questioned existing orthodoxies, particularly with respect to women, marriage, the dowry system, the caste system, and religion. One of the earliest social movements that emerged during this time was the Young Bengal movement, that espoused rationalism and atheism as the common denominators of civil conduct among upper caste educated Hindus.

The parallel socio-religious movement, the Brahmo Samaj, developed during this time period and counted many of the leaders of the Bengal Renaissance among its followers. In the earlier years the Brahmo Samaj, like the rest of society, could not however, conceptualize, in that feudal-colonial era, a free India as it was influenced by the European Enlightenment (and its bearers in India, the British Raj) although it traced its intellectual roots to the Upanishads. Their version of Hinduism, or rather Universal Religion (similar to that of Ramakrishna), although devoid of practices like sati and polygamy that had crept into the social aspects of Hindu life, was ultimately a rigid impersonal monotheistic faith, which actually was quite distinct from the pluralistic and multifaceted nature of the way the Hindu religion was practiced. Future leaders like Keshub Chunder Sen were as much devotees of Christ, as they were of Brahma, Krishna or the Buddha. It has been argued by some scholars that the Brahmo Samaj movement never gained the support of the masses and remained restricted to the elite, although Hindu society has accepted most of the social reform programmes of the Brahmo Samaj. It must also be acknowledged that many of the later Brahmos were also leaders of the freedom movement.

The renaissance period after the Indian Rebellion of 1857 saw a magnificent outburst of Bengali literature. While Ram Mohan Roy and Ishwar Chandra Vidyasagar were the pioneers, others like Bankim Chandra Chatterjee widened it and built upon it. The first significant nationalist detour to the Bengal Renaissance was given by the brilliant writings of Bankim Chandra Chatterjee. Later writers of the period who introduced broad discussion of social problems and more colloquial forms of Bengali into mainstream literature included the great Saratchandra Chatterjee.

The Tagore family, including Rabindranath Tagore, were leaders of this period and had a particular interest in educational reform. Their contribution to the Bengal Renaissance was multifaceted. Indeed, Tagore's 1901 Bengali novella, *Nastanirh* was written as a critique of men who professed to follow the ideals of the Renaissance, but failed to do so within their own families. In many ways Rabindranath Tagore's writings (especially poems and songs) can be seen as imbued with the spirit of the Upanishads. His works repeatedly allude to Upanishadic ideas regarding soul, liberation, transmigration and — perhaps most essentially — about a spirit that imbues all creation not unlike the Upanishadic Brahman. Tagore's English translation of a set of poems titled the Gitanjali won him the Nobel Prize for Literature in 1913. He was the first Asian to win this award. That was the only example at the time but the contribution of the Tagore family is enormous.

Comparison with European Renaissance

The word "renaissance" in European history meant "rebirth" and was used in the context of the revival of the Graeco-Roman learning in the fifteenth and sixteenth centuries after the long winter of the dark medieval period. A serious comparison was started by the dramatis personae of the Bengal renaissance like Keshub Chunder Sen, Bipin Chandra Pal and M. N. Roy. For about a century, Bengal's conscious awareness and the changing modern world was more developed and ahead of the rest of India. The role played by Bengal in the modern awakening of India is thus comparable to the position occupied by Italy in the European renaissance. Very much like the Italian Renaissance, it was not a mass movement; but instead restricted to the upper classes. Though the Bengal Renaissance was the "culmination of the process of emergence of the cultural characteristics of the Bengali people that had started in the age of Hussein Shah, it remained predominantly Hindu and only partially Muslim." There were, nevertheless, examples of Muslim intellectuals such as Saiyed Amir Ali, Mosharraf Hussain, Sake Dean Mahomed, Kazi Nazrul Islam, and Roquia Sakhawat Hussain.

Some scholars in Bangladesh, now hold Bengal Renaissance in a different light. As Professor Muin-ud-Din Ahmad Khan of the department of Islamic History and Culture of Chittagong University, observes:

During nineteenth century A.D., Bengal produced a galaxy of reform movements among the Hindus as well Muslims... the Islamic reform movements such as Faraizi, Tariquah-i-Muhhamadiyah, and Taaiyni and Ahl-i-Hadith, occupied a conspicuous position amongst them. These Islamic movements were revivalist in character... these Islamic movements were born of the circumstances, which had also given birth to the contemporary Hindu reform movements such as Brahmo Samaj and Arya Samaj, which thrived in Bengal side by side with them... Raja Ram Mohan Roy's movement is generally regarded as 'Renaissance movement'. It is called by some as 'Hindu Renaissance' and by others as 'Bengali Renaissance' movement. It should nevertheless be observed that compared with the European 'Renaissance model', it was a Renaissance with a difference, especially, deeply inlaid by a revivalist make-up of pristine Hindu or Aryan religious spirit... Raja Ram Mohan Roy's Renaissance aimed at resuscitating the pristine Aryan spirit, 'Unitarianism of God', with the help of modern Western rationalist spirit."

Science

During the Bengal Renaissance science was also advanced by several Bengali scientists such as Satyendra Nath Bose and Jagadish Chandra Bose. Sir Jagadish Chandra Bose was a polymath: a physicist, biologist, botanist, archaeologist, and writer of science fiction. He pioneered the investigation of radio and microwave optics, made very significant contributions to plant science, and laid the foundations of experimental science in the Indian subcontinent. He is considered one of the fathers of radio science, and is also considered the father of Bengali science fiction. He was the first from the Indian subcontinent to get a US patent, in 1904. Also Satyendra Nath Bose was a physicist, specializing in mathematical physics. He is best known for his work on quantum mechanics in the early 1920s, providing the foundation for Bose-Einstein statistics and the theory of the Bose-Einstein condensate. He is honoured as the namesake of the boson. Although more than one Nobel Prize was awarded for research related to the concepts of the boson, Bose-Einstein statistics and Bose-Einstein condensate—the latest being the 2001 Nobel Prize in Physics, which was given for advancing the theory of Bose-Einstein condensates—Bose himself was never awarded the Nobel Prize.

Bengali Literature

The term Bengali literature refers to literary works written in Bengali language particularly from Bangladesh and the Indian provinces of West Bengal and Tripura. The history of Bengali literature traces back hundreds of years while it is impossible to separate the literary trends of the two Bengals during the pre-independence period. Post independent Bangladesh has given birth to its own distinct set of literature.

History

Early History

The first evidence of Kamrupi literature is known as Charyapada or Chari-Siddha-Pada in dedication on the names of four sons of Brahma, a collection of 8th-12th century CE Buddhist mystic poems from eastern India or ancient Kingdom of Kamarupa now read as Kamrup that provides early examples of Assamese, Oriya and Bengali languages. Poets of these Charyapadas, the Siddhas belonged to the various regions of ancient Kamarupa kingdom or present Assam, Bengal, Orissa and Bihar. Charyapada is also the oldest known written form of Kamrupi. The famous Bengali linguist Harprashad Shastri discovered the palm leaf Charyapada manuscript in the Nepal Royal Court Library in 1907.

In the middle of 19th century, Bengali literature gained momentum. During this period, the Bengali *Pandits* of Fort William College did the tedious work of translating the text books in Bengali to help teach the British some Indian languages including Bengali. This work played a role in the background in the evolution of Bengali prose. In 1814, Raja Ram Mohan Roy arrived in Calcutta and engaged in literary pursuits. Translating from Sanskrit to Bengali, writing essays on religious topics and publishing magazines were some the areas he focused on. He established a cultural group in the name of 'Atmiya Sabha' (Club of Kins) in 1815. Another significant contributor of Bengali literature in its early stage was Ishwar Chandra Bandyopadhyaya.

In 1857, the famous 'Sipahi Bidroha' (Sepoy Mutiny) took place. With the wind of it, 'Nil Bidroho' (Indigo Revolt) scattered all over then Bengal region. This Nil Bidroha lasted for more than a year (In 1859-1860). The literature world was shaken with this revolt. In the light of this revolt, a great drama was published from Dhaka in the name of 'Neel Dorpon' (The Indigo Mirror). Dinabandhu Mitra was the writer of this play.

Michael Madhusudan Dutt

Michael Madhusudan Dutt (Datta), (1824-1873), born Madhusudan Dutt, is a famous 19th century Bengali poet and dramatist. He was born in Sagardari, on the bank of Kopothakho River, a village in Keshobpur Upozila, Jessore District, East Bengal (now in Bangladesh). He was a pioneer of Bengali drama. His famous work *Meghnadh Badh Kabya,* is a tragic epic. It consists of nine cantos and is quite exceptional in Bengali literature both in terms of style and content. He also wrote poems about the sorrows and afflictions of love as spoken by women.

From an early age, Madhusudan desired to be an Englishman in form and manner. Born to a Hindu landed gentry family, he converted to Christianity to the ire of his family and adopted the first name, Michael. However, he was to regret his desire for England and the Occident in later life when he talked ardently of his homeland as is seen in his poems and sonnets from this period.

Madhusudan is widely considered to be one of the greatest poets in Bengali literature and the father of Bangla sonnet. He pioneered what came to be called amitrakshar chhanda (blank verse). Dutt died in Kolkata, India on 29 June 1873.

Early Life

His childhood education started from his neighbour village name Shekpura, There an old mosque, where he went to learn Persian, He was an exceptionally gifted student. Ever since his childhood, young Madhusudan was recognized by his teachers and professors as being a precocious child with a gift of literary expression. He was very imaginative from his boyhood. Early exposure to English education and European literature at home and in Kolkata made him desire to emulate the proverbially stiff upper-lip Englishman in taste, manners and intellect. One of the early impressions were that of his teacher, Capt. D.L.Richardson at Hindu College. In this respect, he was an early Macaulayite without even knowing it. He dreamt of achieving great fame the moment he landed abroad. His adolescence, coupled with the spirit of intellectual enquiry convinced him that he was born on the wrong side of the planet, and that conservative Hindu society in early nineteenth century Bengal (and by extension Indian society) had not yet developed the spirit of rationalistic enquiry and appreciation of greater intellectual sophistry to appreciate his myriad talents. He espoused the view that free thinking and post Enlightenment West would be more receptive to his intellectual acumen and creative genius. In this, perhaps he forgot the colour of his skin, as he was to realize later on in life, much to his consternation and disgust. He composed his early works—poetry and drama—almost entirely in English. Plays like *Sermista, Ratnavali* and translations like *Neel Durpan* and poems like *Captive Ladie* which was written on the mother of his close friend Sri Bhudev Mukhopadhyay, indicate a high level of intellectual sophistication.

In His Own Words

"Where man in all his truest glory lives,
And nature's face is exquisitely sweet;

For those fair climes I heave impatient sigh,
There let me live and there let me die."

Madhusudan embraced Christianity at the church of Fort William in spite of the objections of his parents and relatives on February 9, 1843. Later, he escaped to Madras to escape persecution. He describes the day as:

"Long sunk in superstition's night,
By Sin and Satan driven,
I saw not, cared not for the light
That leads the blind to Heaven.
But now, at length thy grace, O Lord!
Birds all around me shine;
I drink thy sweet, thy precious word,
I kneel before thy shrine!"

On the eve of his departure to England:

"Forget me not, O Mother,
Should I fail to return
To thy hallowed bosom.
Make not the lotus of thy memory
Void of its nectar Madhu."

Later Life

Dutt was particularly inspired by both the life and work of the English Romantic poet Lord Byron. The life of Dutt closely parallels the life of Lord Byron in many respects. Like Byron, Dutt was a spirited bohemian and like Byron, Dutt was a Romantic, albeit being born on the other side of the world, and as a recipient subject of the British imperialist enterprise. However, the lives of the two can be summed up in one word: audacity. These two mighty poets at once remind us of the saying of Georges Danton, the French revolutionist: "L'audace, encore l'audace, toujours l'audace!"

If Lord Byron won over the British literary establishment with *Childe Harold's Pilgrimage*, a comparative analogy may be made for Dutt's heroic epic *Meghnadh Badh Kabya*, although the journey was far from smooth. However, with its publication, the Indian poet distinguished himself as a serious composer of an entirely new genre of heroic poetry, that was Homeric and Dantesque in technique and style, and yet so fundamentally Indian in theme. To cite the poet himself: "I awoke one morning and found myself famous." Nevertheless, it took a few years for this epic to win recognition all over the country.

Linguistic Abilities

Madhusudan was a gifted linguist and polyglot. Besides Indian languages like Bengali, Sanskrit and Tamil, he was well versed in classical languages like Greek and Latin. He also had a fluent understanding of modern European languages like Italian and French and could read and write the last two with perfect grace and ease.

Work with the Sonnet

He dedicated his first sonnet to his friend Rajnarayan Basu, along with a letter which in which he wrote:

"What say you to this, my good friend? In my humble opinion, if cultivated by men of genius, our sonnet in time would rival the Italian."

When Madhusudan later stayed in Versailles, France, the sixth centenary of the Italian poet Dante Alighieri was being celebrated all over Europe. He composed a poem in memory of the immortal poet and translated it into French and Italian and sent it to the court of the king of Italy. Victor Emmanuel II, the then monarch, was enamored of the poem and wrote back to the poet:

"It will be a ring which will connect the Orient with the Occident."

Work in Blank Verse

Sharmistha (spelt as *Sermista* in English) was Madhusudan's first attempt at blank verse in Bengali literature. Sir Ashutosh Mukherjee, while paying a glowing tribute to Madhusudan's blank verse, observed: "As long as the Bengali race and Bengali literature would exist, the sweet lyre of Madhusudan would never cease playing."

He further added: "Ordinarily, reading of poetry causes a soporific effect, but the intoxicating vigour of Madhusudan's poems makes even a sick man sit up on his bed."

In his The Autobiography of an Unknown Indian, Nirad C. Chaudhuri has remarked that during his childhood days in Kishoreganj, a common standard for testing the level of erudition in the Bengali language during family gatherings (like for example, testing the vocabulary stock of a would-be bridegroom as a way of teasing him) was the ability to pronounce and recite the poetry of Dutt, without the trace of an accent.

In France

In his trip to Versailles, France during the 1860s, Madhusudan had to suffer the ignominy of penury and destitution. His friends back home, who had inspired him to cross the ocean in search of recognition, started ignoring him altogether. Perhaps his choice of a lavish lifestyle, coupled with a big ego that was openly hostile to native tradition, was partly to blame for his financial ruin. Except for a very few well-wishers, he had to remain satisfied with many fair-weather friends. It may be argued, not without some obvious irony that during those days, his life oscillated, as it were, between the Scylla of stark poverty and the Charybdis of innumerable loans. He was head over heels in debt. As he was not in a position to clear off his debts, he was very often threatened by imprisonment. Dutt was able to return home only due to the munificent generosity of Ishwar Chandra Vidyasagar. For this, Dutt was to regard Vidyasagar as *Dayar Sagar* (meaning *the ocean of kindness*) for as long as he lived. Madhusudan had cut off all connections with his parents, relatives and at times even with his closest friends, who more often than not were wont to regard him as an iconoclast and an outcast. It was during the course of his sojourn in Europe that Madhusudan then realized his true identity. Perhaps for the first time in his life, he became aware of the colour of his skin and his native language. What he wrote to his friend Gour Bysack from France neatly sums up his eternal dilemma:

> *"If there be any one among us anxious to leave a name behind him, and not pass away into oblivion like a brute, let him devote himself to his mother-tongue. That is his legitimate sphere his proper element."*

Marriage and Relationships

One of the reasons for his decision to leave the religion of his family was his refusal to enter into an arranged marriage that his father had decided for him. He had no respect for that tradition and wanted to break free from the confines of caste-based endogamous marriage. His knowledge of the European tradition convinced him of the superiority of marriages made by mutual consent (or love marriages).

Madhusudan married twice. When he was in Madras, he married *Rebecca Mactavys*. Thru Rebecca, he had four children. Madhusudan wrote to Gour in December 1855:

> *"Yes, dearest Gour, I have a fine English Wife and four children."*

Michael returned from Madras to Calcutta in February 1856, after his father's death. Michael married a French woman named *Henrietta Sophia White*. His second marriage was to last till the end of his life. From his second marriage, he had four children; two sons, one daughter, and a stillborn child.

The tennis player Leander Paes is a direct descendant.

Death

Madhusudan died in Calcutta General Hospital on 27 June 1873 three days after death of Henrietta. Just three days prior to his death, Madhusudan recited a passage from Shakespeare's Macbeth to his dear friend Gour, to express his deepest conviction of life:

> *"...out, out, brief candle!*
>
> *Life's but a walking shadow; a poor player,*
>
> *That struts and frets his hour upon the stage,*
>
> *And then is heard no more; it is a tale Told by an idiot,*
>
> *full of sound and fury, Signifying nothing."*
>
> (Macbeth)

Gour responded with a passage from Longfellow:

> *"Tell me not in mournful numbers,*
>
> *Life is but an empty dream.*
>
> *Life is real! Life is earnest!*
>
> *And the grave is not its goal."*

After Dutt's death, he was not paid a proper tribute for fifteen years. The belated tribute took the form of a shabby makeshift tomb. Madhusudan's life was a mixture of joy and sorrow. Although it could be argued that the loss of self-control was largely responsible for his pitiable fate, his over-flowing poetic originality for joy was to become forever immortalized in his oeuvre.

His epitaph, a verse of his own, reads:

"Stop a while, traveller!
Should Mother Bengal claim thee for her son.
As a child takes repose on his mother's elysian lap,
Even so here in the Long Home,
On the bosom of the earth,
Enjoys the sweet eternal sleep
Poet Madhusudan of the Duttas."

Legacy

In the words of Bankim Chandra Chatterjee, the father of modern Bengali prose, the poet of *Meghnad Badh Kabya* thus:

> *"...to Homer and Milton, as well as to Valmiki, he is largely indebted, and his poem is on the whole the most valuable work in modern Bengali literature."*

In word of Tagore:

> *"The Epic Meghnad-Badh is really a rare treasure in Bengali literature. Through his writings, the richness of Bengali literature has been proclaimed to the wide world."*

Vidyasagar's lofty praise runs:

> *"Meghnad Badh is a supreme poem."*

Rabindranath Tagore would later declare:

> *"It was a momentous day for Bengali literature to proclaim the message of the universal muse and not exclusively its own parochial note. The genius of Bengal secured a place in the wide world overpassing the length and breadth of Bengal. And Bengali poetry reached the highest status."*

In Byron's dramatic poem *Manfred* what the Abbot of St. Maurice spoke of Manfred can equally be applied to the life of Madhusudan:

"This should have been a noble creature: he
Hath all the energy which should have made
A goodly frame of glorious elements,
Had they been wisely mingled, as it is,

It is an awful chaos light and darkness
And mind and dust and passion and pure thoughts
Mixed and contending without end or order,
All dormant or destructive."

In the words of Sri Aurobindo:

"All the stormiest passions of man's soul he [Madhusudan] expressed in gigantic language."

Bankim Chandra Chattopadhyay

Bankim Chandra Chattopadhyay was a Bengali poet, novelist, essayist and journalist, most famous as the author of Vande Mataram or Bande Mataram, that inspired the freedom fighters of India, and was later declared the National Song of India.

Chatterjee is considered as a key figure in literary renaissance of Bengal as well as India. Some of his writings, including novels, essays and commentaries, were a breakaway from traditional verse-oriented Indian writings, and provided an inspiration for authors across India

Chatterjee is considered as a key figure in literary renaissance of Bengal as well as India. Some of his writings, including novels, essays and commentaries, were a breakaway from traditional verse-oriented Indian writings, and provided an inspiration for authors across India.

Early Life and Background

Chattopadhyay was born in the village Kanthalpara in Naihati, in an orthodox Bengali Brahman family, the youngest of three brothers, to Yadav (or Jadab) Chandra Chattopadhyay and Durgadebi. His family was orthodox, and his father, a government official who went on to become the Deputy Collector of Midnapur. One of his brothers, Sanjeeb Chandra Chatterjee, was also a novelist and his known for his famous book "Palamau".

He was educated at the Mohsin College in Hugli-Chinsura and later at the Presidency College, graduating with a degree in Arts in 1857. He was one of the first two graduates of the University of Calcutta. He later obtained a degree in Law as well, in 1869.

He was appointed as Deputy Collector, just like his father, of Jessore, Chatterjee went on to become a Deputy Magistrate, retiring from government service in 1891. His years at work were peppered with incidents that brought him into conflict with the ruling British. However, he was made a Companion, Order of the Indian Empire in 1894.

Literary Career

Chatterjee, following the model of Ishwar Chandra Gupta, began his literary career as a writer of verse. He soon realized, however, that his talents lay in other directions, and turned to fiction. His first attempt was a novel in Bengali submitted for a declared prize. He did not win the prize, and the novelette was never published. His first fiction to appear in print was *Rajmohan's Wife*. It was written in English and was probably a translation of the novelette submitted for the prize. *Durgeshnondini*, his first Bengali romance and the first ever novel in Bengali, was published in 1865.

Kapalkundala (1866) is Chatterjee's first major publication. The heroine of this novel, named after the mendicant woman in Bhavabhuti's *Malatimadhava*, is modelled partly after Kalidasa's Shakuntala and partly after Shakespeare's *Miranda*. However, the partial similarities are only inferential analysis by critics, and Chatterjee's heroine may be completely his original. He had chosen Dariapur in Contai Subdivision as the background of this famous novel. His next romance, *Mrinalini* (1869), marks his first attempt to set his story against a larger historical context. This book marks the shift from Chatterjee's early career, in which he was strictly a writer of romances, to a later period in which he aimed to stimulate the intellect of the Bengali speaking people and bring about a cultural renaissance of Bengali literature. He started publishing a monthly literary magazine *Bangodarshan* in April 1872, the first edition of which was filled almost entirely with his own work. The magazine carried serialized novels, stories, humorous sketches, historical and miscellaneous essays, informative articles, religious discourses, literary criticisms and reviews. *Vishabriksha* (The Poison Tree, 1873) is the first novel of Chatterjee that appeared serially in *Bangodarshan*.

Bangodarshan went out of circulation after 4 years. It was later revived by his brother, Sanjeeb Chandra Chatterjee.

Chatterjee's next major novel was *Chandrasekhar* (1877), which contains two largely unrelated parallel plots. Although the scene is once shifted back to eighteenth century, the novel is not historical. His next novel was *Rajani* (1877), an autobiographical plot, with a blind girl in the title role. Autobiographical plots existed in the techniques of Wilkie Collins' "A Woman in White", and a blind girl in a central role existed in Edward Bulwer-Lytton's Nydia in "The Last Days of Pompeii", though the similarities of *Rajani* with these publications end there. In *Krishnakanter Will* (Krishnakanta's Will, 1878) Chatterjee produced a complex plot. In that complexity, critics saw resemblance of Western novels. The plot is somewhat akin to that of Poison Tree.

The only novel of Chatterjee that can truly be considered historical fiction is *Rajsimha* (1881, rewritten and enlarged 1893). *Anandamath* (The Abbey of Bliss, 1882) is a political novel which depicts a Sannyasi (Brahmin ascetic) army fighting the soldiers of the East India Company. The book calls for the rise of Brahmin/ Hindu nationalism, but does not put forth an alternate to the British Empire. The novel was also the source of the song Vande Mataram (I worship the Mother) which, set to music by Rabindranath Tagore, was taken up by many secular nationalists, and is now the National Song of India. The novel is loosely based on the time of the Sannyasi Rebellion, however in the actual rebellion, Hindus sannyasis and Muslim fakirs both rebelled against the British East India Company. The novel first appeared in serial form in *Bangadarshan*.

Chatterjee's next novel, *Devi Chaudhurani*, was published in 1884. His final novel, *Sitaram* (1886), tells the story of a local Hindu lord, torn between his wife and the woman he desires but unable to attain, makes a series of blunders and takes arrogant, self-destructive decisions. Finally, he must confront his self and motivate the few loyal soldiers that stand between his estate and the Muslim *Nabab*'s army about to take over.

Chatterjee's humorous sketches are his best known works other than his novels. *Kamalakanter Daptar* (From the Desk of Kamalakanta, 1875; enlarged as *Kamalakanta*, 1885) contains half humorous and half serious sketches. Kamalakanta is an opium-addict, similar to De Quincey's Confessions of an English Opium-Eater, but Chatterjee goes much beyond with his deft handling of sarcastic, political messages that Kamalakanta delivers. Some critics, like Pramathnath Bishi, consider Chatterjee as the best novelist in Bangla literature. They believe that few writers in world literature have excelled in both philosophy and art as Bankim has done. They argue that in a colonised nation Bankim could not overlook politics. He was one of the first intellectuals who wrote in a British colony, accepting and rejecting the status at the same time. Bishi also rejects the division of Bankim in 'Bankim the artist' and 'Bankim the moralist'-for Bankim must be read as a whole. The artist in Bankim cannot be understood unless you understand him as a moralist and vice versa.

Personal Life

He was married at a very young of age of eleven, his first wife died in 1859. He later married Rajalakshmi Devi. They had three daughters.

Trivia:

- Ramakrishna Paramahamsa and Chatterjee were very good friends, and both enjoyed humour. Once, the former, playing on the meaning of Bankim (Either *Bright Side of the Moon* or *A Little Bent*), asked him what it was that had bent him. Chatterjee replied that it was the kick from the Englishman's shoe.
- After the *Vishabriksha* (*The Poison Tree*) was published in 1873, The Times of London observed:

"Have you read the Poison Tree

Of Bankim Chandra Chatterjee?"

- When Bipin Chandra Pal decided to start a patriotic journal in August 1906, he named it Bande Mataram, after Chatterjee's song. Lala Lajpat Rai also published a journal of the same name.

Bibliography

Fiction:

- *Durgeshnandini* (March 1865)
- *Kapalkundala* (1866)
- *Mrinalini* (1869)
- *Vishabriksha* (The Poison Tree, 1873)
- *Indira* (1873, revised 1893)
- *Jugalanguriya* (1874)
- *Radharani* (1876, enlarged 1893)

- *Chandrasekhar* (1877)
- *Kamalakanter Daptar* (From the Desk of Kamlakanta, 1875)
- *Rajani*(1877)
- *Krishnakanter Uil* (Krishnakanta's Will, 1878)
- *Rajsimha* (1882)
- *Anandamath* (1882)
- *Devi Chaudhurani* (1884)
- *Kamalakanta* (1885)
- *Sitaram* (March 1887)
- *Muchiram Gurer Jivancharita* (The Life of Muchiram Gur).

Religious Commentaries:

- *Krishna Charitra* (Life of Krishna, 1886)
- *Dharmatattva* (Principles of Religion, 1888)
- *Devatattva* (Principles of Divinity, Published Posthumously)
- *Srimadvagavat Gita*, a Commentary on the Bhagavad Gita (1902-Published Posthumously).

Poetry Collections:

- *Lalita O Manas* (1858).

Essays:

- *Lok Rahasya* (Essays on Society, 1874, enlarged 1888)
- *Bijnan Rahasya* (Essays on Science, 1875)
- *Bichitra Prabandha* (Assorted Essays), Vol 1 (1876) and Vol 2 (1892)
- *Samya* (Equality, 1879).
- This bibliography does not include any of his English works. Indeed his first novel was an English one and he also started writing his religious and philosophical essays in English.

Others

Bangla literature also become rich with its variations. It started to spread its different branches also in poetry Ishwar Chandra Gupta, Biharilal Chakravarty, Kaykobad, in novel Romesh Chunder Dutt, Mir Mosharraf Hossain, in plays Girish Chandra Ghosh, in essays Akshay Kumar Boral, Ramendra Sundar Tribedi and many others contributed to enrich Bangla literature in this time. A lot of literature magazines and newspapers started to come under day light. A number of educational institutes appears all over the region. This helps a lot to nurture the future author and poets of Bangla language.

Rabindranath Tagore

Rabindranath Tagore (7 May 1861 – 7 August 1941), sobriquet Gurudev, was a Bengali polymath. As a poet, novelist, musician, and playwright, he reshaped Bengali literature and music in the late 19th and early 20th centuries. As author of *Gitanjali* and its "profoundly sensitive, fresh and beautiful verse", being the first non-European to win the 1913 Nobel Prize in Literature, Tagore was perhaps the most important literary figure of Bengali literature and a mesmerising representative of the Indian culture whose influence and popularity internationally perhaps could only be compared to that of Gandhi whom Tagore named 'Mahatma' out of his deep admiration for him.

· A Pirali Brahmin from Calcutta, Tagore wrote poems at age eight. At age sixteen, he published his first substantial poetry under the pseudonym *Bhanushingho* ("Sun Lion") and wrote his first short stories and dramas in 1877. Tagore denounced the British Raj and supported independence. His efforts endure in his vast canon and in the institution he founded, Visva-Bharati University.

Tagore modernised Bengali art by spurning rigid classical forms. His novels, stories, songs, dance-dramas, and essays spoke to political and personal topics. *Gitanjali* (*Song Offerings*), *Gora* (*Fair-Faced*), and *Ghare-Baire* (*The Home and the World*) are his best-known works, and his verse, short stories, and novels were acclaimed for their lyricism, colloquialism, naturalism, and contemplation. Tagore was perhaps the only litterateur who penned anthems of two countries: Bangladesh and India: *Amar Shonar Bangla* and *Jana Gana Mana.*

Early Life (1861–1901)

The youngest of thirteen surviving children, Tagore was born in the Jorasanko mansion in Kolkata of parents Debendranath Tagore (1817–1905) and Sarada Devi (1830–1875). Tagore family patriarchs were the Brahmo founding fathers of the Adi Dharm faith. He was largely raised by servants, as his mother had died in his early childhood; his father travelled extensively. Tagore largely declined classroom schooling, preferring to roam the mansion or nearby idylls: Bolpur, Panihati, and others. Upon his *upanayan* initiation at age eleven, Tagore left Kolkata on 14 February 1873 to tour India with his father for several months. They visited his father's Santiniketan estate and stopped in Amritsar before reaching the Himalayan hill station of Dalhousie. There, young "Rabi" read biographies and was home-educated in history, astronomy, modern science, and Sanskrit, and examined the poetry of Kalidasa. He set major works in 1877, one a long poem of the Maithili style pioneered by Vidyapati. Published pseudonymously, experts accepted them as the lost works of Bhnusicha, a newly discovered 17th-century Vaicgava poet. He wrote "Bhikharini" (1877; "The Beggar Woman"—the Bengali language's first short story) and *Sandhya Sangit* (1882)—including the famous poem "Nirjharer Swapnabhanga" ("The Rousing of the Waterfall").

A prospective barrister, Tagore enrolled at a public school in Brighton, East Sussex, England in 1878. He read law at University College London, but left school to explore Shakespeare and more: *Religio Medici, Coriolanus,* and *Antony and Cleopatra;* he returned degreeless to Bengal in 1880. On 9 December 1883 he married Mrinalini Devi (born Bhabatarini, 1873–1900); they had five children, two of whom died before reaching adulthood. In 1890, Tagore began managing his family's vast estates in Shilaidaha, a region now in Bangladesh; he was joined by his wife and children in 1898. In 1890, Tagore released his *Manast* poems, among his best-known work. As "Zamindar Babu", Tagore crisscrossed the holdings while living out of the family's luxurious barge, the *Padma,* to collect (mostly token) rents and bless villagers, who held feasts in his honour. These years—1891–1895: Tagore's *Sadhana* period, after one of Tagore's magazines—were his most fecund. During this period, more than half the stories of the three-volume and eighty-four-story *Galpaguchchha* were written. With irony and gravity, they depicted a wide range of Bengali lifestyles, particularly village life.

Santiniketan (1901–1932)

In 1901, Tagore left Shilaidaha and moved to Santiniketan to found an *ashram* which grew to include a marble-floored prayer hall ("The *Mandir*"), an experimental school, groves of trees, gardens, and a library. There, Tagore's wife and two of his children died. His father died on 19 January 1905, and he received monthly payments as part of his inheritance. He received additional income from the Maharaja of Tripura, sales of his family's jewellery, his seaside bungalow in Puri, and mediocre royalties (Rs. 2,000) from his works. By now, his work was gaining him a large following among Bengali and foreign readers alike, and he published such works as *Naivedya* (1901) and *Kheya* (1906) while translating his poems into free verse. On 14 November 1913, Tagore learned that he had won the 1913 Nobel Prize in Literature, becoming the first Asian Nobel laureate. The Swedish Academy appreciated the idealistic and—for Western readers—accessible nature of a small body of his translated material, including the 1912 *Gitanjali: Song Offerings*. In 1915, Tagore was knighted by the British Crown.

In 1921, Tagore and agricultural economist Leonard Elmhirst set up the Institute for Rural Reconstruction, later renamed Shriniketan—"Abode of Peace"—in Surul, a village near the ashram at Santiniketan. Through it, Tagore bypassed Gandhi's symbolic *Swaraj* protests, which he despised. He sought aid from donors, officials, and scholars worldwide to "free village[s] from the shackles of helplessness and ignorance" by "vitalis[ing] knowledge". In the early 1930s, he targeted India's "abnormal caste consciousness" and untouchability. Lecturing against these, he penned untouchable heroes for his poems and dramas and campaigned—successfully—to open Guruvayoor Temple to Dalits.

Twilight Years (1932–1941)

To the end, Tagore scrutinized orthodoxy. He upbraided Gandhi for declaring that a massive 15 January 1934 earthquake in Bihar—leaving thousands dead—was divine retribution brought on by the oppression of Dalits. He mourned the endemic poverty of Calcutta and the accelerating socioeconomic decline of Bengal, which he detailed in an unrhymed hundred-line poem whose technique of searing double-vision would foreshadow Satyajit Ray's film *Apur Sansar*. Fifteen new volumes of Tagore writings appeared, among them the prose-poems works *Punashcha* (1932), *Shes Saptak* (1935), and *Patraput* (1936). Experimentation continued: he developed prose-songs and dance-dramas, including *Chitrangada* (1914), *Shyama* (1939), and *Chandalika* (1938), and wrote the novels

Dui Bon (1933), *Malancha* (1934), and *Char Adhyay* (1934). Tagore took an interest in science in his last years, writing *Visva-Parichay* (a collection of essays) in 1937. His exploration of biology, physics, and astronomy impacted his poetry, which often contained extensive naturalism that underscored his respect for scientific laws. He also wove the process of science, including narratives of scientists, into many stories contained in such volumes as *Se* (1937), *Tin Sangi* (1940), and *Galpasalpa* (1941).

Tagore's last four years were marked by chronic pain and two long periods of illness. These began when Tagore lost consciousness in late 1937; he remained comatose and near death for an extended period. This was followed three years later in late 1940 by a similar spell, from which he never recovered. The poetry Tagore wrote in these years is among his finest, and is distinctive for its preoccupation with death. After extended suffering, Tagore died on 7 August 1941 (22 Shravan 1348) in an upstairs room of the Jorasanko mansion in which he was raised; his death anniversary is mourned across the Bengali-speaking world.

Travels

Between 1878 and 1932, Tagore visited more than thirty countries on five continents; many of these trips were crucial in familiarising non-Indian audiences to his works and spreading his political ideas. In 1912, he took a sheaf of his translated works to England, where they impressed missionary and Gandhi protege Charles F. Andrews, Anglo-Irish poet William Butler Yeats, Ezra Pound, Robert Bridges, Ernest Rhys, Thomas Sturge Moore, and others. Indeed, Yeats wrote the preface to the English translation of Gitanjali, while Andrews joined Tagore at Santiniketan. On 10 November 1912, Tagore began touring the United States and the United Kingdom, staying in Butterton, Staffordshire with Andrews' clergymen friends. From 3 May 1916 until April 1917, Tagore went on lecturing circuits in Japan and the United States and denounced nationalism. His essay "Nationalism in India" was scorned and praised, this latter by pacifists, including Romain Rolland.

Shortly after returning to India, the 63-year-old Tagore accepted the Peruvian government's invitation to visit. He then travelled to Mexico. Each government pledged US$100,000 to the school at Shantiniketan (Visva-Bharati) in commemoration of his visits. A week after his 6 November 1924 arrival in Buenos Aires, Argentina, an ill Tagore moved into the Villa Miralrío at the behest of Victoria Ocampo. He left for India in January 1925. On 30 May 1926, Tagore reached Naples, Italy; he met Benito Mussolini in Rome the next day. A warm rapport ended when Tagore criticised Mussolini on 20 July 1926.

On 14 July 1927, Tagore and two companions began a four-month tour of Southeast Asia, visiting Bali, Java, Kuala Lumpur, Malacca, Penang, Siam, and Singapore. Tagore's travelogues from the tour were collected into the work "Jatri". In early 1930 he left Bengal for a nearly year-long tour of Europe and the United States. Once he returned to the UK, while his paintings were being exhibited in Paris and London, he stayed at a Friends settlement in Birmingham. There he wrote his Oxford Hibbert Lectures and spoke at London's annual Quaker gathering. There (addressing relations between the British and Indians, a topic he would grapple with over the next two years), Tagore spoke of a "dark chasm of aloofness". He visited Aga Khan III, stayed at Dartington Hall, and toured Denmark, Switzerland, and Germany from June to mid-September 1930, then the Soviet Union. Lastly, in April 1932, Tagore—who was acquainted with the legends and works of the Persian mystic Hafez—was hosted by Reza Shah Pahlavi of Iran. Such extensive travels allowed Tagore to interact with many notable contemporaries, including Henri Bergson, Albert Einstein, Robert Frost, Thomas Mann, George Bernard Shaw, H.G. Wells and Romain Rolland. Tagore's last travels abroad, including visits to Persia and Iraq (in 1932) and Ceylon in 1933, only sharpened his opinions regarding human divisions and nationalism.

Works

Though known mostly for his poetry, Tagore also wrote novels, essays, short stories, travelogues, dramas, and thousands of songs. Of Tagore's prose, his short stories are perhaps most highly regarded; indeed, he is credited with originating the Bengali-language version of the genre. His works are frequently noted for their rhythmic, optimistic, and lyrical nature. Such stories mostly borrow from deceptively simple subject matter: common people.

Novels and Non-fiction

Tagore wrote eight novels and four novellas, among them *Chaturanga*, *Shesher Kobita*, *Char Odhay*, and *Noukadubi*. *Ghare Baire* (*The Home and the World*)—through the lens of the idealistic *zamindar* protagonist Nikhil—excoriates rising Indian nationalism, terrorism, and religious zeal in the *Swadeshi* movement; a frank expression of Tagore's conflicted sentiments, it emerged out of a 1914 bout of depression. The novel ends in Hindu-Muslim violence and Nikhil's (likely mortal) wounding. *Gora* raises controversial questions regarding the Indian identity. As with *Ghore Baire*, matters of self-identity (*jti*), personal freedom, and religion are developed in the context of a family story and love triangle.

In *Jogajog* (*Relationships*), the heroine Kumudini—bound by the ideals of *Shiva-Sati*, exemplified by Dkshyani—is torn between her pity for the sinking fortunes of her progressive and compassionate elder brother and his foil: her exploitative, rakish, and patriarchical husband. In it, Tagore demonstrates his feminist leanings, using *pathos* to depict the plight and ultimate demise of Bengali women trapped by pregnancy, duty, and family honour; simultaneously, he treats the decline of Bengal's landed oligarchy.

Others were uplifting: *Shesher Kobita* (translated twice as *Last Poem* and *Farewell Song*) is his most lyrical novel, with poems and rhythmic passages written by the main character, a poet. It also contains elements of satire and postmodernism; stock characters gleefully attack the reputation of an old, outmoded, oppressively renowned poet who, incidentally, goes by the name of Rabindranath Tagore. Though his novels remain among the least-appreciated of his works, they have been given renewed attention via film adaptations by Satyajit Ray and others: *Chokher Bali* and *Ghare Baire* are exemplary. Their soundtracks often feature Rabindranath Tagore wrote many non-fiction books, writing on topics ranging from Indian history to linguistics. Aside from autobiographical works, his travelogues, essays, and lectures were compiled into several volumes, including *Europe Jatrir Patro* (*Letters from Europe*) and *Manusher Dhormo* (*The Religion of Man*).

Music and Art

Tagore composed roughly 2,230 songs and was a prolific painter. His songs comprise *rabindrasangit*, an integral part of Bengali culture. Tagore's music is inseparable from his literature, most of which—poems or parts of novels, stories, or plays alike—became lyrics for his songs. Influenced by the *thumri* style of Hindustani music, they ran the entire gamut of human emotion, ranging from his early dirge-like Brahmo devotional hymns to quasi-erotic compositions. They emulated the tonal colour of classical *ragas* to varying extents. Though at times his songs mimicked a given raga's melody and rhythm faithfully, he also blended elements of different ragas to create innovative works.

For Bengalis, their appeal, stemming from the combination of emotive strength and beauty described as surpassing even Tagore's poetry, was such that the *Modern Review* observed that "[t]here is in Bengal no cultured home where Rabindranath's songs are not sung or at least attempted to be sung... Even illiterate villagers sing his songs". Arthur Strangways of *The Observer* introduced non-Bengalis to *rabindrasangeet* in *The Music of Hindostan,* calling it a "vehicle of a personality... [that] go behind this or that system of music to that beauty of sound which all systems put out their hands to seize." Among them are Bangladesh's national anthem *Amar Shonar Bangla* and India's national anthem *Jana Gana Mana,* making Tagore unique in having scored two national anthems. He influenced the styles of such musicians as *sitar* maestro Vilayat Khan, and the *sarodiyas* Buddhadev Dasgupta and Amjad Ali Khan.

At age sixty, Tagore took up drawing and painting; successful exhibitions of his many works—which made a debut appearance in Paris upon encouragement by artists he met in the south of France —were held throughout Europe. Tagore—who likely exhibited protanopia ("colour blindness"), or partial lack of (red-green, in Tagore's case) colour discernment—painted in a style characterised by peculiarities in aesthetics and colouring schemes. Tagore emulated numerous styles, including craftwork from northern New Ireland, Haida carvings from the west coast of Canada (British Columbia), and woodcuts by Max Pechstein. Tagore also had an artist's eye for his own handwriting, embellishing the scribbles, cross-outs, and word layouts in his manuscripts with simple artistic leitmotifs, including simple rhythmic designs.

Theatre

At age sixteen, Tagore led his brother Jyotirindranath's adaptation of Molière's *Le Bourgeois Gentilhomme*. At age twenty, he wrote his first drama-opera—*Valmiki Pratibha* (*The Genius of Valmiki*)—which describes how the bandit Valmiki reforms his ethos, is blessed by Saraswati, and composes the *Ramayana*. Through it, Tagore vigorously explores a wide range of dramatic styles and emotions, including usage of revamped *kirtans* and adaptation of traditional English and Irish folk melodies as drinking songs. Another notable play, *Dak Ghar* (*The Post Office*), describes how a child—striving to escape his stuffy confines—ultimately "fall[s] asleep" (which suggests his physical death). A story with worldwide appeal (it received rave reviews in Europe), *Dak Ghar* dealt with death as, in Tagore's words, "spiritual freedom" from "the world of hoarded wealth and certified creeds". During World War II, Polish doctor and educator Janusz Korczak selected "The Post Office" as the play the orphans in his care in the Warsaw Ghetto would perform.

This occurred on 18 July 1942, less than three weeks before they were to be deported to the Treblinka extermination camp. According to his main English-language biographer, Betty Jean Lifton, in her book *The King of Children*, Dr. Korszak thought a great deal about whether one should be able to determine when and how to die. He may have been trying to find a way for the children in his orphanage to accept death.

His other works—emphasizing fusion of lyrical flow and emotional rhythm tightly focused on a core idea—were unlike previous Bengali dramas. His works sought to articulate, in Tagore's words, "the play of feeling and not of action". In 1890 he wrote *Visarjan* (*Sacrifice*), regarded as his finest drama. The Bengali-language originals included intricate subplots and extended monologues. Later, his dramas probed more philosophical and allegorical themes; these included *Dak Ghar*. Another is Tagore's *Chandalika* (*Untouchable Girl*), which was modeled on an ancient Buddhist legend describing how Ananda—the Gautama Buddha's disciple—asks water of an *Adivasi* ("untouchable") girl. Lastly, among his most famous dramas is *Raktakaravi* (*Red Oleanders*), which tells of a kleptocratic king who enriches himself by forcing his subjects to mine. The heroine, Nandini, eventually rallies the common people to destroy these symbols of subjugation. Tagore's other plays include *Chitrangada*, *Raja*, and *Mayar Khela*. Dance dramas based on Tagore's plays are commonly referred to as *rabindra nritya natyas*.

Stories

The "Sadhana" period, 1891–1895, was among Tagore's most fecund, yielding more than half the stories contained in the three-volume *Galpaguchchha*, itself a group of eighty-four stories. They reflect upon Tagore's surroundings, on modern and fashionable ideas, and on mind puzzles. Tagore associated his earliest stories, such as those of the "*Sadhana*" period, with an exuberance of vitality and spontaneity; these traits were cultivated by zamindar Tagore's life in villages such as Patisar, Shajadpur, and Shilaida. Seeing the common and the poor, he examined their lives with a depth and feeling singular in Indian literature up to that point.

In "The Fruitseller from Kabul", Tagore speaks in first person as a town-dweller and novelist who chances upon the Afghani seller. He channels the longing of those trapped in mundane, hardscrabble Indian urban life, giving play to dreams of a different existence in the distant and wild mountains: "There were autumn mornings, the time of year when kings of old went forth to conquest; and I, never stirring from my little corner in Calcutta, would let my mind wander over the whole world. At the very name of another country, my heart would go out to it... I would fall to weaving a network of dreams: the mountains, the glens, the forest.... ". Many of the other *Galpaguchchha* stories were written in Tagore's *Sabuj Patra* period (1914–1917; also named for one of Tagore's magazines).

Tagore's *Golpoguchchho* (*Bunch of Stories*) remains among Bengali literature's most popular fictional works, providing subject matter for many successful films and theatrical plays. Satyajit Ray's film *Charulata* was based upon Tagore's controversial novella, *Nastanirh* (*The Broken Nest*). In *Atithi* (also made into a film), the young Brahmin boy Tarapada shares a boat ride with a village *zamindar*. The boy reveals that he has run away from home, only to wander around ever since. Taking pity, the zamindar adopts him and ultimately arranges his marriage to the *zamindar's* own daughter. However, the night before the wedding, Tarapada runs off—again. *Strir Patra* (*The Letter from the Wife*) is among Bengali literature's earliest depictions of the bold emancipation of women. The heroine Mrinal, the wife of a typical patriarchical Bengali middle class man, writes a letter while she is travelling (which constitutes the whole story). It details the pettiness of her life and struggles; she finally declares that she will not return to her husband's home with the statement *Amio bachbo. Ei bachlum*: "And I shall live. Here, I live".

Haimanti assails Hindu marriage and the dismal lifelessness of married Bengali women, hypocrisies plaguing the Indian middle classes, and how Haimanti, a sensitive young woman, must—due to her sensitiveness and free spirit—sacrifice her life. In the last passage, Tagore directly attacks the Hindu custom of glorifying Sita's attempted self-immolation as a means of appeasing her husband Rama's doubts. *Musalmani Didi* examines Hindu-Muslim tensions and, in many ways, embodies the essence of Tagore's humanism.

Darpaharan exhibits Tagore's self-consciousness, describing a fey young man harboring literary ambitions. Though he loves his wife, he wishes to stifle her own literary career, deeming it unfeminine. Tagore himself, in his youth, seems to have harbored similar ideas about women. *Darpaharan* depicts the final humbling of the man as he acknowledges his wife's talents. As do many other Tagore stories, *Jibito o Mrito* equips Bengalis with a ubiquitous epigram: *Kadombini moriya proman korilo she more nai*—"Kadombini died, thereby proving that she hadn't".

Poetry

Tagore's poetry—which varied in style from classical formalism to the comic, visionary, and ecstatic—proceeds from a lineage established by 15th-and 16th-century Vaishnava poets. Tagore was awed by the mysticism of the *rishi*-authors who—including Vyasa—wrote the Upanishads, the Bhakti-Sufi mystic Kabir, and Ramprasad Sen. Yet Tagore's poetry became most innovative and mature after his exposure to rural Bengal's folk music, which included Baul ballads—especially those of bard Lalon. These—rediscovered and popularised by Tagore—resemble 19th-century Kartbhaj hymns that emphasize inward divinity and rebellion against religious and social orthodoxy. During his Shilaidaha years, his poems took on a lyrical quality, speaking via the *maner manus* (the Bauls' "man within the heart") or meditating upon the *jivan devata* ("living God within"). This figure thus sought connection with divinity through appeal to nature and the emotional interplay of human drama. Tagore used such techniques in his Bhnusicha poems (which chronicle the romance between Radha and Krishna), which he repeatedly revised over the course of seventy years.

Tagore responded to the mostly crude emergence of modernism and realism in Bengali literature by writing experimental works in the 1930s. Examples works include *Africa* and *Camalia*, which are among the better known of his latter poems. He occasionally wrote poems using *Shadhu Bhasha* (a Sanskritised dialect of Bengali); later, he began using *Cholti Bhasha* (a more popular dialect). Other notable works include *Manasi, Sonar Tori* (*Golden Boat*), *Balaka* (*Wild Geese*—the title being a metaphor for migrating souls), and *Purobi. Sonar Tori*'s most famous poem—dealing with the ephemeral nature of life and achievement—goes by the same name; hauntingly it ends: (*"Shunno nodir tire rohinu poºi/Jaha chhilo loe gêlo shonar tori"*—"all I had achieved was carried off on the golden boat—only I was left behind."). Internationally, *Gitanjali* is Tagore's best-known collection, winning him his Nobel Prize.

Tagore's poetry has been set to music by various composers, among them classical composer Arthur Shepherd's triptych for soprano and string quartet, as well as composer Garry Schyman's "Praan", an adaptation of Tagore's poem "Stream of Life" from Gitanjali. The latter was composed and recorded with vocals by Palbasha Siddique to accompany Internet celebrity Matt Harding's 2008 viral video.. In 1917 his words were translated adeptly and set to music by Richard Hageman (an Anglo-Dutch composer) to produce what is regarded as one of the finest art songs in the English language: Do not go my love (Ed.Schirmer NY 1917).

Political Views

Tagore's political thought was complex. He opposed imperialism and supported Indian nationalists. His views have their first poetic release in *Manast*, mostly composed in his twenties. Evidence produced during the Hindu-German Conspiracy trial and later accounts affirm his awareness of the Ghadarite conspiracy, and stated that he sought the support of Japanese Prime Minister Terauchi Masatake and former Premier Ôkuma Shigenobu. Yet he lampooned the Swadeshi movement, denouncing it in "The Cult of the Charka", an acrid 1925 essay. He emphasized self-help and intellectual uplift of the masses as an alternative, stating that British imperialism was a "political symptom of our social disease", urging Indians to accept that "there can be no question of blind revolution, but of steady and purposeful education".

Such views enraged many. He narrowly escaped assassination by Indian expatriates during his stay in a San Francisco hotel in late 1916. The plot failed only because the would-be assassins fell into argument. Yet Tagore wrote songs lionizing the Indian independence movement and renounced his knighthood in protest against the 1919 Jallianwala Bagh Massacre. Two of Tagore's more politically charged compositions, "Chitto Jetha Bhayshunyo" ("Where the Mind is Without Fear") and "Ekla Chalo Re" ("If They Answer Not to Thy Call, Walk Alone"), gained mass appeal, with the latter favoured by Gandhi. Despite his tumultuous relations with Gandhi, Tagore was key in resolving a Gandhi-Ambedkar dispute involving separate electorates for untouchables, ending Gandhi's fast "unto death".

Tagore lampooned rote schooling: in "The Parrot's Training", a bird is caged and force-fed pages torn from books until it dies. These views led Tagore, while visiting Santa Barbara on 11 October 1917, to conceive of a new type of university, desiring to "make Santiniketan the connecting thread between India and the world [and] a world centre for the study of humanity somewhere beyond the limits of nation and geography." The school, which he named Visva-Bharati had its foundation stone laid on 22 December 1918; it was later inaugurated on 22 December 1921. Here, Tagore implemented a *brahmacharya* pedagogical structure employing *gurus* to provide individualised guidance for pupils. Tagore worked hard to fundraise for and staff the school, even contributing all of his Nobel Prize monies. Tagore's duties as steward and mentor at Santiniketan kept him busy; he taught classes in mornings and wrote the students' textbooks in afternoons and evenings. Tagore also fundraised extensively for the school in Europe and the U.S. between 1919 and 1921.

Impact

Tagore's relevance can be gauged by festivals honouring him: *Kabipranam*, Tagore's birth anniversary; the annual Tagore Festival held in Urbana, Illinois, in the United States; *Rabindra Path Parikrama* walking pilgrimages from Calcutta to Shantiniketan; ceremonial recitals of Tagore's poetry held on important anniversaries; and others. This legacy is most palpable in Bengali culture, ranging from language and arts to history and politics. Nobel laureate Amartya Sen saw Tagore as a "towering figure", being a "deeply relevant and many-sided contemporary thinker". Tagore's Bengali-language writings—the 1939 *Rab+ndra Rachanval+*—is also canonised as one of Bengal's greatest cultural treasures. Tagore himself was proclaimed "the greatest poet India has produced".

Tagore was famed throughout much of Europe, North America,

and East Asia. He co-founded Dartington Hall School, a progressive coeducational institution; in Japan, he influenced such figures as Nobel laureate Yasunari Kawabata. Tagore's works were widely translated into English, Dutch, German, Spanish, and other European languages by Czech indologist Vincenc Lesný, French Nobel laureate Andre Gide, Russian poet Anna Akhmatova, former Turkish Prime Minister Bülent Ecevit, and others. In the United States, Tagore's lecturing circuits, particularly those in 1916–1917, were widely attended and acclaimed. Yet, several controversies involving Tagore resulted in a decline in his popularity in Japan and North America after the late 1920s, concluding with his "near total eclipse" outside of Bengal.

Via translations, Tagore influenced Spanish literature: Chileans Pablo Neruda and Gabriela Mistral, Mexican writer Octavio Paz, and Spaniards Jose Ortega—Gasset, Zenobia Camprubí, and Juan Ramón Jimenez. Between 1914 and 1922, the Jimenez-Camprubí spouses translated twenty-two of Tagore's books from English into Spanish and extensively revised and adapted such works as Tagore's *The Crescent Moon*. In this time, Jimenez developed "naked poetry, a landmark innovation. Ortega—Gasset wrote that "Tagore's wide appeal [may stem from the fact that] he speaks of longings for perfection that we all have... Tagore awakens a dormant sense of childish wonder, and he saturates the air with all kinds of enchanting promises for the reader, who... pays little attention to the deeper import of Oriental mysticism". Tagore's works circulated in free editions around 1920 alongside those of Dante Alighieri, Miguel de Cervantes, Johann Wolfgang von Goethe, Plato, and Leo Tolstoy.

Tagore was deemed overrated by some Westerners. Graham Greene doubted that "anyone but Mr. Yeats can still take his poems very seriously." Modern remnants of a past Latin American reverence of Tagore were discovered, for example, by an astonished Salman Rushdie during a trip to Nicaragua.

Quotations

- The danger inherent in all force grows stronger when it is likely to gain success, for then it becomes temptation.
- Our fight is a spiritual fight, it is for Man.
- I say again and again that I am a poet, that I am not a fighter by nature. I would give everything to be one with

my surroundings. I love my fellow beings and I prize their love.

- Creation is an endless activity of God's freedom; it is an end in itself.
- Freedom is true when it is a revelation of truth.
- India has ever declared that Unity is Truth, and separateness is maya.
- I believe in the true meeting of the East and the West.
- It hurts me deeply when the cry of rejection rings loud against the West in my country with the clamour that the Western education can only injure us.
- That which fails to illuminate the intellect, and only keeps it in the obsession of some delusion, is its greatest obstacle.
- After sixty years of self-experience, I have found that out and out hypocrisy is an almost impossible achievement.
- Our country is the land of rites and ceremonials, so that we have more faith in worshipping the feet of the priest than the Divinity whom he serves.
- the religion of economics is where we should above all try to bring about this union of ours...If this field ceases to be one of warfare, if there we can prove, that not competition but cooperation is the real truth, then indeed we can reclaim from the hands of the Evil One an immense territory for the reign of peace and goodwill.
- I have no zeal for life. You know the only thing that concerns me? That I have laboured so hard to build Viswabharati, wouldn't it have no value after my exit?...I think i have one reservation regarding death, and that is Viswabharati, nothing else.
- It's difficult to know a person until he turns twenty-five— difficult to say what would happen to him...but it's easy to recognise a twenty seven years old— it can be said he's become what he's supposed to be, and from now on this is how his life would be guided, there's in left anything in his life to get astonished.
- To enjoy something, it's essential to guard it with the fence of leisure.

Kazi Nazrul Islam

Kazi Nazrul Islam (25 May 1899–29 August 1976) was a Bengali poet, musician and revolutionary who pioneered poetic works espousing intense spiritual rebellion against fascism and oppression. His poetry and nationalist activism earned him the popular title of *Bidrohi Kobi* (Rebel Poet). Accomplishing a large body of acclaimed works through his life, Nazrul is officially recognised as the national poet of Bangladesh and commemorated in India.

Born into a poor Muslim family, Nazrul received religious education and worked as a muezzin at a local mosque. He learned of poetry, drama, and literature while working with theatrical groups. After serving in the British Indian Army, Nazrul established himself as a journalist in Kolkata (then Calcutta). He assailed the British Raj in India and preached revolution through his poetic works, such as "Bidrohi" ("The Rebel") and "Bhangar Gaan" ("The Song of Destruction"), as well as his publication "Dhumketu" ("The Comet"). His impassioned activism in the Indian independence movement often led to his imprisonment by British authorities. While in prison, Nazrul wrote the "Rajbandir Jabanbandi" ("Deposition of a Political Prisoner"). Exploring the life and conditions of the downtrodden masses of India, Nazrul worked for their emancipation.

Nazrul's writings explore themes such as love, freedom, and revolution; he opposed all bigotry, including religious and gender. Throughout his career, Nazrul wrote short stories, novels, and essays but is best-known for his poems, in which he pioneered new forms such as Bengali ghazals. Nazrul wrote and composed music for his nearly 4,000 songs (including gramophone records), collectively known as Nazrul geeti (Nazrul songs), which are widely popular today. At the age of 43 (in 1942) he began suffering from an unknown disease, losing his voice and memory. Eventually diagnosed as Pick's disease, it caused Nazrul's health to decline steadily and forced him to live in isolation for many years. Invited by the Government of Bangladesh, Nazrul and his family moved to Dhaka in 1972, where he died four years later.

Early Life

Kazi Nazrul Islam was born in the village of Churulia in the Burdwan District of Bengal (now located in the Indian state of

West Bengal). He was born in a Muslim family who is second of three sons and a daughter, Nazrul's father Kazi Fakeer Ahmed was the imam and caretaker of the local mosque and mausoleum. Nazrul's mother was Zaheda Khatun. Nazrul had two brothers, Kazi Shahebjan and Kazi Ali Hussain, and a sister, Umme Kulsum. Nicknamed *Dukhu Mia* (Sad Man), Nazrul began attending the *maktab* – the local religious school run by the mosque – where he studied the Qur'an and other scriptures, Islamic philosophy and theology. His family was devastated with the death of his father in 1908. At the young age of ten, Nazrul began working in his father's place as a caretaker to support his family, as well as assisting teachers in school. He later became the muezzin at the mosque, delivering the Athan and calling the people for prayer.

Attracted to folk theatre, Nazrul joined a *leto* (travelling theatrical group) run by his uncle Bazle Karim. Working and travelling with them, learning acting, as well as writing songs and poems for the plays and musicals. Through his work and experiences, Nazrul began learning Bengali and Sanskrit literature, as well as Hindu scriptures such as the Puranas. The young poet composed a number of folk plays for his group, which included "Chasar San" ("The story of a Farmer"), "Shakunibadh" ("The Killing of a Vulture"), "Raja Yudhisthirer San" ("The story of King *Yudhisthir*"), "Data Karna" ("Philanthropic *Karna*"), "Akbar Badshah" ("Emperor *Akbar*"), "Kavi Kalidas" ("Poet *Kalidas*"), "Vidyabhutum" ("The Learned Owl"), "Rajputrer San" ("The story of a Prince"),

In 1910, Nazrul left the troupe and enrolled at the Raniganj Searsole Raj School, and later transferred to the Mathrun High English School, studying under the headmaster and poet Kumudranjan Mallik. Unable to continue paying his school fees, Nazrul left the school and joined a group of kaviyals. Later he took jobs as a cook at the house of a Christian railway guard and at a bakery and tea stall in the town of Asansol. In 1914, Nazrul studied in the Darirampur School (now Jatiya Kabi Kazi Nazrul Islam University) in Trishal, Mymensingh District. Amongst other subjects, Nazrul studied Bengali, Sanskrit, Arabic, Persian literature and classical music under teachers who were impressed by his dedication and skill.

Studying up to Class X, Nazrul did not appear for the matriculation pre-test examination, enlisting instead in the Indian

Army in 1917 at the age of eighteen. He joined the British army mainly for two reasons: first, his youthful romantic inclination to respond to the unknown and, secondly, the call of politics. Attached to the 49th Bengal Regiment, he was posted to the cantonment in Karachi, where he wrote his first prose and poetry. Although he never saw active fighting, he rose in rank from corporal to *havildar*, and served as quartermaster for his battalion. During this period, Nazrul read extensively, and was deeply influenced by Rabindranath Tagore and Sarat Chandra Chattopadhyay, as well as the Persian poets Hafez, Rumi and Omar Khayyam. He learnt Persian poetry from the regiment's Punjabi moulvi, practiced music and pursued his literary interests. His first prose work, "Baunduler Atmakahini" ("Life of a Vagabond") was published in May, 1919. His poem "Mukti" ("Freedom") was published by the "Bangla Mussalman Sahitya Patrika" ("Bengali Muslim Literary Journal") in July 1919.

Rebel Poet

Nazrul left the army in 1920 and settled in Calcutta, which was then the *Cultural capital of India* (it had ceased to be the political capital in 1911). He joined the staff of the "Bangiya Mussalman Sahitya Samiti" ("Bengali Muslim Literary Society") and roomed at 32 College Street with colleagues. He published his first novel "Bandhan-hara" ("Freedom from bondage") in 1920, which he kept working on over the next seven years. His first collection of poems included "Bodhan", "Shat-il-Arab", "Kheya-parer Tarani" and "Badal Prater Sharab" and received critical acclaim.

Working at the literary society, Nazrul grew close to other young Muslim writers including Mohammad Mozammel Haq, Afzalul Haq, Kazi Abdul Wadud and Muhammad Shahidullah. He was a regular at clubs for Calcutta's writers, poets and intellectuals like the Gajendar Adda and the Bharatiya Adda. In October 1921, Nazrul went to Santiniketan with Muhammad Shahidullah and met Rabindranath Tagore. Despite many differences, Nazrul looked to Tagore as a mentor and the two remained in close association. In 1921, Nazrul was engaged to be married to Nargis, the niece of a well-known Muslim publisher Ali Akbar Khan, in Daulatpur, Comilla. But on June 18, 1921—the day of the wedding—upon public insistence by Ali Akbar

Khan that the term *"Nazrul must reside in Daulatpur after marriage"* be included in the marriage contract, Nazrul walked away from the ceremony.

Nazrul reached the peak of fame with the publication of "Bidrohi" in 1922, which remains his most famous work, winning admiration of India's literary classes by his description of the rebel whose impact is fierce and ruthless even as its spirit is deep:.

I am the unutterable grief,

I am the trembling first touch of the virgin,

I am the throbbing tenderness of her first stolen kiss.

I am the fleeting glance of the veiled beloved,

I am her constant surreptitious gaze...

...

I am the burning volcano in the bosom of the earth,

I am the wild fire of the woods,

I am Hell's mad terrific sea of wrath!

I ride on the wings of lightning with joy and profundity,

I scatter misery and fear all around,

I bring earth-quakes on this world! "(8th stanza)" I am the rebel eternal,

I raise my head beyond this world,

High, ever erect and alone! "(Last stanza)" (*English translation by Kabir Choudhary*).

Published in the "Bijli" (*Thunder*) magazine, the rebellious language and theme was popularly received, coinciding with the Non-cooperation movement — the first, mass nationalist campaign of civil disobedience against British rule.

Nazrul explores a synthesis of different forces in a rebel, destroyer and preserver, expressing rage as well as beauty and sensitivity. Nazrul followed up by writing "Pralayollas" ("Destructive Euphoria"), and his first anthology of poems, the "Agniveena" ("Lyre of Fire") in 1922, which enjoyed astounding and far-reaching success. He also published his first volume of short stories, the "Byather Dan" ("Gift of Sorrow") and "Yugbani", an anthology of essays.

Revolutionary

Nazrul started a bi-weekly magazine, publishing the first "Dhumketu" (*Comet*) on August 12, 1922. Earning the moniker of the "rebel poet", Nazrul also aroused the suspicion of British authorities. A political poem published in "Dhumketu" in September 1922 led to a police raid on the magazine's office. Arrested, Nazrul entered a lengthy plea before the judge in the court.

I have been accused of sedition. That is why I am now confined in the prison. On the one side is the crown, on the other the flames of the comet. One is the king, sceptre in hand; the other Truth worth the mace of justice. To plead for me, the king of all kings, the judge of all judges, the eternal truth the living God... His laws emerged out of the realization of a universal truth about mankind. They are for and by a sovereign God. The king is supported by an infinitesimal creature; I by its eternal and indivisible Creator. I am a poet; I have been sent by God to express the unexpressed, to portray the unportrayed. It is God who is heard through the voice of the poet... My voice is but a medium for Truth, the message of God... I am the instrument of that eternal self-evident truth, an instrument that voices forth the message of the ever-true. I am an instrument of God. The instrument is not unbreakable, but who is there to break God?

On April 14, 1923 he was transferred from the jail in Alipore to Hooghly in Kolkata, he began a 40-day fast to protest mistreatment by the British jail superintendent. Nazrul broke his fast more than a month later and was eventually released from prison in December 1923. Nazrul composed a large number of poems and songs during the period of imprisonment and many his works were banned in the 1920s by the British authorities.

Kazi Nazrul Islam became a critic of the Khilafat struggle, condemning it as hollow, religious fundamentalism. Nazrul's rebellious expression extended to rigid orthodoxy in the name of religion and politics. Nazrul also criticised the Indian National Congress for not embracing outright political independence from the British Empire. He became active in encouraging people to agitate against British rule, and joined the Bengal state unit of the Congress party. Nazrul also helped organise the Sramik Praja Swaraj Dal, a political party committed to national independence and the service of the peasant masses. On December 16, 1925 Nazrul started publishing the weekly "Langal", with himself as chief editor. The "Langal" was the mouthpiece of the Sramik Praja Swaraj Dal.

During his visit to Comilla in 1921, Nazrul met a young Hindu woman, Pramila Devi, with whom he fell in love and they married on April 25, 1924. Pramila belonged to the Brahmo Samaj, which criticised her marriage to a Muslim. Nazrul in turn was condemned by Muslim religious leaders and continued to face criticism for his personal life and professional works, which attacked social and religious dogma and intolerance. Despite controversy, Nazrul's popularity and reputation as the "rebel poet" rose significantly.

Weary of struggles, I, the great rebel,

Shall rest in quiet only when I find

The sky and the air free of the piteous groans of the oppressed.

Only when the battle fields are cleared of jingling bloody sabres

Shall I, weary of struggles, rest in quiet,

I the great rebel.

Mass Music

With his wife and young son Bulbul, Nazrul settled in Krishnanagar in 1926. His work began to transform as he wrote poetry and songs that articulated the aspirations of the downtrodden classes, a sphere of his work known as "mass music." Nazrul assailed the socioeconomic norms and political system that had brought upon misery. From his poem *Daridro* (Pain or Poverty):

O poverty, thou hast made me great.

Thou hast made me honoured like Christ

With his crown of thorns. Thou hast given me

Courage to reveal all. To thee I owe

My insolent, naked eyes and sharp tongue.

Thy curse has turned my violin to a sword...

O proud saint, thy terrible fire

Has rendered my heaven barren.

O my child, my darling one

I could not give thee even a drop of milk

No right have I to rejoice.

Poverty weeps within my doors forever

As my spouse and my child.

Who will play the flute?

In what his contemporaries regarded as one of his greatest flairs of creativity, Nazrul began composing the very first ghazals in Bengali, transforming a form of poetry written mainly in Persian and Urdu. Nazrul for the first introduced Islam into the larger mainstream tradition of Bengali music. The first record of Islamic songs by Nazrul Islam was a commercial success and many gramophone companies showed interest in producing these. A significant impact of Nazrul was that it drew made Muslims more comfortable in the Bengali Arts, which used to be dominated by Hindus. Nazrul also composed a number of notable *Shamasangeet, Bhajan* and *Kirtan,* combining Hindu devotional music. Arousing controversy and passions in his readers, Nazrul's ideas attained great popularity across India. In 1928, Nazrul began working as a lyricist, composer and music director for His Master's Voice Gramophone Company. The songs written and music composed by him were broadcast on radio stations across the country. He was also enlisted/attached with the Indian Broadcasting Company.

Nazrul professed faith in the belief in the equality of women—a view his contemporaries considered revolutionary. From his poet *Nari* (Woman):

I don't see any difference

Between a man and woman

Whatever great or benevolent achievements

That are in this world

Half of that was by woman,

The other half by man. (Translated by Sajed Kamal)

His poetry retains long-standing notions of men and women in binary opposition to one another and does not affirm gender similarities and flexibility in the social structure:

Man has brought the burning, scorching heat of the sunny day;

Woman has brought peaceful night, soothing breeze and cloud.

Man comes with desert-thirst; woman provides the drink of honey.

Man ploughs the fertile land; woman sows crops in it turning it green.

Man ploughs, woman waters; that earth and water mixed together, brings about a harvest of golden paddy.

However, Nazrul's poems strongly emphasise the confluence of the roles of both sexes and their equal importance to life. He stunned society with his poem "Barangana" ("Prostitute"), in which he addresses a prostitute as "mother". Nazrul accepts the prostitute as a human being, reasoning that this person was breast-fed by a noble woman and belonging to the race of "mothers and sisters"; he assails society's negative notions of prostitutes.

Who calls you a prostitute, mother?

Who spits at you?

Perhaps you were suckled by someone

as chaste as Seeta.

And if the son of an unchaste mother is 'illegitimate',

so is the son of an unchaste father.

("Barangana" ("Prostitute") Translated by Sajed Kamal)

Nazrul was an advocate of the emancipation of women; both traditional and non-traditional women were portrayed by him with utmost sincerity. Nazrul's songs are collectively called as *Nazrul geeti.*

Exploring Religion

Nazrul's mother died in 1928, and his second son Bulbul died of smallpox the following year. His first son, Krishna Mohammad had died prematurely. His wife gave birth to two more sons — Savyasachi in 1928 and Aniruddha in 1931 — but Nazrul remained shaken and aggrieved for a long time. His works changed significantly from rebellious expositions of society to deeper examination of religious themes. His works in these years led Islamic devotional songs into the mainstream of Bengali folk music, exploring the Islamic practices of *namaz* (prayer), *roza* (fasting), *hajj* (pilgrimage) and *zakat* (charity). This was regarded by his contemporaries as a significant achievement as Bengali Muslims had been strongly averse to devotional music. Nazrul's creativity diversified as he explored Hindu devotional music by composing *Shama Sangeet, bhajans* and *kirtans,* often merging Islamic and Hindu values. Nazrul's poetry and songs explored the philosophy of Islam and Hinduism.

Let people of all countries and all times come together. At one great union of humanity. Let them listen to the flute music of one great unity. Should a single person be hurt, all hearts should feel it equally. If one person is insulted; it is a shame to all mankind, an insult to all! Today is the grand uprising of the agony of universal man.

Nazrul's poetry imbibed the passion and creativity of Shakti, which is identified as the Brahman, the personification of primordial energy. He wrote and composed many *bhajans, shyamasangeet, agamanis* and *kirtans*. He also composed large number of songs on invocation to Lord Shiva, Goddesses Lakshmi and Saraswati and on the theme of love of Radha and Krishna.

Nazrul assailed fanaticism in religion, denouncing it as evil and inherently irreligious. He devoted many works to expound upon the principle of human equality, exploring the *Qur'an* and the life of Islam's prophet Muhammad. Nazrul has been compared to William Butler Yeats for being the first Muslim poet to create imagery and symbolism of Muslim historical figures such as Qasim, Ali, Umar, Kamal Pasha, Anwar Pasha and the prophet Muhammad. His vigorous assault on extremism and mistreatment of women provoked condemnation from Muslim and Hindu fundamentalists.

In 1920, Nazrul expressed his vision of religious harmony in an editorial in *Yuga Bani,*

"Come brother Hindu! Come Musalman! Come Buddhist! Come Christian! Let us transcend all barriers, let us foresake forever all smallness, all lies, all selfishness and let us call brothers as brothers. We shall quarrel no more".

In another article entitled *Hindu Mussalman* published in *Ganabani* on September 2, 192 he wrote-

"I can tolerate Hinduism and Muslims but I cannot tolerate the Tikism (Tiki is a tuft of never cut hair kept on the head by certain Hindus to maitain personal Holiness) and beardism. Tiki is not Hinduism. It may be the sign of the pundit. Similarly beards is not Islam, it may be the sign of the pundit. Similarly beard is not Islam, it may be the sign of the mollah. All the hair-pulling have originated from those two tufts of hair. Todays fighting is alos between the Pundit and the Mollah: It is not between the Hindus and the Muslims. No prophet has said, "I have come for Hindus I have come for Muslims I have come for Christians." They have said, "I have come for the humanity for everyone, like light". But the devotees of Krishna says, "Krishna is for Hindus". The followers of Muhammad (Sm) says, "Muhammad (Sm) is for the Muslims". The Disciple of Christ is for Christian". Krishna-Muhammad-Christ have become national property. This property is the root of all trouble. Men do not quarrel for light but they quarrel over cattles."

Nazrul was an exponent of humanism. Although a Muslim, he named his sons with both Hindu and Muslim names: Krishna Mohammad, Arindam Khaled (bulbul), Kazi Sazbyasachi and Kazi Aniruddha.

Later Life and Illness

Nazrul, in the 1930s

In 1933, Nazrul published a collection of essays titled "Modern World Literature", in which he analyses different styles and themes of literature. Between 1928 and 1935 he published 10 volumes containing 800 songs of which more than 600 were based on classical *ragas*. Almost 100 were folk tunes after *kirtans* and some 30 were patriotic songs. From the time of his return to Kolkata until he fell ill in 1941, Nazrul composed more than 2,600 songs, many of which have been lost. His songs based on *baul, jhumur,* Santhali folksongs, jhanpan or the folk songs of *snake charmers, bhatiali* and *bhaoaia* consist of tunes of folk-songs on the one hand and a refined lyric with poetic beauty on the other. Nazrul also wrote and published poems for children.

Nazrul's success soon brought him into Indian theatre and the then-nascent film industry. The first picture for which he worked was based on Girish Chandra Ghosh's story "Bhakta Dhruva" in 1934. Nazrul acted in the role of Narada and directed the film. He also composed songs for it, directed the music and served as a playback singer. The film "Vidyapati" ("Master of Knowledge") was produced based on his recorded play in 1936, and Nazrul served as the music director for the film adaptation of Tagore's novel *Gora*. Nazrul wrote songs and directed music for Sachin Sengupta's bioepic play "Siraj-ud-Daula". In 1939, Nazrul began working for Calcutta Radio, supervising the production and broadcasting of the station's musical programmes. He produced critical and analytic documentaries on music, such as "Haramoni" and "Navaraga-malika". Nazrul also wrote a large variety of songs inspired by the raga *Bhairav*. Nazrul sought to preserve his artistic integrity by condemning the adaptation of his songs to music composed by others and insisting on the use of tunes he composed himself.

Nazrul's wife Pramila Devi fell seriously ill in 1939 and was paralysed from waist down. To provide for his wife's medical treatment, he resorted to mortgaging the royalties of his gramophone records and literary works for 400 rupees. He returned to journalism in 1940 by working as chief editor for the daily newspaper "Nabayug" ("New Age"), founded by the eminent Bengali politician A. K. Fazlul Huq.

Nazrul also was shaken by the death of Rabindranath Tagore on August 8, 1941. He spontaneously composed two poems in Tagore's memory, one of which, "Rabihara" (loss of Rabi or without Rabi) was broadcast on the All India Radio. Within months, Nazrul himself fell seriously ill and gradually began losing his power of speech. His behaviour became erratic, and spending recklessly, he fell into financial difficulties. In spite of her own illness, his wife constantly cared for her husband. However, Nazrul's health seriously deteriorated and he grew increasingly depressed. He underwent medical treatment under homeopathy as well as Ayurveda, but little progress was achieved before mental dysfunction intensified and he was admitted to a mental asylum in 1942. Spending four months there without making progress, Nazrul and his family began living a silent life in India. In 1952, he was transferred to a mental hospital in Ranchi. With the efforts of a large group of admirers who called themselves the "Nazrul Treatment Society" as well as prominent supporters such as the Indian politician Syama Prasad Mookerjee, the treatment society sent Nazrul and Promila to London, then to Vienna for treatment. Examining doctors said he had received poor care, and Dr. Hans Hoff, a leading neurosurgeon in Vienna, diagnosed that Nazrul was suffering from Pick's disease. His condition judged to be incurable, Nazrul returned to Calcutta on 15 December 1953. On June 30, 1962 his wife Pramila died and Nazrul remained in intensive medical care. In 1972, the newly independent nation of

Bangladesh obtained permission from the Government of India to bring Nazrul to live in Dhaka and accorded him honorary citizenship. Despite receiving treatment and attention, Nazrul's physical and mental health did not improve. In 1974, his youngest son, Kazi Aniruddha, an eminent guitarist died, and Nazrul soon succumbed to his long-standing ailments on August 29, 1976. In accordance with a wish he had expressed in one of his poems, he was buried beside a mosque on the campus of the University of Dhaka. Tens of thousands of people attended his funeral; Bangladesh observed two days of national mourning and the Indian Parliament observed a minute of silence in his honour.

Criticism and Legacy

Nazrul's poetry is characterised by an abundant use of rhetorical devices, which he employed to convey conviction and sensuousness. He often wrote without care for organisation or polish. His works have often been criticized for egotism, but his admirers counter that they carry more a sense of self-confidence than ego. They cite his ability to defy God yet maintain an inner, humble devotion to Him. Nazrul's poetry is regarded as rugged but unique in comparison to Tagore's sophisticated style. Nazrul's use of Persian vocabulary was controversial but it widened the scope of his work. Nazrul's works for children have won acclaim for his use of rich language, imagination, enthusiasm and an ability to fascinate young readers.

Nazrul is regarded for his secularism. He was the first person to cite of Christians of Bengal in his novel Mrityukhudha. He was also the first user of folk terms in Bengali literature. He first printed the Sickle and Hammer in any Indian magazine. Nazrul pioneered new styles and expressed radical ideas and emotions in a large body of work. Scholars credit him for spearheading a cultural renaissance in Muslim-majority Bengal, "liberating" poetry and literature in Bengali from its medieval mould. Nazrul was awarded the Jagattarini Gold Medal in 1945 — the highest honour for work in Bengali literature by the University of Calcutta — and awarded the Padma Bhushan, one of India's highest civilian honours in 1960. The Government of Bangladesh conferred upon him the status of being the "national poet". He was awarded the Ekushey Padak by the Government of Bangladesh. He was awarded Honorary D.Litt. by the University of Dhaka. Many centres of learning and culture in India and Bangladesh have been founded and dedicated to his memory. The Nazrul Endowment is one of several scholarly institutions established to preserve and expound upon his thoughts and philosophy, as well as the preservation and analysis of the large and diverse collection of his works. The Bangladesh Nazrul Sena is a large public organization working for the education of children throughout the country.

Other Notable Names

Novelists

Sarat Chandra Chattopadhyay was one of the most popular novelists of early 20th century whose speciality was exploring life and sufferings of women in contemporary rural Bengal. His sympathy towards the common rural folks in "pallisamaj" and a trademark simplified Bengali as a writing style made him one of the most popular writer in his time. Even long after his death many Bengali and Bollywood blockbusters were based on his novels. After him Tarashankar Bandopadhyay, Bibhutibhushan Bandopadhyay, Manik Bandopadhyay, are the three Bandopadhyays who broke out into a new era of realistic writing style. Where the two of the above Bibhutibhusan and Manik had long standing influence on the two of the most brilliant film directors from Bengal, Satyajit Ray and Ritwik Ghatak respectively. Other famous Bengali novelists are Jagadish Gupta, Satinath Bhaduri, Balai Chand Mukhopadhyay (Banophool), Saradindu Bandopadhyay, Kamal Kumar Majumdar, Sunil Gangopadhyay, Sandipan Chattopadhyay, Shumotho Nath Ghosh, Gagendra Kumar Mitra, Bimal Mitra, Bimal Kar, Samaresh Basu, Mani Shankar Mukherjee (Shankar), etc. Seeds of Bengali science fiction could be observed in the writings of Jagadish Chandra Bose, which was later put into a definite genre by writers such as Jagadananda Roy, Hemlal Dutta, Begum Roquia Sakhawat Hussain, Premendra Mitra, Satyajit Ray. Where Satyajit Ray is also notable for his short stories where he revives the tradition of Thakurmar Jhuli into a mixture of fantasy, mystery, science, and fairy tale.

The genre of parallel novel-writing started from the 1960s with the Hungryalist Movement. Malay Roy Choudhury, Subimal Basak and Basudeb Dasgupta are known to be the most experimental novelists belonging to this movement. Basudeb is known to his readers for his only novel Kheladhula. Malay is famous for his Dubjaley trilogy and Subimal for his broken narrative Chhatamatha.

More experimental novelists who came into the scene in the midst of surging change in Bengali Literature are: Udayan Ghosh, Rabindra Guha, Kamal Chakraborty, Barin Ghoshal, Subimal Mishra, Arupratan Basu, Nabarun Bhattacharya.

In the New Age (21st Century), Arupratan Ghosh can be considered the only novelist of this genre with his novel Suryaheen (published in 2007).

Sharat Chandra Chatterji

Sharat Chandra Chatterji, also known as Sarat Chandra Chattopadhyay or Sharat Chandra Chatterjee (15 September 1876-16 January 1938) was a legendary Bengali novelist from India. He was one of the most popular Bengali novelists of the early 20th century.

Background and Writing

Sarat Chandra was born into poverty in Debanandapur, Hooghly, India. Though his family was occasionally supported by other family members, Saratchandra's lack of financial stability would influence his writing in years to come. Although he began as a fine arts student, Chatterji left his studies due to his persistent state of poverty. He got his early education residing at his paternal uncle's house.

His work represented rural Bengali society and he often wrote against social superstitions and oppression. For a short period, he was a *sannyasi*, a Hindu ascetic who abandons the material and social worlds. His first published story was, 'Mandir'. He was particularly sensitive to the cause of women in general.

He died in Kolkata of liver cancer in 1938.

After the death of this parents, Sarat Chandra left his college education midway and went to Burma in 1903. There he found employment with a Government Office as Clerk. He did not continue his job in Burma for long time and decided to come back, but before his departure he submitted a short story for a prize competition, but in his uncle's name, Surendranath Ganguli. It won the first prize in 1904. Sarat Chandra was also a fond disciple of Swami Vivekananda. There is a biography of Sharat babu written by Vishnu Prabhakar a Hindi writer named Awara Masiha. Prabhakar travelled for fourteen years continuously to collect material for this book

Bartaman Hindu-Mussalman Samasya

Bartaman Hindu-Mussalman Samasya (literally, Contemporary Hindu-Muslim Problem) is an essay by Sarat Chandra first presented at the Bengal Provincial Conference of 1926. In the essay the author decries the Muslims as lacking culture from birth whereas the Hindus are claimed to be born with culture. According to noted historian K. N. Panikkar this manner of thinking contributed to the "construction of a new communal consciousness". The author re-invented a traditional category of "mlech" (impure) in order to achieve the contemporary purpose of undermining the Gandhian political ideal of Hindu-Muslim unity.

Works

- *Baradidi,* (The Elder Sister) 1907
- *Bindur Chhele,* (Bindu's Son) 1913
- *Parinita/Parineeta,* 1914
- *Biraj Bou,* (Mrs. Biraj) 1914
- *Ramer Shumoti,*(Ram Returning to Sanity) 1914
- *Palli Shomaj,* 1916
- *Arakhsanya,* 1916
- *Debdas/Devdas,* 1917 (written in 1901)
- *Choritrohin,* (Characterless) 1917
- *Srikanto,* (4 parts, 1917, 1918, 1927, 1933)
- *Datta,* 1917-19
- *Grihodaho,* 1919
- *Dena Paona,*(Debts and Demands) 1923
- *Pather Dabi,*(Demand for a pathway) 1926
- *Ses Prasna,* (The Final Question) 1931.
- *Bipradas,* 1935
- Nishkriti
- Mejho didi
- Chandranath

- Bilashi
- Mandir
- Pandit Mashay
- Adhare alo
- Naba Bidhan
- Shesher parichoy
- Boikanter will
- Shubhoda.

Tarashankar Bandopadhyay

Tarashankar Bandopadhyay was one of the leading Bengali novelists. He wrote 65 novels, 53 story-books, 12 plays, 4 essay-books, 4 autobiographies and 2 travel stories. A notable man of wisdom, he was awarded Rabindra Puraskar, Sahitya Akademi award, Jnanpith Award, and Padma Bhushan.

Personal Life and Education

Bandopadhyay was born at Labhpur, Birbhum district, West Bengal. He was born to Haridas Bandopadhyay and Prabhabati Debi. He passed the Matriculation examination in 1916 and took admission in the intermediate class at St. Xavier's College, Calcutta.

While studying in intermediate at St. Xavier's College, he joined the non-cooperation movement and was interned in 1921. He was again jailed for a year in 1930. After the release from the prison in 1931, he decided to devote himself to literature.

Bandopadhyay married Uma Shashi Debi and they had two sons and two daughters. The Elder son was Sanat Bandopadhyay & Younger son Sarit Bandopadhyay. The elder daughter Ganga and younger was Bani. Ganga is alive as in January 2010.

Literary Career

Literary Achievements: The realism in Literature is well substituted when the writers indulge in introducing romance in it. Tarashankar Bandopadhyay is grouped with those writers of the third decades of the twentieth centuries who broke the poetic tradition in novels but took to writing prose with the world around them adding romance to human relationship breaking the indifference of the so called conservative people of the society who dare to call a spade a spade. Tarashankar's novels, so to say, do not look back to the realism in rejection, but accepted it in a new way allowing the reader to breath the truth of human relationship restricted so far by the conservative and hypocrisy of the then society.

He learned to see the world from various angles. He seldom rose above the matter soil and his Birbhum exists only in time and place. He had never been a worshipper of eternity. Tarashankar's chief contribution to Bengal literature is that he dared writing unbiased. He wrote what he believed. He wrote what he observed.

His novels are rich in material and potentials. He preferred sensation to thought. He was ceaselessly productive and his novels are long, seemed unending and characters belonged to the various classes of people from zaminder down to pauper. Tarashankar experimented in his novels with the relationships, even so called illegal, of either sexes. He proved that sexual relation between man and women sometimes dominate to such an extent that it can take an upperhand over the prevailing laws and instructions of society. His novel 'Radha' can be set for an example in this context.

His historical novel 'Ganna Begum' is an attempt worth mentioning for it's traditional values. Tarashankar ventured into all walks of Bengali life and it's experience with the happenings of socio-political milieu. Tarashankar will be remembered for his potential to work with the vast panorama of life where life is observed with care and the judgment is offered to the reader and long ones, then any other author. He is a *region* novelist, his country being the same Birbhum.

Works

Tarashankar mainly flourished during the war years, having produced in that period a large number of novels. His celebrated novels are Dhatridebta, Kalindi, Panchagrm, Ganadebata, Kabi, Arogyaniketan, Jalsaghar, Raskali, Hansulibaker Upakatha and so on.

Awards

In 1957, he led the Indian delegation of writers at the Asian Writers' Conference in Tashkent. For his novel *Arogya Niketan,* he received the Rabindra Puraskar in 1955 and the Sahitya Akademi Award in 1956. In 1966, he received the Jnanpith Award for his novel *Ganadebata.* He was honoured with the Padma Shri in 1962 and the Padma Bhushan in 1969. He also received the *Sharat Smriti Puraskar* and the *Jagattarini Gold Medal* from the Calcutta University. In 1970, he was elected the president of the Bangiya Sahitya Parishad. He was a member of the West Bengal Vidhan Parishad from 1952-60 and the Rajya Sabha from 1960-66.

Bibliography

Novels:

- Chaitali Ghurni (*1931*)
- Raikamal (*1933*)
- Aagun (*1937*)
- Dhatridevata (*1939*)
- Ganadevata (*1942*)
- Panchagram (*1944*)
- Hansuli Banker Upakatha (*1947*)
- Naginikanyar Kahini (*1955*)
- Kalindi
- Janapada
- Padachinha
- Kalantar
- Kirtihater Karcha
- Kabi
- Abhijan
- Chanpadangar Bou (*1945*)
- Manjuri Opera (*1964*)
- Fariyad
- Radha
- Gannabegum
- Saptapadi
- Bipasha
- Dakharkara
- Shatabdir Mrityu (*1972*).

Bibhutibhushan Bandopadhyay

Bibhutibhushan Bandopadhyay (12 September 1894-1 November 1950) was a Bengali novelist and writer. His most well known book is the autobiographical novel, *Pather Panchali* (The Song of the Road), incorporated (along with *Aparajito*, the sequel) into the memorable Apu Trilogy films by Satyajit Ray.

Personal Life and Education

Bandopadhyay was born in Kalyani, Muratipur village (Under Kanchapara Gram Panchayet), in the Nadia of Bengal, British India at his maternal uncle's house in a Hindu Brahmin family. His father, Mahananda Bandopadhyay, was a Sanskrit scholar and a *Kathak*, one who tells stories for a living.

His early days were spent in abject poverty. Nevertheless, he fought his way to complete his undergraduate degree in History, at the Surendranath College, Kolkata; although he could not afford to enroll for the postgraduate course at the University of Calcutta. The economic burden of his family rested squarely on his shoulders.

He married Gouri Devi, but she died in childbirth after only a year of their marriage. The tragic theme of death and loneliness is a recurrent factor in his early writings.

At 46, Bibhutibhushan married Rama Chattopadhyay. Their only son, Taradas, was born in 1947.

Bandopadhyay died on 1 November, 1950, of a heart attack while staying at Ghatshila.

Career

Bandopadhyay, before becoming a writer, took up various jobs to make ends meet. He taught school, became a secretary, managed an estate. Finally, in 1921 he published his first short story, "Upekshita," in *Probasni,* one of the leading literary magazines of Bengal at that time. However, it was not until 1928, when his first novel, *Pather Panchali* (also known in English as *Song of the Little Road*), was published, that Bibhutibhushan got critical attention. With *Pather Panchali* Bibhutibhushan became, instantly, a prominent name in Bengali literature.

Bandopadhyay had a stout constitution and walked miles in the woods every day. He usually took his notebook with him and loved to write surrounded by the wilderness.

Critical Acclaim

Pather Panchali is considered to be Bibhutibhushan's masterpiece. It has been included in the CBSE syllabus for students choosing to study Bengali. He has 16 novels and over two hundred short stories to his credit.

Humayun Azad opined that the novel is superior to its cinematic rendition. This is not necessarily a commonly held view in the West, as the Apu Trilogy is considered to be among the finest films in the history of cinema, and the unavailability of a complete translation of *Pather Panchali* into English makes it an issue hard for the English-speaking audience to resolve: the available translation (by T. W. Clark and Tarapada Mukherji) is a truncated version of the novel. However, in the Bengali-speaking world, the stature of the novel is not seriously in doubt. Martin Seymour-Smith, in his *Guide to Modern World Literature* (1973), calls Bandopadhyay (he uses the form Banerji) "perhaps the best of all modern Indian novelists" and says "probably nothing in twentieth-century Indian literature, in prose or poetry, comes to the level of *Pather Panchali*".

Apart from the translation of the truncated text by T. W. Clark and Tarapada Mukherji, Amit Chaudhuri has translated a few excerpts for inclusion in the anthology *The Picador Book of Modern Indian Literature*. In his introduction to these excerpts, Chaudhuri writes: "Unique for its tenderness and poetry... *Pather Panchali* rejects both nineteenth-century realism and social realism (the social milieu described in it would have logically lent itself to the latter) for an enquiry into perception and memory."

The complete text of *Aparajito*, the sequel to *Pather Panchali*, has been translated into English by Gopa Majumdar.

Bibhutibhushan's works are mostly concerned with the lives of people from rural Bengal. His writings come alive with vibrant and thoroughly normal characters from the countryside.

Bibliography

Complete list of novels:

- *Pather Panchali* (Song of the Road)
- *Aparajito* (Unvanquished; sequel to *Pather Panchali*)
- *Aranyak* (In the Forest)
- *Adarsha Hindu Hotel*
- *Ichhamati*
- *Dristi Pradeep*

- *Chander Pahar*
- *Heera Manik Jale*
- *Debjan*
- *Bipiner Sangsar*
- *Anubartan*
- *Ashani Sanket*
- *Kedar Raja*
- *Dampati*
- *Sundarbane Sat Batsar-Not completed by him*
- *Dui Bari*
- *Kajol—Sequel of Aparajito-Completed By His Son Taradas*
- *Mismider Kabach*
- *Kosi Pranganeyer Chitthi.*

Partial short Story Collections

- *MeghaMallar*
- *Mauriphool*
- *Jatrabadol.*

Manik Bandopadhyay

Manik Bandopadhay or Manik Banerjee (19 May 1908 – 30 November 1956) Born as Prabodh Kumar Bandhopadhay to Harihar Bandhopadhay and Neeroda Devi, is one of the founding fathers of modern Bangla fiction. During a short life of forty eight years, plagued simultaneously with ailment and financial crisis, he produced forty two novels and more than two hundred short-stories. His important works include Padma Nadir Majhi (Tr. The Boatman of Padma River) and Putul Nacher Etikatha (Tr. The Tale of Puppet Dance) and Chatushkone (Tr. Quadrilateral).

Life

Manik Bandopadhyay was born on 19 May 1908 in a small town called Dumka in the district of Santal Paragona in the state of Bihar in India. His original name is Prabodh Kumar Bandhopaddhay. His pen name is derived from his family nick 'Manik'. He was the fifth of the fourteen children (eight sons and six daughters) of his parents. His father was Harihar Bandopadhyay and his mother was Niroda Devi. Harihar was a government official and travelled across undivided Bengal in connection with his service which gave the author to experience life and living of different peoples of Bengal, in his early life.

Since his childhood Manik was carefree and adventurous in character. But he also possessed a very sensitive soul. He lost his mother on 28 May 1924 when he was only sixteen and this berevement left a deep mark in his psyche. After his mother's death, Manik became reckless and tie with his family grew thin.

The writer married Kamala Devi, the third daughter of Surendranath Chattopadhay. He had two sons and two daughters.

Education

Manik passed Entrance examinaiton from the Midnapore Zilla School in 1926 securing first division with letter marks in both compulsory and optional Mathematics. In the same year he got admitted in Welleslyan Mission College at Bankura. Earlier he has also studied in Kanthi Model School in Tangail.

In Welleslyan College Manik came in contact with a professor called Jackson.Being influenced by him Manik read Bible and got rid of religious inferiority. In 1928 he passed I. Sc. with first division.

He got admitted to the B.Sc. course in Mathematics at the Presidency College, Calcutta with the inspiration of his father.

Living

Writing was the only source of income for Manik Bandopadhyay throughout his life and hence he languished perpetual poverty. However, for a short while he tried to enhance his earning through involvement with one or two literary magazines. He worked as editor of *Nabarun* for a few months in 1934. During 1937-38, he worked as Assisatnt Editor of literary magazine Bangasree. Also he had established a printing and publishing house in 1939 which turned out to be a short-lived endeavour. Also, he worked as Publicity Assistant for the Government of India in 1943.

Death

Manik died in 1956, at age 48. His funeral took place at Nimtala Shmashan Ghat. Since early life he had struggled with poverty and epilepsy. The signs of epilepsy first surfaced when he was engaged in writing *Padma Nadir Majhi* and *Putul Nacher Etikatha.* Continued and unabated ailment, problems and crises devastated his mental disposition and eventually he resorted to alcohol for respite, adding to his misery. On 30 November 1956, the author collapsed and fell into a coma. He was admitted to the Nilratan Government Hospital on 2nd of December where he died the next day. Following his death, a mourning meeting was held on 7 December, attended by a huge crowd.

Literary Life

One day when he was sitting with his friends in their college canteen one of his friend told could he publish the story in "Bichitra" paper he said that he could publish his first story "Atshi mami". In those days "Bichitra" paper was famous & only famous writer could write. One day he went to "Bichitra" paper's office & posted the story on the editor's letter box.At the end of the story he wrote his name as Manik Bandhopadhay. After four months the story was published & the story became famous in Kolkata & from then he was popularly known as Manik Bandhopadhay.

His stories and novels were published in various literary magaziens of the then Bengal. They included Bichitra, Bangasree, Purbasha, AnandaBazaar Patrika, Jugantor, Satyajug, Probashi, Desh, Chaturanga, NoroNari, Notun Jiban, Bosumati, Golp-Bharati, Mouchak, Pathshala, Rang-Mashal, NoboShakti, Swadhinata, Agami, Kalantar, Parichaya, Notun Sahitya, Diganta, Sanskriti, Mukhopotro, Provati, Ononnya, Ultorath, Elomelo, Bharatbarsha, Modhyabitta, Sharodi, Sonar Bangla, Agami, Ononya, Krishak, Purnima, Rupantar and Swaraj.

During his lifetime, Manik published as many as fifty seven titles. He has also taken shots at composing poetry.

Theme & Style

His writing stands in stark contrast to that of other contemporary luminaries like Bibhutibhushan Bandopadhyay who portrayed life in rural Bengal in a gentle, lyrical light. Although he had some common grounds with Tarashanker Bandopadhyaya, he distinguished himself with profouond and scientific into the lives of ordinary people. Manik's writing dealt with the pettiness and wretchedness of existence in a village context. His primary concern was the dark alleyways of the human mind, even among the supposedly simple village folk, and not the serene beauty of nature that was always in the background in his novels. In Putulnacher Etikatha he took on rather savagely the touchy topic of hypocrisy in villages: an elderly couple are canonised as saints after committing morpheine-induced suicide; the daughter of one of the village's elders gets married off to a wealthy businessman in Kolkata who treats her as a 'kept' woman, she develops a drinking habit and comes back to her old home just a shadow of her former self. However, the people around her keep pretending that nothing untoward has happened. Numerous other examples abound.

A Pioneer of Bengali Novel

Shortly after making his debut in the world of fiction in 1935 through a short story titled *Atshi Mami*, Manik Bandopadhay embarked upon writing novels. Publication of *Diba-Ratrir Kabya* in 1935 and Padma Nadir Majhi and Putul Nacher Itikotha in 1936 established him as the most notable novelist Bengali literature since Bankimchandra, Rabindranath and Saratchandra. He distinguished himself with focus on the life of ordinary rural and urban people, with the colloquial language and with a neat narrative. He was a great story-teller who perfected his fiction with insight into human mind. In the earlier works he took a Freudian approach. In the later life, he showed influence of Marxist theory. His treatment of human sexuality in *Chatushkone* is path-breaking.

Putul Nacher Etikatha

Putul Nacher Etikatha is one of the most outstanding works of Manik Bandopadhyaya. In one of his letters Manik informed that this novel is an humble protest to those who tend to play with the life of human beings as if they are puppets.

It was serialized in the *Bharatbarsha* from Poush 1341 to Agrahayana 1342. D. M. Library of Calcutta published it in book form first in 1936. A movie was produced based on this great novel in 1949. The film was directed by Asit Bandopadhyay and produced by K. K. Productions.

Social and Political Views

Manik carefully read Marx and Engels and became a Marxist. He became an active politician of Marxism by joining the Communist Party of India in 1944.

Works

Novels

He wrote 34 novels and around 180 short-stories in his short,stormy yet intensely prolific litarary career of 27 years.

- Janani (Tr. Mother-1935)
- Diba-Ratrir Kabya (Tr. Poetry of Days and nights-1935)
- Padma Nadir Majhi (Tr. The Boatman of River Padma-1936)
- Putul Nacher Itikatha (Tr.The Tale of Puppet Dance-1936)
- Jiboner Jotilota (Complicacies of Life-1936)
- Ahinsa (1941)
- Dhorabandha Jiban (Tr. Routine Life-1941)
- Chatushkone (Tr. Quadrilateral-1942)
- Protibimbo (Tr. The Reflection-1943)
- Drapan (Tr. The Mirror-1945)
- Shorobasher Itikotha (Tr. A Tale of City Life-1946)
- Chinha (Tr. The Sign-1947)
- Jiyonto (Tr. Alive-1950)
- Pesha (Tr. The Profession-1951)
- Swadhinotar Swad (Tr. Taste of Freedom-1951)
- Pashapashi (Tr. Side by side-1952)
- Sarbojonin (Tr. Universal-1952)
- Nagpash (Tr. Serpent's Grasp-1953)
- Feriwala (Tr. Vendor on foot-1953)
- Arogya (Tr. Recovery-1953)
- Chalcholon (Tr. Life style-1953)
- Haraf (Tr. The Alphabet-1954)
- Holud Nodi Sobuj Bon (Tr. Yellow River Green Woods-1956)
- Mashul (Tr. The Penalty-1956)
- Majhir Chele(a novel for the adolescent readers).

Short Stories

- Atashi Mami (1935)
- Pragoitihashik (Tr. Pre-historic-1937)

- Mihi O Mota Kahini (1938)
- Sarisrip (Tr. Amphibian-1939)
- Bou (Tr. The Bride-1940)
- Shamudrer Swad (Tr. The Taste of the Seas-1943)
- Bhejal (Tr. Adulterated-1944)
- Holudpora (1945)
- Poristhiti (Tr. The Situation-1946)
- Khotian (Tr. The Report-1947)
- Matir Mashul (Tr. Earthen Penalty-1948)
- Choto Boro (Tr. The Big and the Small-1948)
- Lajuklota (Tr. A shy creeper-1953).

Play

- Bhite-Mati (Tr. The Homestead-1946).

Essay

- Lekhoker Katha (Tr. The Writer's Statement-1957).

Poetry

- Manik Bandopadhyay-er Kobita (Tr. The poems of Manik Bandopadhyay-1970).

1.Diner kobita 2.Raater kobita 3.Dibaraatrir kabyo 4.Uttor dokkhin 5.gaachtolae 6.Buro santrasbadi 7.Cha 7.Prothom kobitar kahini 8.Raja o proja 8.Sundor 9.Shrabon maas 10.kishori 11.Adim kobita 12.Mod je khae se matal 13.Nastiker kotha 14.Rupkotha 15.Hae go hae

Quotation

- I write to communicate those things which can't be expressed other than through writing.
- Never wrote a single line, but read a lot.May not be literature, may not be creativity, but editor-catering stories possible.
- It's cruel to forbid someone to love
- Religion! Religion is curse
- I have always been a loner
- Need to learn humilty..have to love human beings. I'm a communist.

- Same reason behind the Partition and worsening of Indo-Pak relation. So that British-American imperialism could eat up both.

Jagadish Gupta

Jagadish Gupta (1886-1957), was a renowned Bangla writer and poet. He was born in Kushtia, Bengal (now in Bangladesh).

Life

He studied in Kolkata City School and Ripon College.

Works

Jagadish Gupta started his writing career as a poet and later, became a famous short story writer.

His literary works were included in the curriculum of school level, secondary, higher secondary and graduation level Bengali Literature in Bangladesh.

Books

- *Binodini*
- *Ruper Bahire*
- *Srimoti*
- *Swanirbachito Golpo*
- *Osadhu Sidhartho*
- *Dulaler Dola.*

Banaphool

Banaphool (sometimes translated as *Banaphool* or *Bonoful* literally meaning The Wild Flower in Bengali) is the pen name of the Bengali author, playwright and poet, Balai Chand Mukhopadhyay (1899–1979).

Born in Manihari (or Purnia) Bihar, Mukhopadhyay began writing as a teenager and adopted the his pen name (*wild-flower* in Bengali) to hide his work from his tutors. He is most noted for his short vignettes, often just one page long, but his body of work spanned sixty five years and included "thousands of poems, 586 short stories, 60 novels, 5 dramas, a number of one-act plays, an autobiography, and numerous essays."

In addition to his literary works, Mukhopadhyay was also a

physician, and practised medicine throughout his life. He died in 1979 and, on the 100th anniversary of his birth, India issued a postage stamp featuring his image.

Selected Works

Novels:

- *Trinokhondo*
- *Boitorini Tire*
- *Kichukhon*
- *Se O Ami*
- *Jangam*
- *Ogni*
- *Doiroth*
- *Mrigoya*
- *Nirmok*
- *Mandonda*
- *Nobodigondo*
- *Koshtipathar*
- *Sthabor*
- *Pancha Parba*
- *Lokhir Agomon*
- *Dana.*

Short Story Collection

- *Bonofuler Golpo*
- *Bonofuler Aro Golpo*
- *Bahullo*
- *Bindu Bishorgo*
- *Adrisholok*
- *Anugamini*
- *Tonni*
- *Nobomonjori*
- *Urmimala*
- *Soptomi*
- *Durbin*
- *Bonofuler Sreshto Golpo*

- *Bonofuler Golpo Songroho-1*
- *Bonofuler Golpo Songroho-2.*

Short Story Writers

Bengali literature is also famous for short stories. Some of the famous short story writers are Rabindranath Tagore, Manik Bandopadhyay, Jagadish Gupta, Tarashankar Bandopadhyay, Bibhuti Bhushan Bandopadhyay, Rajshekhar Basu (Parasuram), Premendra Mitra, Kamal Kumar Majumdar, Shibram Chakrabarti, Saradindu Bandopadhyay, Subodh Ghosh, Narendranath Mitra, Jyotirindra Nandi, Bimal Kar, Narayan Gangopadhyay, Shumotho Nath Ghosh, Gagendra Kumar Mitra, Santosh Ghosh, Debesh Roy, Anish Deb,Abhijnan Roychowdhury, Satyajit Roy, Lila Majumder, Shiresendu Mukhopaddhyay, Ratan Lal Basu, Sayed Walliullaha, Sandipan Chattopadhyay, Basudeb Dasgupta, Subimal Mishra, Arupratan Basu, Kamal Chakraborty, Aboni Dhar, Nabarun Bhattacharya, Akhtaruzzaman Ilias, Mahmudul Huq, Hasan Azizul Huq, etc. Malay Roy Choudhury has introduced a completely new genre of Bengali short story writing called 'Atibastab' or 'Hyperreal' during 1990s.

New writers and experimental short stories (apart from the mainstream ones) were not in the scene over the last two decades (1980's and 90's). A revival of new experimental short stories is observed in the New Age (21st Century). Pratishedhak, a New Age magazine (which first revived the experimental short story culture in early 2000), has played a major influential role to promote further revival of the experimental short story writing culture. Some New Age short story writers are:

Souptik Chakraborty, Arko Chattopadhyay, Arupratan Ghosh, Sudeshna Majumdar and Ratul Paul.

The first New Age short story book-Napoleoner Nabobarsho by Souptik Chakraborty-was published in 2008.

Poets

Jatindramohan Bagchi, Kazi Nazrul Islam, Jibanananda Das, along with Buddhadeva Bose, marks the beginning of the major move to transcend the Tagore legacy. Even though Jibanananda went through a terbulent and difficult financial troubles and met an unfortunate accident caliming his life early in his writing career, he remains to be the most influential poet of post-Rabindranath era. The new genre of Bengali poets departed considerably from Tagore's ideological style and adopted various themes and philosophies such as Marxism, Freudian interpretation of mind, which were avoided and often criticized by Rabindranath Tagore. These three marked the beginning of the era that will burst with activities and urge to merge with the greater world of poetry absorbing elements from them. Commonly called polli-kobi (*pastoral poet*) Jasimuddin, Shamsur Rahman, widely known for his 'playing with words' are also notable.

Hungryalism

There has been only one pathbreaking literary movement in West Bengal, namely The Hungry generation or Hungryalism. The famous poets of this movement are Malay Roy Choudhury, Shakti Chattopadhyay, Benoy Majumdar, Samir Roychoudhury, Falguni Ray, Saileswar Ghose, Pradip Chowdhuri, Subo Acharya, Arunesh Ghose, Tridib Mitra and Debi Ray. The fiction writers are Sandipan Chattopadhyay, Basudeb Dasgupta, Subimal Basak, Malay Roy Choudhury and Samir Roychoudhury. The painters are Anil Karanjai and Karunanidhan Mukhopadhyay.

Prakalpana Movement

The Prakalpana Movement of Kolkata was sparked off in the Bengali language on September 6, 1969 by Vattacharja Chandan with the assistance of Dilip Gupta and Asish Deb. They later declared the day as "Prakalpana Day," because to them "the earth stood still" on the natal day of the movement. *Swatotsar*, the journal of the movement was published by Vattacharja Chandan and named by Dilip Gupta. *Swatotsar* was dubbed to be an "anti-magazine," for, in keeping with its iconoclastic content, the magazine was printed to be read in Asian style—i.e. from back to front. In addition, *Swatotsar* was shaped like an axe blade—an axe (according to its editors) to be used against the roots of conventionalism. Up to that time, modern Bengali literature and art had been over-burdened by colonial styles, adaptations and ideas such as Surrealism, Absurdist literature, the Beat Generation, Existentialism, Concrete poetry, free verse, blank verse, etc. Consequently, the Prakalpana Movement has as its goal the defining and promulgating of a brand new, indigenous genre of literature for the literary world of the new millennium.

A Tiny Literary Revolution

Steve LeBlanc who interviewed Vattacharja Chandan in the beginning of the nineties, wrote:

> *"For all the cliches, deserved or not, and despite its ponderous social problems, Calcutta has, for the past 20 years or so nurtured a tiny literary revolution by the mysterious name of Prakalpana Literature. Championed by its founder and chief conspirator Vattacharja Chandan, Prakalpana Literature—the name of the movement and the title of its own bilingual (Bengali and English) chapbook lit-zine has tried to define a whole new kind of writing, one that draws from all genres, drama to poetry to fiction. For an obscure literary movement, Prakalpana has drawn fans far outside the borders of India including underground American writers and mail art fans from around the globe"...*

Vattacharja Chandan, the creator of the concept of this movement initially coined the term Prakalpana, deriving it from Pra*bandha* (essay)+ Ka*bita* (poetry)+ *Ga*lpa (story)+ Na*tak* (drama). But later in order to make the new form globally more acceptable and perceptible, he extended the purview, span and scope of Prakalpana as the convergence of: P for prose, poetry, opera + R for story, drama + A for art, essay + K for kinema + L for culture + N for song, novel...etc.

Influence

Since visuals are frequently used in Prakalpana, some critics think that the movement features concrete or visual poetry. Actually, Prakalpana is more narrative fiction than poetry, though poetry and visuals might be used in parts of Prakalpana if the concerned writer finds it suitable to mix genres in the same piece of writing. The resulting form is Prakalpana only—not any other of the discrete ingredients. Moreover, *Swachhando* or *Flow verse*, the rhythm of Sabangin Poetry, is also not concrete poetry, visual poetry, free verse or other pre-conceived forms or meters, but was created from a mixing of prosaic and poetic rhythms and got its name from the pioneering, similarly named Bengali and English poems by Chandan.

Prakalpana World

Prakalpana Sahitya:Prakalpana Literature magazine began its journey in 1977 to bring all the forms of Prakalpana literature and Sarbangin poetry movement under a single umbrella, as *Swatotsar* was publishing mostly Prakalpana.

So *Swatotsar* was closed after more than ten years of its existence in 1979 having published twenty issues, in favour of *Kobisena* and *Prakalpana Literature*. Bilingual *Prakalpana Literature* has been publishing Prakalpana, Sarbangin Poetry and all other kinds experimental and avant-garde poetry, apart from essay, review, literary news, letter and artwork from around the globe. It has published sporadically twenty three issues so far. Ashish Deb had left Swatotsar after the first issue and he came back for a short stint in 2005.

Dilip Gupta had deserted the movement in 1978 and returned after almost eight years in the eighties. From the very beginning of the movement it did not solely depend on the contributions from the members of the group only as usually like other movements. On the contrary over all these long years, countless non-commercial Indian as well as writers and artists from around the world have contributed to this movement, which have always fertilized and revitalized the movement with longer life and global ambience.

To name some of them are: Dilip Gupta, Asish Deb, Sukla Mojumdar, Hitabrata Roychoudhury, Rabindra Bhattacharya, Satya Ranjan Biswas, Bablu Roy Choudhury, Shyamoli Mukherjee Bhattacharjee, Ramratan Mukhopadhyay, Nikhil Bhaumik, Baudhayan Mukhopadhyay, Braja Chattopadhyay, Arun Kumar Chakraborty, Paresh Mandal, Rishin Mitra, Debkumar Basu, Laxmi Paul, Utpal, Tapas Bandopadhyay, Syed Asrar Ahmed, Ashok Bosu, Kashinath Mandal, Amar Das, Sandip Chattopadhyay, Amit Kashyap, Bandopadhyay Soumitra, Tapon Ghosh and Tapas Ghosh (brothers), Bibhu Padhi, Ramtanu Datta, Niva De, Shaswata Shikdar, Vattacharja Chandan, Ruj Sukumar, Banhisikha Bhattacharya, Goutam Mitra, Sidhartha Ranjan Choudhury, Uttar Basu, Nasim A Alam, &c....(India); and Fern C J Carr, Mary Rudbeck Stanko, (Canada); Hugo Pontes, Jose Roberto Sechi (Brazil); Alfred A Walker, Gerald England, John Light (UK); Amari Hamadane (Algeria); Giovanni Malito, (Ireland); Carla Bertola, Gloria Persiani (Italy); Jesse Glass, (Japan); Michael Scherba (Kazakhstan); Christian Burgaud (France); Jorge Ignacio Nazavel Cowan (Cuba); and John Byrum, Richard Kostelanetz, Don Webb, John M. Bennett, Madison

Morrison, Sheila Murphy, Guy R Beining, Susan Smith Nash, Jessica Manack, Margarita Engle, Ray Succre, Charlene Mary-Cath Smith, Geof A. Huth, Jeramy Dodds, t winter-damon, Derek White, Holden, Brett K. Fletcher, Mick Cusimano, Jim Dewitt &c.....(USA).

Reviews of *Kobisena* and *Prakalpana Literature* in the much-read US review magazine Factsheet Five and currently in Zine World and other reviews on line along with the enlistment in the *International Directory of Little Magazines and Small Presses*, and *Poet's Market*, enabled the movement to get submissions from different parts of the world. In 1997 Vattacharja Chandan, representing Bengali Literature with Sunil Gangopadhyay and a few others, participated in the Asian Literary Leaders' Conference in Washington DC,USA, where he had informal discussions with some international writers on the movement. When he presented *Kobisena* to poet Derek Walcott, the Nobel laureate wrote on it:'With thanks'. His visit to some other countries including Bangladesh helped spread to some extent the gospel of this movement abroad. To reach the common non-literary audience, several issues of *Kobisena* and *Prakalpana Literature* were published with consumer datebooks which proved popular. In addision to the artists and mail artists like Jorge Ignacio Nazavel Cowan, Syamoli Mukherjee Bhattacharjee, Mick Cusimano, Christian Burgaud, Carla Bertola, Vattacharja Chandan, Norman J. Olson, Hugo Pontes etc., they have also published the works of eminent artists like Rabindranath Tagore, Ramkinkar Baij, Mukul Dey, Sunil Das, Rabin Mandal, Ramananda Bandopadhyay, Pranabesh Maity &c.

Here are samples how the international neutral critics are viewing this movement

"...the other day, I received a brilliant small press mag from India, Prakalpana Literature, written half in Bengali and half in English, and filled with oddities from around the world. I am not sure that I can describe the delirious enthusiasm of this magazine, it begins with "Global Litmosphere", a report on various obscure works from France, Ireland, Taiwan, Ukraine, UK, US, India and even Canada. This leads into a hundred pages of tightly-packed prose, poetry, comics, drawings, and commentaries, some in Bengali, some in English....."

"A collaborative effort by Indian writers and western writers.... It seems a positive gesture in establishing communication between different literary and geographical worlds."

Kobisena the Poet Troop

In September 1972 at a convention in Vidyasagar Hall in Kolkata, triggered off a new outfit named *Kobisena* (meaning Poet troop) of the poetry by the poetry and for the poetry. Accordingly a pamphlet of four pages, edited by Vattacharja Chandan and published by Rabindra Bhattacharya was out in December, being the mouthpiece of the Sarbangin Poetry Movement—the poetry front of Prakalpana Movement. About Sarbangin Poetry (Kobita) Steve LeBlanc observed:

" In order to separate prakalpana from collage poetry and other forms of experimental literature, Chandan introduces the concept of 'Sarbangin Kobita'— poetry that grows out of proper imagination, feeling and realization. Sarbangin Kobita reveals what Chandan describes as chetanavyasism (wholeness of cosmic matter and revealed sense) while utilizing the wholesome and artful repetition of words and visuals, sonorous and mathematical effects in Flow Verse rhythm. The term Sarbangin itself derives from Chandan's poem 'Kobitaay Sarbangin Amritakharan' and an accompanying theoritical essay 'Sarbangin Kobita Jagga' published in Kobisena, a sister publication of Prakalpana Literature."

Rabindra Bhattacharya left the movement thereafter soon. But Kobisena has been continuing its run still today piloted by the same editor to publish its new kind of Sarbangin Poetry and to popularize poetry through public performances of poetry reading even in unlikely places like outside the corn field in village, in front of book stalls of Bengal Cultural Conference, Kolkata Book Fair, Kolkata Art Fair, in spite of being encountered by other stall owners which hampered their sales due to the gathering of large crowd attracted by their open readings. In 1973 Kobisenas even stormed into the East Zone Cultural Conference convened by the government, in procession with posters and festoons and questioned the organizers as to why the new poetry and poets had not been included as the subject of discourses, which resulted in pandemonium and hurried closure of the day's session and thereafter the capture of the dias by the Kobisenas and rejuvenate the session. Besides they kicked off crazy extempore readings at fairs, train, street, beneath the statue, even on the merry go round as well as at countless literary fests and seminars in different grounds and halls. Just as one was the Prakalpana Litfest 2009 on 6 September, the Prakalpana Day in Jibanananda Sabhaghar,

Kolkata. Many eminent persons had graced these occasions in different times, to name some of them: Nagarjun, Monindra Roy, Sunil Gangopadhyay, Prakash Karmakar, Madison Morrison, Amitava Dasgupta, Ananda Ghoshhajra, Sandipan Chattopadhyay...&c. On several occasions Kobisenas used painted hats, belts and peculiar attires and musical instruments to attract the audience.

The performers of poetry who in different times made their marks were Bablu Roy Choudhury, Rabindra Bhattacharya, Kashinath Mandal, Narak Das, Ashok Bosu, Arun Kumar Chakraborty and Vattacharja Chandan. Chandan even uses his music and songs with his performance of poetry. Since the eighties Kobisena has been published bilingual to reach the global shore. So far it has fortyfour issues infrequently published. And this small pamphlet has been an avid traveller around the world. But as to how it has fared, let us read a bit of unaffiliated independent reactions:

" This is an eight sided issues focusing avant garde/ experimental poetry which frequently includes graphics in the body of the work. The pamphlet is unusual in several ways, It is bilingual, printed in Bengali and English, and it carries the exhortation Please copy this issue and distribute anywhere in the globe....The poetry found in Kobisena is full of the same concerns poets write of everywhere: relationship and family, life and love, existence and imagination. This small pamphlet provides some interesting work, strong enough to make the reader pause for reflection."

"...there's a definite charge that comes with having something this weird show up in your mailbox. The poems are adorned with faces and illustrations that have been xeroxed and xeroxed to the point where their resolution is beginning to degenerate: I can't tell you if these are part of the poem or just layout ornamentation together, which, far from detracting, is part of the appeal some people in India cobbled this fragile packet of meaning together and somehow it travelled from person to person until a stranger sent it to me in Chicago and I put the words on the Internet and they found way to you. Musing on this process makes this strange document a potent testament to both the durability and the ephermerality of human communication. Like holding a grain of sand that came from halfway around the world".

Literature that Crosses the Boundaries

We are not sure how many, or if any other movement in the modern literary world can be found like Prakalpana Movement that has been running even after crossing the hurdles of four decades. Still the humble impact of Prakalpana Movement as arguably perhaps one of the most important among the experimental and avant garde literary scene in India that has a global presence at this point of time, is evident from the fact that the experimental short stories in Bengali literature seem to have been arranged and deranged on the lines of prakalpana form, which paradoxically is not at all short story. And also the sporadic use of signs, symbols, pictures and henceforth considered unliterary material are being used now in some literature as has been used by Prakalpanites and Kobisenas long ago. Now a days adopting the western ways and styles is the trendy high tide, rampant and go with the flow downstream everywhere else as in Bengali Literature and art since the colonial days.

But being based in Bengali literature, export of the indigenous new concepts of Prakalpana, Chetanavyasism, Sarbangin Poetry, Flow Verse... etc. into the global literary arena in reverse swing from India is an arduous task in the low tide against strong high tides to the upstream. This is more so especially for a non-commercial non-conforming yet non-confronting alternative movement like Prakalpana, being completely independent of the myth of main stream establishment and anti-establishment and new media communications.

This goal might seem however implausible and ambitious to be achieved by an independent alternative literary and art movement like Prakalpana, but not to its artificer and mentor Vattacharja Chandan, who has been spearheading the Movement in each and every theory and practice so far without bothering for any obstacles from the very beginning. And with his world vision catalog, he still wants to gear up this movement, simply and solely banking on the virtual latent support of some independent, known and unknown brand new and old band of writers, artists and readers scattered around the world. His immediate associate Prakalpanite teammates currently include Dilip Gupta, Ramratan Mukhopadhyay, Nikhil Bhaumik, Bablu Roy Choudhury, Syamoli Mukherjee Bhattacharjee, Boudhayan Mukhopadhyay, Kalyan Bandopadhyay, Debjani Das and Utpal.

The Prakalpanites simply want to plant and spread the seeds of a few new Chetanavyasist species in the literary and art world. But whether they will weather the storm or wither away in some unfavorable literary climate, or forest and flower in a new earth in the new millennium, only the future will say. But so far their spirit is, as one daily newspaper once commented:

" The blue blood of the Kobisenas' pen never dries up".

And as of this time,

"For literature that crosses the boundaries this is a good place to look".

Parallel Poetry and Poets Since 1970

Kaurab Cult

Some major changes occurred in the 1970s in the Bengali Poetry, chiefly around Kaurab-a literary & cultural magazine nearly four decades old. Prime cult-figures of Kaurab are :

Swadesh Sen, Kamal Chakraborty, Barin Ghosal, Debajyoti Dutta, Shankar Lahiri, Shankar Chakraborty, Pranabkumar Chattopadhayay and Aryanil Mukhopadhyay.

Poets who Lead Left-Movement Since 1970

Biplab Majee, Ananya Ray, Tusar Roy, Monibhushan Bhattacharya, Pranab Chattopadhya, Saroj Dutta.

New Poetry (Natun Kabita)

Since the mid 80's Bengali Literature experienced a new genre of Bengali poetry called New Poetry. From the early 90's a Kolkata based poetry journal Kabita Campus has organized various workshops and poetry-camps focusing on this genre. In 2003 some poets of that journal have separately started another one named Natun Kabita containing their ideas and poems, through both online and print media. Another new age poetry magazine in the same sphere is Boikhoribhashya. Poets associated with this literary movement are: Barin Ghosal, Ranjan Maitra, Swapan Roy, Dhiman Chakraborty, Alok Biswas, Pronob Pal, Soumitra Sengupta, Arupratan Ghosh, Indranil Ghosh, Amitava Praharaj and Debanjan Das.

Rajarshi Chattopadhyay, Atanu Bandopadhyay, Pradip Chakraborty are the poets who joined this movement in mid 90's.

The first decade of this century (2000-09) is considered to be the period of a *New Age* of Bengali poetry.

Prominent poets rising from the period are: Sankha Subhra Devbarman, Arindam Ray, Arup Ghosh, Tanmay Mandal, Arjun Bandopadhyay, Susnata Jana, Himalay Jana, Kaushik Bhowmik, Pallab Chakrabarti, Sanghamitra Haldar, Himadri Mukhopadhyay, Somnath Ghosal, Swagata Dasgupta, Nabendu Bikash Ray, Ripon Fio, Atanu Sinha, Sandip Kumar, Paramita Das.

Musicians

Seminal Hindu religious works in Bangla include the many songs of Ramprasad Sen. His works (still sung today) from the 17th century cover an astonishing range of emotional responses to the goddess Kali, detailing complex philosophical statements based on Vedanta teachings and more visceral pronouncements of his love of the goddess. They are known as *Shyama Sangeet* and were the literary inspiration for Kazi Nazrul Islam's later, famed Shyama Sangeet. There are also the laudatory accounts of the lives and teachings of the Vaishnava saint Chaitanya Mahaprabhu (the *Choitanyo Choritamrit*) and Shri Ramakrishna (the *Ramakrishna Kathamrita*, translated roughly as Gospel of Ramakrishna). There is also a large body of Islamic literature, that can be traced back at least to *Noornama* by Abdul Hakim. *Bishad Sindhu* depicting the death of Hussain in Karbala is very popular novel written by Mir Mosharraf Hossain. Later works influenced by Islam include devotional songs written by Nazrul, and popularized by Abbas Uddin, among others.

Bauls and Traditional Singers

The mystic Bauls of the Bengal countryside who preached the boundless spiritual truth of *Sôhoj Pôth* (the Simple, Natural Path) and *Moner Manush* (The Man of The Heart) drew on Vedantic philosophy to propound transcendental truths in song format, traveling from village to village proclaiming that there was no such thing as Hindu, Muslim or Christian, only *moner manush.*

The literature discussed so far can be more or less regarded as the common heritage of both Bangladesh and West Bengal. Since the partition of Bengal in 1947, the east and west parts of Bengal have also developed their own distinctive literatures. For example, the Naxalite movement has influenced much of West

Bengal's literature, whereas the Liberation War has had a similarly profound impact on Bangladeshi literature.

Major Literary Figures in Bangladesh

Shawkat Osman, Shamsur Rahman, Sufia Kamal, Al Mahmud, Abubakar Siddique, Ghulam Murshid,Hasan Azizul Huq, Selina Hossain, Shawkat Ali, Akhtaruzzaman Ilias, Nirmalendu Goon, Mahadev Saha, Abul Hasan, Humayun Azad, Shaheedul Jahir, Humayun Ahmed, Imdadul Haque Milon, Anisul Hoque, Taslima Nasrin, Rabbani Choudhury and Tahmima Anam to name a few.

Major Literary Figures in West Bengal

Nihar Ranjan Gupta, Ashutosh Mukhopadhyay, Sunil Gangopadhyay, Nabaneeta Dev Sen, Syed Mustafa Siraj, Baren Gangopadhyay, Shirshendu Mukhopadhyay, Amiya Bhushan Mazumdar, Lokenath Bhattacharya, Debesh Roy, Atin Bandopadhyay, Shankha Ghosh, Sandipan Chattopadhyay, Samir Roychoudhury, Subimal Basak, Shakti Chattopadhyay, Mahasweta Devi, Moti Nandi, Kamal Kumar Majumdar, Subimal Mishra, Shankar, Suchitra Bhattacharya, Vattacharja Chandan, Bani Basu, Buddhadeb Guha, Shiersendu Mukhopaddhyay, Suchitra Bhattacharya etc.

Literay Figures Since 1970's

Swadesh Sen, Barin Ghosal, Pranabkumar Chattopadhayay, Biplab Majee, Ananya Roy, Subimal Mishra, Vattacharja Chandan, Kamal Chakraborty, Ranjan Maitra, Swapan Roy, Shankar Lahiri, Dhiman Chakraborty, Anirban Mukhopadhyay, Aryanil Mukhopadhyay, Sarthak Roychowdhury, Sharmi Pandey, Shubhankar Das, Rajarshi Chattopadhyay, Arupratan Ghosh, Indranil Ghosh, Amitava Praharaj, Souptik Chakraborty, Animikh Patra, Paramita Das, Himadri Mukhopadhyay, Arindam Ray, Anamitra Roy, Tanmay Mandal, Deb Maity, Swagata Dasgupta, Kaushik Bhowmik, Debanjan Das, Arjun Bandopadhyay, Souva Chattopadhyay, Atanu Sinha, Arup Ghosh.

Bengali Science Fiction

Bengali science fiction is a rich part of Bengali literature. Although it is not as established as other genres in the Bengali language, it is gaining popularity among Bengali readers, especially in Bangladesh.

Earliest Writers

Bengali writers wrote various science fiction works in the 19th and early 20th centuries during the British Raj, before the partition of India. Isaac Asimov's assertion that "true science fiction could not really exist until people understood the rationalism of science and began to use it with respect in their stories" is true for the earliest science fiction written in the Bengali language.

The earliest notable Bengali science fiction was Jagadananda Roy's *Shukra Bhraman* (*Travels to Venus*), published in 1879. This story is of particular interest to literary historians, as it described an interstellar journey to another planet; its description of the alien creatures that are seen in Uranus used an evolutionary theory similar to the origins of man: "They resembled our apes to a large extent. Their bodies were covered with dense black fur. Their heads were larger in comparison with their bodies, limbs sported long nails and they were completely naked." This story was published a decade before H. G. Wells's *The War of the Worlds* (1898) in which Wells describes the aliens from Mars.

Some specialists credit Hemlal Dutta as one of the earliest Bengali science fiction writers for his *Rohosso* ("The Mystery"). This story was published in two instalments in 1882 in the pictorial magazine *Bigyan Dorpon* ("Mirror of Science").

Jagadish Chandra Bose, now considered as the father of Bangla science fiction, wrote "Niruddesher Kahini" in 1896. This tale of weather control, one of the first Bangla science fiction works, features getting rid of a cyclone using a little bottle of hair oil (Kuntol Keshori). Later, he submitted the story to *Obbakto* as "Polatok Tufan" ("Run Away Cyclone").

Roquia Sakhawat Hussain (Begum Rokeya), an early Islamic feminist, wrote "Sultana's Dream", one of the earliest examples of feminist science fiction in any language. It depicts a feminist utopia of role reversal, in which men are locked away in seclusion, in a manner corresponding to the traditional Muslim practice of purdah for women. The short story, written in English, was first published in the Madras-based *Indian Ladies Magazine* in 1905, and three years later appeared as a book.

Premendra Mitra wrote the first novel, *Kuhoker Deshe* ("In the Land of Mystery"). Hemendra Kumar Ray wrote *Meghduter Morte Agomon*.

Science Fiction in Bangladesh

After Qazi Abdul Halim's *Mohasunner Kanna* ("Tears of the Cosmos"), Humayun Ahmed wrote the first modern Bangla SF novel, *Tomader Jonno Valobasa* ("Love For You All"). It was published in 1973. This book is treated as the first full-fledged Bangladeshi science fiction novel. Then he wrote *Tara Tinjon* ("They were Three"), *Irina, Anonto Nakshatra Bithi* ("Endless Galaxy"), *Fiha Somikoron* ("Fiha Equation") etc.

But Bangla science fiction leaves its cocoon phase holding the hands of Muhammed Zafar Iqbal. Mr. Iqbal wrote a story named "Copotronic Sukh Dukho" when he was a student of Dhaka University. This story was later included in a compilation of Iqbal's work in a book by the same name. Muktodhara, a famous publishing house of Dhaka was the publisher of this book. This collection of sci-fi stories gained huge popularity and the new trend of science fiction emerged among Bangla writers and readers. After his first collection, Mr. Iqbal transformed his own science fiction cartoon strip "Mohakashe Mohatrash" ("Panic in the Cosmos") into a novel. All told, Muhammed Zafar Iqbal has written the greatest number of science fiction works in Bangla sci-fi.

Following the footsteps of the ancestors, more and more writers, especially young writers started writing Science Fiction and a new era started in Bangla literature.

Moulik, the first and longest-running Bangladeshi science fiction magazine, was first published in 1997, with famous cartoonist Ahsan Habib as the editor. This monthly magazine plays an important role in the development of Bangla science fiction in Bangladesh. A number of new and very promising sci-fi writers like Rabiul Hasan Avi, Anik Khan, Asrar Masud, Sajjad Kabir, Russel Ahmed and Mizanur Rahman Kallol came of age while working with the magazine.

Other Writers of Bangladesh

Other notable writers in the genre include: Nipun Alam, Ali Imam, Qazi Anwar Hussain, Altamas Pasha, Anirudha Alam, Ahsanul Habib, Kamal Arsalan, Dr. Ahmed Mujibar Rahman, Moinul Ahsan Saber, Swapan Kumar Gayen, Mostafa Tanim, Vobdesh Ray, Jubaida Gulshan Ara Hena, Amirul Islam, Touhidur Rahman, Zakaria Swapan and Qazi Shahnur Hussain.

Writers from West Bengal

A number of writers from West Bengal, India have written science fiction, as well. But almost all of the writers of West Bengal (excepting Premendra Mitra) actually wrote science fantasy rather than science fiction.

Adrish Bardhan is one of the most notable names among West Bengal's sci-fi writers. He also was the editor of *Ashchorjo,* the first Bangla science fiction magazine. After a six year run, this magazine ceased publishing. Later, Mr. Bardhan became editor of the magazine *Fantastic,* but it did not last long. Another Sci-Fi magazine "Vismoy Science Fiction" was edited by Sujit Dhar and Ranen Ghosh but it lasted only about two years.

A short story known as *The Alien* written by Satyajit Ray about an alien named "Mr. Ang" gained popularity among Bengalis in the early 1960s. He virtually pioneered the genre of Indian Science Fiction. It is alleged that the script for Steven Spielberg's film *E.T.* was based on a script for *The Alien* that Ray had sent to the film's producers in the late 1960s.

Other notable science fiction writers of West Bengal include: Lila Majumdar, Sunil Ganguly, Kinnor Ray, Abhijnan Roychowdhury, Anish Deb, Shirshendu Mukherjee, Said Mustafa Siraj, Samarjit Kor, Swapan Banarjee and Somoresh Majumder.

Bangla science fiction was given a magic realism worldview by the Hungryalist writers Malay Roy Choudhury in his novel *Kuharbhumey Nishidishi* and *Jinnatulbilader Rupkatha,* and by Basudeb Dasgupta in his short story collection *Randhanshala.*

2

The Asiatic Society

The Asiatic Society was founded by Sir William Jones (1746-1794) on January 15, 1784 in a meeting presided over by Sir Robert Chambers, the Chief Justice of the Supreme Court at the Fort William in Calcutta, then capital of the British Raj, to enhance and further the cause of Oriental research. At the time of its foundation, this Society was named as "Asiatick Society". In 1825, the antique *k* was dropped without any formal resolution and the Society was renamed as "The Asiatic Society". In 1832 the name was changed to "The Asiatic Society of Bengal" and again in 1936 it was renamed as "The Royal Asiatic Society of Bengal." Finally, on July 1, 1951 the name of the society was changed to its present one. The Society is housed in a building at Park Street in Kolkata (Calcutta). The Society moved into this building during 1808. In 1823, the Medical and Physical Society of Calcutta was formed and all the meetings of this society were held in the Asiatic Society.

History

In January, 1784 Sir William Jones sent out a circular-letter to a selected number of British residents of Calcutta with a view to establish a society for the Asiatic studies. At his inivitation, thirty British residents met in the Grand Jury Room of the Supreme Court (in the Fort william) on January 15, 1784. The meeting was presided over by Sir Robert Chambers. At this meeting, Jones explained the aims of the Society, he would establish. The *Memorandam of Aritcles* of the Asiatick Society, prepared by Jones said:

The bounds of investigations will be the geographical limits of Asia, and within these limits its enquiries will be extended to whatever is performed by man or produced by nature. Initially, the Grand Jury Room of the Supreme Court was used for the meetings of the members, who had to pay a quarterly fee of two mohurs. The members were elected through ballot-voting. On September 29, 1796 the Society decided to have its own building. J.H. Harrington, then Vice-President selected the corner of Park Street and Chowringhee Road (present location) for the Society's house. The site was granted to the society on May 15, 1805. The original plan for the new building was prepared by Captain Thomas Preston. The French architect, Jean Jacques Pichon (or Jean Jacques Pissaun) made certain modifications to it and constructed a two storeyed building at the site. This 15,071 ft.^{2} building was built at a cost of Rs.30,000.00. The first quarterly meeting of the Society for 1808 was held at its new building on February 3, 1808.

From 1784 to 1828, only Europeans were elected members of the Society. In 1829, at the initiative of H.H. Wilson, a number of Indians were elected members, which include Dwarakanath Tagore, Sivchandra Das, Maharaja Baidyanath Roy, Maharaja Bunwari Govind Roy, Raja Kalikrishna Bahadur, Rajchunder Das, Ram Comul Sen and Prasanna Coomar Tagore. On December 12, 1832 Ram Comul Sen was elected 'Native Secretary'. Later, Rajendralal Mitra became the first Indian President in 1885.

Library

At present, the library of the Asiatic Society has a collection of about 1,17,000 books and 79,000 journals printed in almost all the major languages of the world. It has also a collection of 293 maps, microfische of 48,000 works, microfilm of 387,003 pages, 182 paintings, 2500 pamphlets and 2150 photographs. The earliest printed book preserved in this library is Juli Firmici's *Astronomicorum Libri* published in 1499. It has in its possession a large number of books printed in India in the late 18th and early 19th centuries. The library also possesses many rare and scarcely available books. The library has a rich collection of about 47,000 manuscripts in 26 scripts. The most notable amongst them are an illustrated manuscript of the *Quran*, a manuscript of the *Gulistan* text, and a manuscript of *Padshanamah* bearing the signature of Emperor Shahjahan. The number of journals in the possession of the library is about 80,000 at present. The early collection of this library was enriched by the contributions it received from its members. In March 25, 1784 the library received seven Persian manuscripts from Henri Richardson. The next contribution came from William Marsden, who donated his book, *History of Island of Sumatra* (1783) on November 10, 1784. Robert Home, the first Library-in-Charge (1804) donated his small but valuable collection of works on art. The first accession of importance was a gift from the Seringapatam Committee on February 3, 1808 consisting of a collection from the Palace Library of Tipu Sultan. The library received the Surveyor-General Colonel Mackenzie's collection of manuscripts and drawings in December 1822.

Museum

The museum of the Society was founded in 1814 under the superintendence of N. Wallich. The rapid growth of its collection is evident from its first catalogue, published in 1849. When the Indian Museum of Calcutta was established in 1814, the Society handed over most of its valuable collections to it. The Society however still has a museum of its own which possesses a rock edict of Asoka (c. 250 BCE) and a significant collection of copper plate inscriptions, coins, sculptures, manuscripts and archival records. Some masterpieces, like Joshua Reynolds' *Cupid asleep on Cloud,* Guido Cagnacci's *Cleopatra,* Thomas Daniell's *A Ghat at Benares* and Peter Paul Rubens' *Infant Christ* are also in the possession of this museum.

William Jones (Philologist)

Sir William Jones (28 September 1746 – 27 April 1794) was an English philologist and scholar of ancient India, particularly known for his proposition of the existence of a relationship among Indo-European languages. He was also the founder of the Asiatic Society.

Biography

Jones was born in London at Beaufort Buildings, Westminster; his father (also named William Jones) was a mathematician from Anglesey in north Wales, noted for devising the use of the symbol pi. The young William Jones was a linguistic prodigy, learning Greek, Latin, Persian, Arabic, Hebrew and the basics of Chinese writing at an early age. By the end of his life he knew thirteen languages thoroughly and another twenty-eight reasonably well, making him a hyperpolyglot.

Though his father died when he was only three, Jones was still able to go to Harrow in September 1753 and on to Oxford University. He graduated from University College, Oxford in 1768 and became M.A. in 1773.

Too poor, even with his award, to pay the fees, he gained a job tutoring the seven-year-old Lord Althorp, son of Earl Spencer and as such an ancestor of Princess Diana.

He embarked on a career as a tutor and translator for the next six years. During this time he published *Histoire de Nader Chah* (1770), a French translation of a work originally written in Persian by Mirza Mehdi Khan Astarabadi. This was done at the request of King Christian VII of Denmark who had visited Jones-who by the age of 24 had already acquired a reputation as an orientalist. This would be the first of numerous works on Persia, Turkey, and the Middle East in general.

In 1770, he joined the Middle Temple and studied law for three years, which would eventually lead him to his life-work in India; after a spell as a circuit judge in Wales, and a fruitless attempt to resolve the issues of the American Revolution in concert with Benjamin Franklin in Paris, he was appointed puisne judge to the Supreme Court of Bengal in March 1783. In April 1783 he married Anna Maria Shipley, the eldest daughter of Dr. Jonathan Shipley, Bishop of Landaff and Bishop of St. Asaph. On 25 September 1783 he arrived in Calcutta.

In the Subcontinent he was entranced by Indian culture, an as-yet untouched field in European scholarship, and on 15 January 1784 he founded the Asiatic Society in Calcutta. Over the next ten years he would produce a flood of works on India, launching the modern study of the subcontinent in virtually every social science. He also wrote on the local laws, music, literature, botany, and geography, and made the first English translations of several important works of Indian literature. He died in Calcutta on 27 April 1794 at the age of 47.

Scholarly Contributions

Of all his discoveries, Jones is best known today for making and propagating the observation that Sanskrit bore a certain resemblance to classical Greek and Latin. In *The Sanscrit Language* (1786) he suggested that all three languages had a common root, and that indeed they may all be further related, in turn, to Gothic and the Celtic languages, as well as to Persian. His third annual discourse before the Asiatic Society on the history and culture of the Hindus (delivered on 2 February 1786 and published in 1788) with the famed "philologer" passage is often cited as the beginning of comparative linguistics and Indo-European studies. This is Jones' most quoted passage, establishing his tremendous find in the history of linguistics:

The *Sanscrit* language, whatever be its antiquity, is of a wonderful structure; more perfect than the *Greek*, more copious than the *Latin*, and more exquisitely refined than either, yet bearing to both of them a stronger affinity, both in the roots of verbs and the forms of grammar, than could possibly have been produced by accident; so strong indeed, that no philologer could examine them all three, without believing them to have sprung from some common source, which, perhaps, no longer exists; there is a similar reason, though not quite so forcible, for supposing that both the *Gothic* and the *Celtic*, though blended with a very different idiom, had the same origin with the *Sanscrit*; and the old *Persian* might be added to the same family.

This common source came to be known as Proto-Indo-European.

As early as the mid-17th century Dutchman Marcus Zuerius van Boxhorn (1612–1653) and others had been aware that Ancient Persian belonged to the same language group as the European languages. Similarly, American colonist Jonathan Edwards Jr. published in 1787 a work where he demonstrated that the Algonquian languages across northeastern North America were related to each other, and so were the Iroquoian languages. Nevertheless, it was Jones' discovery that caught the imagination of later scholars and became the semi-mythical origin of modern historical and comparative linguistics.

In 1789 he was the first to translate the Abhijnna [kuntalam, an Indian play (written in a mix of Sanskrit and Prakrit) into a Western language under the title of *Sacontalá or The Fatal Ring; An Indian Drama by Cálidás* (Kalidasa). He encouraged his colleague Charles Wilkins to make the first translation of the Bhagavad Gita into English.

Jones is also indirectly responsible for some of the sensibility of the poetry of the English Romantic movement (particularly that of Lord Byron and Samuel Taylor Coleridge), as his translations of "eastern" poetical works were a source for that style.

Latin Chess Poem

In 1763, at the age of 17, Jones wrote the poem *Caissa* in Latin hexameters, based on a 658-line poem called "Scacchia, Ludus" published in 1527 by Marco Girolamo Vida, giving a mythical origin of chess that has become well known in the chess world. He also published an English language version of the poem.

In the poem the nymph Caissa initially repels the advances of Mars, the god of war. Spurned, Mars seeks the aid of the god of sport, who creates the game of chess as a gift for Mars to win Caissa's favour. Mars wins her over with the game.

Caissa has been since been characterised as the "goddess" of chess, her name being used in several contexts in modern chess playing.

Schopenhauer's Citation

On page two of his main work of 1819, Schopenhauer referred to one of Sir William Jones's publications. Schopenhauer was trying to support the doctrine that "everything that exists for knowledge, and hence the whole of this world, is only object in relation to the subject, perception of the perceiver, in a word, representation." He quoted Sir William Jones's original English:

...how early this basic truth was recognized by the sages of India, since it appears as the fundamental tenet of the Vedanta philosophy ascribed to Vyasa, is proved by Sir William Jones in the last of his essays: "On the Philosophy of the Asiatics" (*Asiatic Researches*, vol. IV): "The fundamental tenet of the Vedanta school consisted not in denying the existence of matter, that is solidity, impenetrability, and extended figure (to deny which would be lunacy), but in correcting the popular notion of it, and in contending that it has no essence independent of mental perception; that existence and perceptibility are convertible terms."

Schopenhauer used Jones's authority to relate the basic principle of his philosophy to what was, according to Jones, the most important underlying proposition of Vedanta. He referred to Sir William Jones's writings in a few other places in his works, but this was the most extensive citation.

Fort William College

Fort William College (also called the College of Fort William) was an academy and learning centre of Oriental studies established by Lord Wellesley, then Governor-General of British India. It was founded on July 10, 1800 within the Fort William complex in Calcutta. Thousands of books have been translated from Sanskrit, Arabic, Persian, Bengali, Hindi and Urdu at this institution.

The College

The College of Fort William emerged as both a centre of research and a publication unit, a cradle of creativity as well as scholarship. Planned originally to train probationer British civilians in the languages and cultures of the subjugated country, the college rendered services tantamount to those of a university in promoting modern Indian literatures, Bengali in particular... Under the leadership of William Carey, the College could also claim credit for drawing together Sanskrit pandits and Perso-Arabic munshis to reshape Bengali prose... The variety of the College's publication also deserve note. From colloquies and popular stories, chronicles and legends, to definitive editions of literary texts. —Majumdar, Swapan

Fort William College aimed at training British officials in Indian languages and in the process it fostered the development of languages such as Bengali and Hindi. The period is of historical importance. In 1815, Ram Mohan Roy settled in Calcutta. It is considered by many historians to be starting point of the Bengal renaissance. The establishment of The Calcutta Madrassa in 1781, the Asiatic Society in 1784 and the Fort William College in 1800, completed the first phase of Kolkata's emergence as an intellectual centre.

Teaching of Asian languages dominated: Arabic, Hindustani, Persian, Sanskrit, Bengali; and later Marathi and even Chinese were added. Each department of the college was staffed by notable scholars. The Persian department was headed by Neile B. Edmonstone, Persian translator to the government. His assistant teacher was John H. Harington, a judge of Sadar Diwani Adalat and Francis Gladwin, a soldier diplomat. For Arabic studies, there was Lt. John Baillie, a noted Arabist. The Hindustani language department was entrusted to John Borthwick Gilchrist, an Indologist of great repute. H.T. Colebroooke, the famous orientalist, was head of the Sanskrit department. William Carey, a non-civilian missionary and a specialist in many Indian languages, was selected to head the department of vernacular languages. While notable scholars were identified and appointed for different languages, there was no suitable person in Kolkata who could be appointed to teach Bengali. In those days the Brahmin scholars learnt only Sanskrit, considered to be the language of the gods, and did not study Bengali. The authorities decided to appoint Carey, who was with the Baptist Mission in Serampore. He, in turn, appointed Mrityunjoy Vidyalankar as head pandit, Ramnath Bachaspati as second pandit and Ramram Bose as one of the assistant pandits.

Along with teaching, translations were organized. The college employed more than one hundred local linguists. At that time there were no textbooks available in Bengali. On 23 April 1789, *Calcutta Gazette* published the humble request of several Natives of Bengal for a Bengali grammar and dictionary.

Location

It was located at the corner of Council House Street. The house was subsequently occupied by Messrs. Mackenzie Lyall & Co., and known as *The Exchange*. Still later, it housed the offices of Bengal Nagpur Railway. In those days, it was at one corner of the parade ground, now known as the Maidan. The Raj Bhavan (then known as Government House) was opened a little later.

Library

For teaching purposes the College of Fort William accumulated a library of old manuscripts (from all over South Asia) and added multiple copies of its own imprints. The list of books recommended later for preservation includes many books of historical value. Subsequently, when the college was wound up, it gave away the magnificent collection in the library to the newly formed Calcutta Public Library, now the National Library.

Hurdles

The court of directors of the British East India Company were never in favour of a training college in Kolkata and as such there always was a fund crunch for running the college. Subsequently a separate college for the purpose, The East India Company College at Haileybury (England), was established in 1807. However Fort William College continued to be a centre of learning languages.

With the British settling down in the seat of power, their requirements changed. Bentinck announced his educational policy of public instruction in English in 1835, mostly to cater to the growing needs of administration and commerce. He clipped the wings of Fort William College and the Dalhousie administration formally dissolved the institution in 1854.

Eminent Scholars

Fort William College was served by a number of eminent scholars. They contributed enormously towards development of Indian languages and literature. Some of them are noted below.

- William Carey (1761–1834) was with Fort William College from 1801 to 1831. During this period he published a Bengali grammar and dictionary, numerous text books, the Bible, grammar and dictionary in other Indian languages.
- John Borthwick Gilchrist (June 1759-1841)
- Mrityunjay Vidyalankar (1762?–1819) was First Pandit at Fort William College. He wrote a number of text books and is considered the first 'conscious artist' of Bengali prose. Although a Sanskrit scholar he started writing Bengali as per the needs of Fort William College. He published *Batris Singhasan* (1802), *Hitopodesh* (1808) and *Rajabali* (1808). The last named book was the first published history of India. Mrityunjoy did not know English and as such the contents were possibly provided by the English-knowing scholars of Fort William College.
- Tarini Charan Mitra (1772–1837), a scholar in English, Urdu, Hindi, Arabic and Persian, was with the Hindustani department of Fort William College. He had translated many stories into Bengali.
- Lallulal (also spelt as Lalloolal or Lallo Lal), the father of Hindi Khariboli prose, was instructor in Hindustani at Fort William College. He printed and published in 1815 the first book of old Hindi literature, Tulsidas's *Vinaypatrika*.
- Ramram Basu (1757–1813) was with the Fort William College. He assisted William Carey, Joshua Marshman and William Ward in the publication of the first Bengali translation of the Bible.

- Ishwar Chandra Vidyasagar (1820–91) was head pandit at Fort William College from 1841 to 1846. He concetrated on English and Hindi while serving in the college. After discharging his duties as academician, and engagements as a reformer he had little time for creative writing. Yet through the text books he produced, the pamphlets he wrote and retelling of Kalidas's *Shakuntala* and Shakespeare's *A Comedy of Errors* he set the norm of standard Bengali prose.
- Madan Mohan Tarkalankar (1817–58) taught at Fort William College. He was one of the pioneers of text book writing.

Serampore College

Serampore College is located in Serampore Town, in Hooghly District, West Bengal, India.

The college consists of two entities:

- The theological faculty
- A separate college with faculties of arts, science, commerce

The Senate of Serampore College (University) runs the academic administration of all the theological colleges affiliated with it. The council of Serampore College holds a Danish charter and had the power to confer degrees in any subject, which it currently exercises only for conferring theological degrees as recommended by the senate.

Degrees are awarded for arts, science and commerce students of the Serampore College by the University of Calcutta

For theology, the college is affiliated to the Senate of Serampore College (University). Several theological colleges and seminaries all over India including Nepal, Bangladesh and Sri Lanka are affiliated to the Senate of Serampore College (University).

The present principal is Dr. Lalchungnunga.

Motto

The Latin name of the college motto is *Gloriam Sapientes Possidebunt* which derives from chapter 3, verse 35 of the Latin Vulgate-Book of Proverbs, meaning, the wise shall possess glory.

Authority to Issue Degrees and Accreditation

King Frederick VI of Denmark originally granted a Royal Charter giving Serampore College the status of a university to confer degrees.

With the later establishment of the University of Calcutta in 1857 the arts, science and commerce parts of Serampore College were affiliated to the University of Calcutta.

However, Serampore College still today continues to enjoy the privilege of conferring its own degrees in theology under the power vested by the Charter and Act of Serampore College. It is a private Grant-in-aid Minority College. The college is recognized by the University Grants Commission under Section 2(f) and 12(b) of the UGC Act, 1956.

History

Principals:

- William Carey, 1818-1832
- Joshua Marshman, 1832-1837
- John Mack, 1837-1845
- W. H. Denham, 1845-1858
- John Trafford, 1858-1879
- Albert Williams, 1879-1882
- E.S. Summers, 1883-1906
- George Howells, 1906-1929
- G. H. C. Angus, 1929-1949
- C. E. Abraham, 1949-1959
- William Stewart, 1959-1966
- S. J. Samartha, 1966-1968
- A. K. Mundle, 1968-1969
- M. N. Biswas, 1969-1972
- S. K. Chatterjee, 1972-1976
- R. L. Rodrigues, 1976-1977
- S. Mukhopadhyay, 1977-1987
- T. K. Swarnakar, 1988-1989
- J. T. K. Daniel, 1990-1998
- Dr. Lalchungnunga, 1999.

Founding by English Missionaries

Serampore College was founded in 1818 by the English missionaries known as the Serampore Trio):

- William Carey
- Joshua Marshman
- William Ward.

Their aim was to give an education in arts and sciences to students of every "caste, colour or country" and to train people for ministry in the growing church in India.

From its beginning the college has been ecumenical but this means that it has no automatic basis of support from any one branch of the Christian church. Prior to 1818, the Serampore Trio had worked together in providing education for their own children and the children, including females, of the native Indians.

Original Charter from Denmark

The status accorded by the Danish charter has since been reaffirmed for the study of theology and now forms the basis for degrees of all levels conferred by over forty theological colleges throughout India and is administered by the senate. It was incorporated by Royal Charter in 1827 and the Bengal Government Act IV of 1918.

Control Passed Back to the British

After February 22, 1845 when Denmark sold all of its Indian assets to Britain the management and operation of the college continued without interruption under the direction of a master and council. In 1856 the Baptist Missionary Society in England took over the management of the college and, in 1857, the college became affiliated with the newly established University of Calcutta and became a constituent college of that university.

Arts College Closes to Become Full-Time Seminary

In 1883 the college closed as an arts college and began functioning as a Christian Training Institution and a theological institute for the Baptist churches in Bengal. Affiliating again with the University of Calcutta in 1911, Serampore College, in 1913, was authorised to award the Bachelor of Arts degree. The college faculty was interdenominational.

Twentieth Eentury

On December 4, 1915, the first group of Bachelor of Divinity students graduated:

- The Reverend I. W. Johory, Professor in the Canadian Mission College, Indore;
- The Reverend N. G. Kuriakos, a priest in the Orthodox Syrian Church; and
- Mr. D. M. Devasahayam, London Missionary Society, South India.

Between 1916 and 1927, sixty-nine further students earned their Bachelor of Divinity degrees through Serampore College.

The name of the college and its founders are honoured today more widely than just within Christian circles – the Carey Library at Serampore houses 16,000 rare volumes and is used by scholars from across the world.

Serampore Trio

The "Serampore Trio" was the name given to three pioneering missionaries to India in the 18th century, who set up, amongst other things Serampore College.:

- Joshua Marshman
- William Carey &
- William Ward.

Joshua Marshman

The Reverend Dr. Joshua Marshman (1768-1837) was born in Westbury Leigh, Wiltshire, England and died in Serampore, India.

His Family

Of his family little is known, except that they traced their descent from an officer in the Army of Cromwell: one of a band who, at the Restoration, relinquished, for conscience-sake all views of worldly aggrandisement, and retired into the country to support himself by his own industry.

His father John passed the early part of his life at sea and was engaged in the "Hind" Sloop of War, commanded by Captain Bond at the Capture of Quebec. Shortly after this he returned to England and in 1764 married Mary Couzener. She was a descendant of a French family who had sought refuge in England following the revocation of the Edict of Nantes; after his marriage he lived in Westbury Leigh and took up the trade of a weaver.

This occupation didn't pay well and he was unable to afford his son any education beyond that supplied in the village.

Early Days

In 1791, Joshua married Hannah Marshman and in 1794 they moved from Westbury Leigh in Wiltshire to Bristol. In Bristol they joined the Broadmead Baptist Church and Marshman taught in a local Charity School supported by the church. At this time he also studied at Bristol Baptist College.

On 29 May 1799, Joshua, Hannah and their then two children set out from Portsmouth for India aboard the ship "Criterion". Although there was a threat of a French naval attack the family landed safely at the Danish settlement of Serampore (a few miles north of Calcutta) on the 13th October 1799.

The couple had 12 children; of these only five lived longer than their father. Their youngest daughter Hannah married Henry Havelock, who became a British General in India, and whose statue is in Trafalgar Square, London.

A Talented Scholar

Like the pioneer missionary William Carey with whom he had come to work, Marshman was a talented and gifted scholar. Marshman and Carey together translated the Bible into many Indian Languages as well as translating much classical Indian literature into English.

Marshman at this time also translated the Bible into Chinese- and had an important role in the development of Indian newspapers. He was a keen proponent of the new developments in educational practice and was keen to encourage school teaching in local languages, even though the colonial authorities preferred that lessons be given in English.

The Founding of Serampore College

On 5 July 1818, William Carey, Joshua Marshman and William Ward (another member of their missionary team) issued a prospectus (written by Marshman) for a proposed new "College for the instruction of Asiatic, Christian, and other youth in Eastern literature and European science". Thus was born Serampore College-which still continues to this day.

At times funds were tight, and after a brief and false rumour alleging misapplication of funds caused the flow of funds being raised by Ward in America dried up, Carey wrote, "Dr. Marshman is as poor as I am, and I can scarcely lay by a sum monthly to relieve three or four indigent relatives in Europe. I might have had large possessions, but I have given my all, except what I ate, drank, and wore, to the cause of missions, and Dr. Marshman has done the same, and so did Mr. Ward."

Carey's Children Looked after

Marshman was appalled by the neglect with the way in which Carey looked after his four boys when he first met them in 1800. Aged 4, 7, 12 and 15, they were unmannered, undisciplined, and even uneducated. Carey had not spoiled, but rather simply ignored them. Marshman, his wife Hannah, and their friend the printer William Ward, took the boys in tow. Together they shaped the boys as Carey pampered his botanical specimens, performed his many missionary tasks and journeyed into Calcutta to teach at Fort William College. They offered the boys structure, instruction and companionship. To their credit-and little to Carey's-all four boys went on to useful careers.

The Family Tradition Passes down to his Son John Clark Marshman

Joshua's son, John Clark Marshman (1794-1877), was also to become an important part of the missionary work at the College; he was also an official Bengali translator and published a Guide to the Civil Law which, before the work of Macaulay, was the civil code of India; he also wrote a "History of India" (1842).

In his book "Carey, Marshman and Ward" John Marshman states that by his death his father had spent over £400,000 of his own money on his missionary related works in India.

William Carey (Missionary)

William Carey (17 August 1761 – 9 June 1834) was an English Baptist missionary and Baptist minister, known as the "father of modern missions."Template:Gonzalez, Justo L. The Story of Christianity Vol. 2 pg. 306 Carey was one of the founders of the

Baptist Missionary Society. As a missionary in the Danish colony, Serampore, India, he translated the Bible into Bengali, Sanskrit, and numerous other languages and dialects.

Childhood and Early Adulthood

Carey, the eldest of five children, was born to Edmund and Elizabeth Carey, who were weavers by trade in the village of Paulerspury in Northamptonshire. William was raised in the Church of England; when he was six, his father was appointed the parish clerk and village schoolmaster. As a child he was naturally inquisitive and keenly interested in the natural sciences, particularly botany. He possessed a natural gift for language, teaching himself Latin.

At the age of 14, Carey's father apprenticed him to a shoemaker in the nearby village of Hackleton, Northamtonshire. His master, Clarke Nichols, was a churchman like himself, but another apprentice, John Warr, was a Dissenter. Through his influence Carey would eventually leave the Church of England and join with other Dissenters to form a small Congregational church in Hackleton. While apprenticed to Nichols, he also taught himself Greek with the help of a local villager who had a college education.

When Nichols died in 1779, Carey went to work for another local shoemaker, Thomas Old; he married Old's sister-in-law Dorothy Plackett in 1781.

Unlike William, Dorothy was illiterate; her signature in the marriage register is a crude cross. William and Dorothy Carey had six children, four sons and two daughters; both girls died in infancy, as well as their son Peter, who died at the age of 5. Old himself died soon afterward, and Carey took over his business, during which time he taught himself Hebrew, Italian, Dutch, and French, often reading while working on his shoes.

Founding of the Baptist Missionary Society

Carey became involved with a local association of Particular Baptists that had recently formed, where he became acquainted with men such as John Ryland, John Sutcliff, and Andrew Fuller, who would become his close friends in later years. They invited him to preach in their church in the nearby village of Barton every other Sunday. On 5 October 1783, William Carey was baptized by Ryland and committed himself to the Baptist denomination.

In 1785, Carey was appointed the schoolmaster for the village of Moulton. He was also invited to pastor the local Baptist church. During this time he read Jonathan Edwards' *Account of the Life of the Late Rev. David Brainerd* and the journals of the explorer James Cook, and became deeply concerned with propagating the Christian Gospel throughout the world. His friend Andrew Fuller had previously written an influential pamphlet in 1781 titled "The Gospel Worthy of All Acceptation", answering the hyper-Calvinist belief then prevalent in the Baptist churches, that all men were not responsible to believe the Gospel. At a ministers' meeting in 1786, Carey raised the question of whether it was the duty of all Christians to spread the Gospel throughout the world. J. R. Ryland, the father of John Ryland, is said to have retorted: "Young man, sit down; when God pleases to convert the heathen, he will do it without your aid and mine." However, Ryland's son, John Ryland Jr., disputes that his father made this statement.

In 1789 Carey became the full-time pastor of a small Baptist church in Leicester. Three years later in 1792 he published his groundbreaking missionary manifesto, *An Enquiry into the Obligations of Christians to use Means for the Conversion of the Heathens*. This short book consists of five parts. The first part is a theological justification for missionary activity, arguing that the command of Jesus to make disciples of all the world (Matthew 28:18-20) remains binding on Christians. The second part outlines a history of missionary activity, beginning with the early Church and ending with David Brainerd and John Wesley. Part 3 comprises 26 pages of tables, listing area, population, and religion statistics for every country in the world. Carey had compiled these figures during his years as a schoolteacher. The fourth part answers objections to sending missionaries, such as difficulty learning the language or danger to life. Finally, the fifth part calls for the formation by the Baptist denomination of a missionary society and describes the practical means by which it could be supported. Carey's seminal pamphlet outlines his basis for missions: Christian obligation, wise use of available resources, and accurate information.

Carey later preached a pro-missionary sermon (the so-called Deathless Sermon), using Isaiah 54:2-3 as his text, in which he repeatedly used the epigram which has become his most famous quotation: "Expect great things from God; attempt great things for God."

Carey finally overcame the resistance to missionary effort, and the *Particular Baptist Society for the Propagation of the Gospel Amongst the Heathen* (subsequently known as the *Baptist Missionary Society* and since 2000 as BMS World Mission) was founded in October 1792, including Carey, Andrew Fuller, John Ryland, and John Sutcliff as charter members. They then concerned themselves with practical matters such as raising funds, as well as deciding where they would direct their efforts. A medical missionary, Dr. John Thomas, had been in Calcutta and was currently in England raising funds; they agreed to support him and that Carey would accompany him to India.

Early Indian Period

Carey, his eldest son Felix, Thomas and his wife and daughter sailed from London aboard an English ship in April 1793. Dorothy Carey had refused to leave England, being pregnant with their fourth son and having never been more than a few miles from home; but before they left they asked her again to come with them and she gave consent, with the knowledge that her sister Kitty would help her give birth. En route they were delayed at the Isle of Wight, at which time the captain of the ship received word that he endangered his command if he conveyed the missionaries to Calcutta, as their unauthorized journey violated the trade monopoly of the British East India Company. He decided to sail without them, and they were delayed until June when Thomas found a Danish captain willing to offer them passage. In the meantime, Carey's wife, who had by now given birth, agreed to accompany him provided her sister came as well. They landed at Calcutta in November.

During the first year in Calcutta, the missionaries sought means to support themselves and a place to establish their mission. They also began to learn the Bengali language to communicate with the natives. A friend of Thomas owned two indigo factories and needed managers, so Carey moved with his family north to Midnapore. During the six years that Carey managed the indigo plant, he completed the first revision of his Bengali New Testament and began formulating the principles upon which his missionary community would be formed, including communal living, financial self-reliance, and the training of indigenous ministers. His son Peter died of dysentery, causing Dorothy to suffer a nervous breakdown from which she never recovered. Meanwhile, the missionary society had begun sending more missionaries to India. The first to arrive was John Fountain, who arrived in Midnapur and began teaching school. He was followed by William Ward, a printer; Joshua Marshman, a schoolteacher; David Brunsdon, one of Marshman's students; and William Grant, who died three weeks after his arrival. Because the East India Company was still hostile to missionaries, they settled in the Danish colony at Serampore and were joined there by Carey on 10 January 1800.

Late Indian Period

Once settled in Serampore, the mission bought a house large enough to accommodate all of their families and a school, which was to be their principal means of support. Ward set up a print shop with a secondhand press Carey had acquired and began the task of printing the Bible in Bengali. In August 1800 Fountain died of dysentery. By the end of that year, the mission had their first convert, a Hindu named Krishna Pal. They had also earned the goodwill of the local Danish government and Richard Wellesley, then Governor-General of India.

The conversion of Hindus to Christianity posed a new question for the missionaries concerning whether it was appropriate for converts to retain their caste. In 1802, the daughter of Krishna Pal, a Sudra, married a Brahmin. This wedding was a public demonstration that the church repudiated the caste distinctions.

Brunsdon and Thomas died in 1801. The same year, the Governor-General founded Fort William, a college intended to educate civil servants. He offered Carey the position of professor of Bengali. Carey's colleagues at the college included pundits, whom he could consult to correct his Bengali testament. He also wrote grammars of Bengali and Sanskrit, and began a translation of the Bible into Sanskrit. He also used his influence with the Governor-General to help put a stop to the practices of infant sacrifice and suttee, after consulting with the pundits and determining that they had no basis in the Hindu sacred writings (although the latter would not be abolished until 1829).

Dorothy Carey died in 1807. She had long since ceased to be a useful member of the mission, and in fact was actually a hindrance to its work. John Marshman wrote how Carey worked away on his studies and translations, "...while an insane wife, frequently wrought up to a state of most distressing excitement, was in the next room...". Carey re-married a year later to Charlotte Rhumohr, a Danish member of his church who, unlike Dorothy, was his intellectual equal. They were married for 13 years until her death.

From the printing press at the mission came translations of the Bible in Bengali, Sanskrit, and other major languages and dialects. Many of these languages had never been printed before; William Ward had to create punches for the type by hand. Carey had begun translating literature and sacred writings from the original Sanskrit into English to make them accessible to his own countryman. On 11 March 1812, a fire in the print shop caused £10,000 in damages and lost work. Amongst the losses were many irreplaceable manuscripts, including much of Carey's translation of Sanskrit literature and a polyglot dictionary of Sanskrit and related languages, which would have been a seminal philological work had it been completed. However, the press itself and the punches were saved, and the mission was able to continue printing in six months. In Carey's lifetime, the mission printed and distributed the Bible in whole or part in 44 languages and dialects.

Also, in 1812, Adoniram Judson an American Congregational missionary enroute to India studied the scriptures on baptism in preparation for a meeting with Carey. His studies led him to become a Baptist. Carey's urging of American Baptists to take over support for Judson's mission, led to the foundation in 1814 of the first American Baptist Mission board, the *General Missionary Convention of the Baptist Denomination in the United States of America for Foreign Missions*, later commonly known as the Triennial Convention. Most American Baptist denominations of today are directly or indirectly descended from this convention.

In 1818, the mission founded Serampore College to train indigenous ministers for the growing church and to provide education in the arts and sciences to anyone regardless of caste or country. The King of Denmark granted a royal charter in 1827 that made the college a degree-granting institution, the first in Asia. In 1820 Carey founded the The Agri Horticultural Society of India at Alipore, Kolkata, supporting his enthusiasm for botany.

Carey's second wife, Charlotte, died in 1821, followed by his eldest son Felix. In 1823 he married a third time, to a widow named Grace Hughes.

Internal dissent and resentment was growing within the Missionary Society as its numbers grew, the older missionaries died, and they were replaced by less experienced men. Some new missionaries arrived who were not willing to live in the communal fashion that had developed, one going so far as to demand "a separate house, stable and servants." Unused to the rigorous work ethic of Carey, Ward, and Marshman, the new missionaries thought their seniors-particularly Marshman-to be somewhat dictatorial, assigning them work not to their liking.

Andrew Fuller, who had been secretary of the Society in England, had died in 1815, and his successor, John Dyer, was a bureaucrat who attempted to reorganize the Society along business lines and manage every detail of the Serampore mission from England. Their differences proved to be irreconcilable, and Carey formally severed ties with the missionary society he had founded, leaving the mission property and moving onto the college grounds. He lived a quiet life until his death in 1834, revising his Bengali Bible, preaching, and teaching students. The couch on which he died, on 9 June 1834, is now housed at Regent's Park College, the Baptist hall of the University of Oxford.

Family History

Biographies of Carey, such as those by F.D. Walker and J.B. Myers, only allude to Carey's distress caused by the mental illness and subsequent breakdown suffered by his wife, Dorothy, in the early years of their ministry in India. More recently, Beck's biography of Dorothy Carey paints a more detailed picture: William Carey uprooted his family from all that was familiar and sought to settle them in one of the most unlikely and difficult (for an uneducated eighteenth century English peasant woman) cultures in the world. Dorothy faced enormous difficulties in adjusting to all of this change; she failed to make the adjustment emotionally and ultimately, mentally, and her husband seemed to be unable to help her through all of this because he just did not know what to do about it. Carey even wrote to his sisters in England on 5 October 1795, that "I have been for some time past in danger of losing my wife. Jealousy is the great evil that haunts her mind."

Dorothy's mental breakdown ("at the same time William Carey was baptizing his first Indian convert and his son Felix, his wife was forcefully confined to her room, raving with madness") led inevitably to other family problems. Joshua Marshman was appalled by the neglect with which Carey looked after his four boys when he first met them in 1800. Aged 4, 7, 12 and 15, they were unmannered, undisciplined, and even uneducated. Carey had not spoiled, but rather simply ignored them.

Eschatology

Besides Iain Murray's study, *The Puritan Hope,* less attention has been paid in Carey's numerous biographies to his postmillennial eschatology as expressed in his major missionary manifesto, notably not even in Bruce J. Nichols' article "The Theology of William Carey." Carey was a Calvinist and a postmillennialist. Even the two dissertations which discuss his achievements (by Oussoren and Potts) ignore large areas of his theology. Neither mention his eschatological views, which played a major role in his missionary zeal. One exception, found in James Beck's biography of his first wife, mentions his personal optimism in the chapter on "Attitudes Towards the Future," but not his optimistic perspective on world missions, which he derived from Postmillenial theology.

Schools

Carey has at least four colleges named after him: William Carey International University in Pasadena, California, Carey Theological College in Vancouver, British Columbia, Carey Baptist College, Carey Baptist Grammar School in Melbourne, Victoria and William Carey University, Hattiesburg, Mississippi. William Carey Academy of Chittagong, Bangladesh teaches both Bangladeshi and expatriate children, from Kindergarten to grade 10.

Legacy and Influence

William Carey has been referred to as the "father of modern missions" and was a significance influence to the Protestant missionary movement of the 19th century.

Chronology

- 1761 Born at Paulerspury, Northampton. England; 17 August.
- 1777 Apprenticed to the shoemaking trade.
- 1779 Attended prayer-meeting that changed his life, 10 February.

- 1783 Baptized by Mr. Ryland, 5 October.
- 1786 Called to the ministry at Olney, August 10.
- 1792 Pamphlet "An Inquiry" published;
    - o Baptist Missionary Society in England formed, 2 October.
- 1793 Appointed missionary to India, 10 January;
    - o Arrived in Calcutta, 11 November.
- 1786 5-year-old son Peter dies on 11 October.
- 1796 Baptized a Portuguese, his first convert.
- 1800 Moved to Serampore, 10 January;
    - o Baptized Krishna Pal, first Bengali convert, 28 December;
    - o Elected Professor of Sanskrit and Bengali languages at Fort Williams College.
- 1801 Completed New Testament in Bengali, 7 February.
- 1803 Self-supporting missionary organization founded.
- 1807 Doctor of Divinity conferred by Brown University of U.S.A.;
    - o Member of Bengali Asiatic Society.
    - o Dorothy Carey died.
- 1808 New Testament in Sanskrit published;
    - o Married Charlotte Emilia Rumohr.
- 1809 Completed translation of Bible in Bengali, 24 June.
- 1811 New Testament in Marathi published.
- 1815 New Testament in Punjabi published.
- 1818 His father died, 15 June.
- 1818 Old Testament in Sanskrit published.
- 1820 Founded the Agricultural and Horticultural Society, 4 September;
    - o Danish King granted charter for college at Serampore;
    - o Marathi Old Testament published.
- 1821 Serampore college opened;
    - o Second wife Charlotte died.
- 1823 Married Grace Hughes.
- 1825 Completed Dictionary of Bengali and English.

- 1826 Government gave Carey "Grant in Aid" for education.
- 1829 Sati prohibited through Carey's efforts, 4 December.
- 1834 Died at Serampore, 9 June.
- 1835 Third wife Grace died.

William Ward (Missionary)

William Ward (1769-1823) was an English pioneer Baptist missionary, author, printer and translator. On 10 May 1802 he was married at Serampore to the widow of John Fountain, another missionary, by whom he left two daughters.

Early Life

Ward was born at Derby on 20 October 1769, and was the son of John Ward, a carpenter and builder of that town, and grandson of Thomas Ward, a farmer at Stretton, near Burton in Staffordshire. His father died while he was a child, and the care of his upbringing fell to his mother. He was placed with a schoolmaster named Mr. Congreve, near Derby, and afterwards with another named Mr. Breary.

On leaving school he was apprenticed to a Derby printer and bookseller Mr. Drewry, with whom he continued two years after the expiry of his indentures, assisting him to edit the Derby Mercury. He then removed to Stafford, where he assisted Joshua Drewry, a relative of his former master, to edit the Staffordshire Advertiser and in either 1794 or 1795 proceeded to Hull, where he followed his business as a printer, and was for some time editor of the Hull Advertiser.

Religion

Ward early in life became an Anabaptist, and on 26 August 1796 he was baptised at Hull. Preaching constantly in the neighbouring villages, he became known as a man of promise, and, with the assistance of a member of the baptist community named Mr. Fishwick, he proceeded in August 1797 to Ewood Hall, near Halifax in Yorkshire, the theological academy of John Fawcett (1740-1817), where he studied for a year and a half.

Missionary Work

In the autumn of 1798, the baptist mission committee visited Ewood, and Ward offered himself as a missionary, influenced perhaps by a remark made to him in 1793 by William Carey concerning the need for a printer in the Indian mission field.

Ward sailed from England in the Criterion in May 1799, in company with Joshua Marshman. On arriving at Calcutta he was prevented from joining Carey by an order from the Government, and was thereby obliged to proceed to the Danish settlement of Serampore, where he was then joined by Carey.

In India, Ward's time was chiefly occupied in overseeing the community's printing press, which was used to disseminate the scriptures, once they had been translated into Bengali, Mahratta, Tamil, and twenty-three other languages. Numerous philological works were also issued and Ward still found time to both keep a copious diary and to preach the gospel to the natives.

Until 1806, he made frequent tours amongst the towns and villages of the province, but after that year the increasing claims of the press on his time, and the extension of the missionary labours in Serampore and Calcutta, prevented him quitting headquarters. In 1812 the printing office was destroyed by fire. It contained the types of all the scriptures that had been printed, to the value of at least ten thousand pounds. The moulds for casting fresh type, however, were recovered from the debris, and with the help of friends in Great Britain the loss was soon repaired.

Serampore College

In 1818, Ward, having been for some time in bad health, revisited England. Here he was entrusted with the task of pleading for funds with which to endow a new college at Serampore which he had founded along with Joshua Marshman & William Carey, for the purpose of instructing natives in European literature and science. He undertook a series of journeys throughout England and Scotland, and also visited Holland and North Germany. In October 1820 he embarked for New York, and travelled through the United States, returning to England in April 1821. On 28 May he sailed for India in the Alberta, carrying funds for Serampore College; as a result, Ward, Marshman & Carey became known as the Serampore trio.

Death

Ward died of cholera at Serampore on 7 March 1823, and was interred in the mission burial-ground.

Written Works

Besides his sermons, Ward was also the author of:

- 'Account of the Writings, Religion, and Manners of the Hindoos,' Serampúr, 1811, 4 vols. 4to; 5th edit., abridged, Madras, 1863, 8vo.
- 'Farewell Letters in Britain and America on returning to Bengal in 1821,' London, 1821, 12mo; 2nd edit. 1821.
- 'Brief Memoir of Krishna-Pal, the first Hindu, in Bengal, who broke the Chain of the Cast by embracing the Gospel;' 2nd edit., London, 1823, 12mo.

He was also the author of several sonnets and short poems which were printed as an appendix to a memoir of him by Samuel Stennett. A portrait, engraved by R. Baker from a painting by Overton, is prefixed to the same work.

Hannah Marshman

Hannah Marshman (13 May 1767, Bristol-5 March 1847, Serampore, India) was a missionary.

She was the daughter of John Shepherd, a farmer, and his wife Rachel, and the granddaughter of John Clark, pastor of the Baptist church at Crockerton, Wiltshire.

Her mother died when she was eight. In 1791 Hannah Shepherd married Joshua Marshman. In 1794, the married young couple moved from Westbury Leigh in Wiltshire to Bristol, where they joined the Broadmead Baptist Church. The couple were to eventually have 12 children; of these only five lived longer than their mother.

Hannah is considered to be the first woman missionary in India.

Leaving for India

On 29 May 1799, Hannah and Joshua, and their two children set out from Portsmouth for India aboard the ship *Criterion*. Although there was a threat of a French naval attack the family landed safely at the Danish settlement of Serampore (a few miles north of Calcutta) on 13 October 1799. They had chosen to land here because the East India Company was still hostile to missionaries, they settled in the Danish colony at Serampore and were joined there by William Carey on 10 January 1800.

The Missionary Settlement

On 1 May 1800, Joshua and Hannah Marshman opened two boarding schools at Serampore. The two schools became the most popular in the Presidency and their son John Clark Marshman received his education from his parents. He was part of the growing mission family, eating at the communal table and joining with other children in mission life. As with all other mission family members he was encouraged to become a fluent Bengali speaker.

Meanwhile, the Missionary Society had begun sending more missionaries to India. The first to arrive was John Fountain, who arrived in Mudnabatty and began a teaching school. He was followed by William Ward, a printer; David Brunsdon, one of Marshman's students; and William Grant, who died three weeks after his arrival.

The spirit of the early community's unity was somewhat broken when some new missionaries arrived and who were not willing to live in the communal fashion that had developed. One missionary even went as far as to demand "...a separate house, stable and servants." There were also other differences, as the new missionaries found their seniors-particularly Joshua Marshman, to be somewhat dictatorial, assigning them duties which were not to their liking.

In 1800, when she first met them, Marshman was appalled by the neglect with the way in which William Carey looked after his four boys; aged 4, 7, 12 and 15, they were unmannered, undisciplined, and even uneducated. Carey had not spoiled, but rather simply ignored them. Marshman, her husband and their friend the printer William Ward, took the boys in tow. Together they shaped the boys as Carey pampered his botanical specimens, performed his many missionary tasks and journeyed into Calcutta to teach at Fort William College. They offered the boys structure, instruction and companionship. To their credit-and little to Carey's-all four boys went on to useful careers.

At one point, Hannah wrote about Carey, "The good man saw and lamented the evil but was too mild to apply an effectual remedy."

Serampore College and the Serampore Girls' School

On 5 July 1818, William Carey, Joshua Marshman and William

Ward issued a prospectus (written by Marshman) for a proposed new "College for the instruction of Asiatic, Christian, and other youth in Eastern literature and European science". Thus was born Serampore College-which still continues to this day.

Hannah herself went onto to found the local girls' school.

Death and Memorial

The following Inscription to her memory is placed in the Mission Chapel at Serampore: "In Memory of Hannah Marshman, widow of Joshua Marshman, D. D. the last surviving Member of the Mission Family at Serampore, she arrived in this settlement in October 1799, and opened a seminary to aid in the support of the Mission in May 1800, after having consecrated her life and property to the promotion of this sacred cause and exhibited an example of humble piety and energetic benevolence for forty-seven years. She died at the age of eighty, March 5, 1847."

The full text of her obituary in the Bengal Obituary can be found here.

Sanskrit College

Principals:

- Ramkamal Sen
- Pandit Ishwar Chandra Vidyasagar
- Mahamahopadhyay Pandit Mahesh Chandra Nyayratna Bhattacharya, C.I.E.
- Surendranath Dasgupta.

Sanskrit College is an Institute of Higher Education and one of the affiliated colleges of the University of Calcutta. Founded on 1st January 1824, Sanskrit College, is one of the oldest educational institutions in the subcontinent. A traditional college that specializes in the scholarship of Indian tradition, philosophy and religion, with undergraduate programs in philosophy, history and other humanities subjects, it is located on College Street (now renamed Bidhan Sarani) in central Kolkata. Its centrality is heightened by its proximity to Presidency College, Kolkata, which is located on the other side of the road. It was established during the Governor-Generalship of Lord Amherst, based on a recommendation by HT James Prinsep and Thomas Babington Macaulay among others.

Mahamahopadhyay Pandit Mahesh Chandra Nyayratna Bhattacharya, C.I.E., the eminent scholar of Sanskrit was the principal of the college for over 18 years. He was a Companion of the Indian Empress (C.I.E.), and a member of the Most Eminent Order of the Indian Empire.

He played a crucial role in Bengal's educational reformation. He revived the "Tol" system in Sanskrit education, and introduced titles or "Upadhi".

The institution rose to prominence during the principalship by Ishwar Chandra Vidyasagar in 1851, who admitted students from other than the Brahman caste. In particular the *tol* or traditional Indian training school model was incorporated as a department in the 1870s. In the pre-independence era, it was one of the finest seats of academic excellence in matters pertaining to Hinduism, eastern philosophy, ancient Indian history and ancient Indian languages like Pali and Prakrit. It is particularly well known for the contribution of its faculty and students in the social, cultural and religious transformation in nineteenth century Bengal in what came to be popularly regarded as the Bengal Renaissance. In terms of scholarship and intellectual output, it contributed hugely to enriching the knowledge of ancient Indian society and interpretation of ancient Indian texts.

In post-independence era, the college has not attracted meritorious students (like Krishna Kanta Handique) although it still houses some of India's leading scholars of traditional Hindu scholarship. Bimal Krishna Matilal was a teacher here from 1957 to 1962.

Medical College Kolkata

Medical College Kolkata (also known as Calcutta Medical College) was established 1835 as Medical College, Bengal in Kolkata, India as the first college of European medicine in Asia. The purpose of establishing this college was to train native youths irrespective of caste and creed in the principles and practices of medical science in accordance with the mode adopted in Europe. Medical College Bengal was established on 28 January 1835, soon followed by Madras Medical College [1] on 2 February 1835.

The college now imparts the degrees Bachelors of Medicine and Surgery (MBBS) after completion of 5 and half years of medical training. Also specialization degrees like MD and MS are given to post-graduate students. Besides there are nursing and several para-medical courses. The hospital associated with the college is one of the largest hospitals in Kolkata and houses several specialty and super-specialty departments.

History

Principals:

- MJ Bramley, 1835 – 1837
- David Hare, 1837 – 1841
- FJ Mouat, 1841 – 1851
- E Goodeve, 1851 – 1856
- WCB Eatwell, 1857 – 1859
- Normal Chevers, 1861 – 1873
- DB Smith, 1874 – 1880
- JM Coates, 1880 – 1890
- EA Birch, 1890 – 1893
- G Bomford, 1893 – 1905
- CP Lukis, 1905 – 1909
- FJ Drury, 1910 – 1912
- JT Calvert, 1912 – 1919
- BH Deare, 1919 – 1922
- AF Barnardo, 1922 – 1928
- AD Stewart, 1928 – 1930
- DP Goil, 1930 – 1932
- T Crawford Boyd, 1932 – 1939
- J.C.De, 1939 – 1941
- UP Basu, 1941 – 1945
- R Linton, 1945 – 1947
- AC Ukil, 1947 – 1948
- DC Chakraborty, 1948-1953
- MN Sarkar, 1953 – 1957
- SC Bose, 1957 – 1960
- KC Sarbadhikary, 1960 – 1968
- AK Duttagupta, 1968 – 1969
- D Roymahasay, 1969 – 1973

- BK Chakraborty, 1973 – 1977
- JB Mukherjee, 1977 – 1984
- RN Roy, 1984 – 1985
- KK Bhattacharya, 1985 – 1986
- AK Chandra, 1986 – 1987
- SK Biswas, 1988
- S Chowdhury, 1889 – 1991
- PB Pathak, 1991 – 1998
- SK Basu, 1998 – 2001
- SN Banerjee, 2001 – 2002
- Jayasree Mitra (Ghosh), 2002 – 2005
- Indrajit Ray, 2005-present.

The Planning

Calcutta Medical College was the first institution in India imparting a systematic education in western medicine. The British East India Company established the Indian Medical Service (IMS) as early as 1764 to look after Europeans in British India. IMS officers headed military and civilian hospitals in Bombay, Calcutta and Madras, and also accompanied the Company's ships and army. A utilitarian approach and the need to provide expert apothecaries, compounders, and dressers in different hospitals prompted the earliest official involvement with medical education in India. These subordinate assistants would help European doctors and surgeons who looked after the health of European civilians and military employees and also reduce the company's financial burdens by limiting the appointment of European doctors.

On 9 May 1822 the government laid down a plan for the instruction of up to twenty young Indians to fill the position of native doctors in the civil and military establishments of the Presidency of Bengal. The outcome was the establishment of "The Native Medical Institution"(NMI) in Calcutta (21 June 1822), where medical teaching was imparted in the vernacular. Treatises on anatomy, medicine, and surgery were translated from European languages for the benefit of the students. From 1826 onwards, classes on Unani and Ayurvedic medicine were held respectively at the Calcutta madrasa and the Sanskrit college. In 1827 John Tyler, an Orientalist and the first superintendent of the NMI started lectures on Mathematics and Anatomy at the Sanskrit College. In general, the medical education provided by the colonial state at this stage involved parallel instructions in western and indigenous medical systems. Translation of western medical texts was encouraged and though dissection was not performed, clinical experience was a must. Trainee medical students had to attend different hospitals and dispensaries. Successful native doctors were absorbed into government jobs.

Towards the end of 1833 a Committee was appointed by the government of William Bentinck in Bengal to report on the state of medical education and also to suggest whether teaching of indigenous system should be discontinued. The Committee consisted of Dr John Grant as President and J C C Sutherland, C E Trevelyan, Thomas Spens, Ram Comul Sen and M J Bramley as members. The Committee criticised the medical education imparted at the NMI for the inappropriate nature of its training and the examination system as well as for the absence of courses on practical anatomy. The Committee submitted a report on October 20, 1834, where the Anglicists' point of view finally prevailed over the Orientalists. The Committee recommended that the state found a medical college 'for the education of the natives'. The various branches of medical science cultivated in Europe should be taught in this college. The intending candidates should possess a reading and writing knowledge of the English language, similar knowledge of Bengali and Hindustani and a proficiency in Arithmetic. This recommendation, soon followed by Macaulay's minute and Bentinck's resolution, sealed the fate of the school for native doctors and medical classes at the two leading oriental institutions of Calcutta. The NMI was abolished and the medical classes at the Sanskrit College and at the Madrasa were discontinued by the government order of 28 January 1835.

The Beginning

The proposed new college, known as the Calcutta Medical College (CMC), which was established by an order of 20 February 1835 ushered in a new era in the history of medical education in India. Its stated purpose was to train native youths aged between 14 and 20 irrespective of caste and creed in the principles and practices of medical science in accordance with the mode adopted in Europe. This marked the end of official patronage of indigenous medical learning which in its turn evoked long-term reaction among the Indian practitioners of indigenous medicine and later the nationalists who strongly criticised the government for the withdrawal of patronage to the Indian system. Different sections of the Indian population responded differently to this newly founded system of education. Among the Hindus the Brahmins, Kayasthas, Vaidyas, were particularly enthusiastic about medical education.

The activities of the college started on 20 February 1835 with the process of admission of students. Twenty students were selected through a preliminary examination of about one hundred students. These boys had received their education either at the Hindu College, Hare School or the General Assembly's Institution. Twenty-nine more students had already been selected. All of these 49 students were to receive a monthly stipend of Rs 7 from the government, but it was to be raised gradually. The students were to remain in the College for a period of not less than 4 years and not more than 6 years. On completion of their studies the students had to sit for a final examination. Successful candidates were to receive from the President of the Committee of education certificates of qualifications to practise surgery and medicine. They could also enter public service where they would be called 'Native Doctors' receiving an initial pay of Rs 30 per month which would be raised to Rs 40 after 7 years and to 50 after 14 years of service.

The College was placed under the charge of a full-time Superintendent who was assisted by a European Assistant. The government was required to provide a suitable building, a library, anatomical materials and other objects necessary for the education of the students. For practical clinical experience the students had to visit the General Hospital, the Native Hospital, The Hon'ble Company's Dispensary, the dispensaries for the Poor and the Eye Infirmary. Dr MJ Bramley was appointed Superintendent and Dr HH Goodeve and WBO'Shaughnessy were appointed professors. Only one member of the staff of the Native Medical Institution, Madhusudan Gupta (an Ayurvedic practitioner trained in western medicine), was transferred to the new college.

The First Batches

The classes were started in an old house at the rear of the Hindu College. In May 1835, new premises were built on land donated by Mutty Lal Seal. These are the premises that the College has since occupied. During the first year of study, a series of lectures on anatomy and physiology was given.

O'Shaughnessy delivered an elementary course of lectures on Chemistry from January to March 1836 and a second course from April to September. During 1837 and 1838, the staff of the College was extended and enriched by the appointment of CC Eggerton as Professor of Surgery and Clinical Surgery, Nathaniel Wallich as Professor of Botany and R O'Shaughnessy as demonstrator of Anatomy.

The year 1836 was a landmark in the history of the growth of western medicine in British India since it witnessed the first dissection of a human corpse by Indian students. Madhusudan Gupta is often given the credit of being the first person in modern India to have dissected a human body. But many accounts state that Umacharan Set, Rajkrishna De, Dwarakanath Gupta and Nabin Chandra Mitra comprised the first batch of students to take part in dissection. They passed the first examination held on 30 October 1838 and were declared fit to practise medicine and surgery. They consequently represented the first group of Indians qualified in western medicine and given government appointments as Sub-Assistant Surgeons to the hospitals at Dhaka, Murshidabad, Patna and Chittagong.

Many luminaries of Calcutta including Dwarkanath Tagore and Ram Comul Sen enthusiastically supported medical education at the CMC by instituting scholarships and prizes for brilliant students. Four students of the College were sent to England through the financial help of Dwarakanath Tagore, Professor Goodeve and partly of the government.

Three of them, including Dwaraka Nath Bose, Bhola Nath Bose, and Gopal Chunder Seal passed the examination for MRCS (Member of the Royal College of Surgeons) in 1846 and returned to India to join the uncovenanted Medical Service. Soorjo Coomar Goodeve Chuckerbutty remained there, obtained the MD degree of the University College of London and became the first Indian to pass the examination for the Indian Medical Service and join the covenanted Medical Service. He also became a distinguished professor of the Medical College holding the Chair of Materia Medica from 1864 till his death in 1874.

Changes

In 1842, a Council of Education, which introduced many changes in the curriculum and system of examinations, replaced the Committee of Public Instruction. The new courses of study, based on the advice of the Royal College of Surgeons in London, were introduced in 1844, and were ultimately recognised by them, by the London University and the Society of Apothecaries in 1846. After the foundation of the university of Calcutta in 1857 and its faculty of medicine for the award of medical degrees, the courses of study were revised to a certain extent. The University conferred three medical degrees, Licentiate in Medicine and Surgery (LMS), Bachelor in Medicine (MB), and Doctor of Medicine (MD).

Other changes brought about in the College aimed at fulfilling the needs of the state to supply an increased number of medical personnel for employment in the army and for combating epidemic diseases among the civilians. The government order of August 1839 instituted medical classes through the medium of Urdu and Hindustani. Lessons were imparted in Anatomy, Materia Medica, Medicine and Surgery. Dissections and teaching methods followed western principles. Fifty students were selected initially. They received a monthly allowance of Rs 5 each and had to undergo clinical training by discharging hospital duties at the Medical College Hospital, founded in 1838. In 1838, a large female (lying in) hospital started functioning under the benevolence of Mutty Lal Seal. This was followed by the opening of a large hospital in 1853, designed to accommodate 350 patients. Other hospitals were: the Eden Hospital (1881-82), the Ezra Hospital (1887), the Shama Charan Laha Eye Hospital (1891) and the Prince of Wales Surgical Block, opened in March 1911.

Before 1857 the number of students taking admission in the Maternity class fluctuated between 28 and 69. After 1857 the number increased slowly. At the end of their period of study the students were examined in anatomy, materia medica, surgery and medicine for the diploma of Native Doctor.

To meet the rising demand for native doctors, the Government introduced a Bengali class at the Calcutta Medical College in 1851. Proficiency in Bengali was an essential prerequisite for admission to this class. The theoretical and practical courses were almost the same as in the Hindustani class. 21 students admitted in this class were examined in 1853. Qualified students filled the ranks of the subordinate medical services as Hospital Apprentices or Vernacular Licentiates in Medicine and Surgery (VLMS) or found employment under Deputy Magistrates attached to Charitable Dispensaries and Jail Hospitals. In 1856-57, the class had 88 students and the number went on increasing until it touched the figure of 635 in 1872. The students mostly belonged to the Brahmin, Kayastha and Vaidya castes.

In 1864, the Bengali class was divided into two sections: The Native Apothecary section, which trained students for government employment, and the Vernacular Licentiate section which gave instructions in medicine and surgery in order to enable the students to practise among the less affluent sections of Indians. In 1873, both these classes were transferred to a new school called the Sealdah Medical School or the Campbell Medical School. The Hindu bhadralok class, Europeans and Eurasians dominated the student population. Although during 1880-1890 there was a small increase in the number of Muslim students, their proportion was very small.

A resolution of 29 June 1883 allowed the admission of women into the CMC after doing FA. Kadambini Ganguly, a Bengali Brahmo became the first woman admitted to the CMC. In 1884 the government offered scholarships of Rs 20 per month to all female students. Bidhu Mukhi Bose and Virginia Mary Mitter received these scholarships and became the first Indian women to graduate during 1888-89.

Growth

The growth of the CMC as reflected in the number of students presents an interesting pattern. A period of modest rise in the number of students was followed by rapid increase from 1891-92 till 1901-02, and then a fall in 1906-07, exactly during the period of the turmoil of the swadeshi movement in Bengal. Thereafter the increase continued unabated. The number rose from 612 in 1911-12 to 1030 in 1921-22. From the mid-1920s there was a downward trend which was reversed in the thirties.

An important change occurred in 1906 when the Calcutta University decided to discontinue the LMS examination held since 1861 and henceforth confer only the degrees of MB and MD. The last batch of LMS students was examined in 1911.

During the 1930s, the system of reservation of seats was introduced, based on the relative population of different classes of people. Further it was decided that of the 100 students taken, 5 were to be female candidates. Most of the female students belonged to the Anglo-Indian, Christian, Brahmo or Parsi communities. In 1940 the duration of study was reduced from 6 to 5 years, to be followed by a six-month period of Pre-Registration Clinical Assistantship. The year 1940 also saw the conversion of the Students' Club of the CMC into the Students' Union.

Presidency College, Kolkata

Presidency College, Kolkata is a co-founding, semi-autonomous, arts and sciences çollege affiliated to the University of Calcutta. Initially it was called Hindu College. It is the oldest college in India, and was set up in 1817. It continues to be one of the most eminent educational institutions in the Indian subcontinent. It has been consistently rated, since rating of Indian colleges was started, as one of the top ten colleges of the country: in 2002 it was ranked number one by the weekly news magazine *India Today*. It offers undergraduate and postgraduate degrees as well as Ph.D. degrees in the natural sciences, humanities and the social sciences.

History

Principals:

- J.Kerr, 1842-1848
- D.L. Richardson, 1848-1849
- E.Lodge, 1849-1852
- J.Sutcliff, M.A., 1852-1856
- Leonidas Clint, 1856-1857 (acting)
- E.Lodge, 1857-1858 (acting)
- J.Sutcliffe, M.A., 1858-1863
- W.Grapel, 1863-1864 (acting)
- J.Sutcliffe, M.A., 1864-1875
- H.Woodrow, 1875 (acting)
- C.H.Tawney, 1875 (acting)
- J.Sutcliffe, M.A., 1875
- Alefred Croft, 1876 (acting)

- C.H.Tawney, 1876-1881
- G.Bellet, 1881-1882
- John Elliot, 1882-1883
- Alexander Pedler, 1883 (acting)
- John Elliot, 1883 (acting)
- G.Bellet, 1883
- John Elliot, 1884-1885 (acting)
- C.H.Tawney, 1885
- W.Griffiths, 1885-1886 (acting)
- C.H.Tawney, 1886-1887
- Alexander Pedler, 1887 (acting)
- C.H.Tawney, 1887
- Alexander Pedler, 1887-1889 (acting)
- C.H.Tawney, 1889
- Alexander Pedler, 1889 (acting)
- F.J.Rowe, 1889 (acting)
- C.H.Tawney, 1889
- W.Griffiths, 1892-1896
- Alexander Pedler, 1896-1897
- J.H.Gilliland, 1897 (acting)
- F.J.Rowe, 1897-1898 (acting)
- J.H.Gilliland, 1898 (acting)
- F.J.Rowe, 1898 (acting)
- William Booth, 1898 (acting)
- A.Clarke Edwards, 1899-1900 (acting)
- A.Clark Edwards, 1900-1902
- P.K.Roy, 1902 (acting)
- A. Clarke Edwards, 1902-1903
- P.K.Roy, 1903 (acting)
- A.Clarke Edwards, 1903
- M.G.D.Prothero, 1904-1905 (acting)
- P.K.Roy, 1905-1906 (acting)
- Alexander Macdonnell, 1906
- A.Clarke Edwards, 1906-1907

- Henry Rosher James, 1907-1909
- Hugh Melville Percival, 1909 (acting)
- Henry Rosher James, 1909-1911
- C.W.Peake, 1911-1912 (acting)
- Henry Rosher James, 1912-1916
- W.C.Wordsworth, 1916-1917
- John Rothney Barrow, 1917-1924 (acting)
- W.C.Wordsworth, 1924
- H.E.Stapleton, 1924-1925 (acting)
- H.E.Stapleton, 1925-1926
- T.S.Sterling, 1926-1927 (acting)
- H.E.Stapleton, 1927-1928
- R.B.Ramsbotham, 1928-1929
- John Rothney Barrow, 1929-1930
- Jahangir C. Coyajee, 1930-1931
- Bhupatimohan Sen, 1931-1934 (acting)
- Bhupatimohan Sen, 1934-1936
- P.C.Mahalanobis, 1936 (acting)
- Bhupatimohan Sen, 1936-1942
- P.C.Mahalanobis, 1942 (acting)
- Bhupatimohan Sen, 1942-1943
- Apurbakumar Chanda, 1943
- Jyotirmoy Ghosh, 1943-1944 (acting)
- Apurbakumar Chanda, 1944
- P.C.Mahalanobis, 1945-1946 (acting)
- P.C.Mahalanobis, 1946-1947
- Muhammad Qudrut-i-Khuda, 1947 (acting)
- P.C.Mahalanobis, 1947
- Jogischandra Sinha, 1947 (acting)
- P.C.Mahalanobis, 1948
- Jyotirmoy Ghosh, 1948-1950
- J.C.Sengupta, 1950 (acting)
- Jyotirmoy Ghosh, 1950-1951
- J.C.Sengupta, 1951-1956

- F.J.Friend-Pereira, 1956-1958
- Sanat Kumar Basu, 1958-1967
- Rajendralal Sengupta, 1967-1969
- Samerendranath Ghoshal, 1969-1970
- Sudhir Chandra Shome, 1970
- Pratul Chandra Mukherjee, 1970-1975
- Sudhir Chandra Shome, 1975-1976
- Pratul Chandra Mukherjee, 1976-1979
- Bijoy Shankar Basak, 1979-1982
- Achinta Kumar Mukherjee, 1982-1986
- Sunil Kumar Rai Chaudhuri, 1986-1991
- Amal Kumar Mukhopadhyay, 1991-1997
- Nitai Charan Mukherjee, 1997-2000
- Amitabha Chatterjee, 2001-2005
- Mamata Ray, 2005-2008
- Sanjib Ghosh, 2008-present.

Origin

With the creation of the Supreme Court of Calcutta in 1773 many Hindus of Bengal showed eagerness to learn the English language. David Hare, in collaboration with Raja Radhakanta Deb had already taken steps introduce English education in Bengal. Babu Buddinath Mukherjee advanced the introduction of English as a medium of instruction further by enlisting the support of Sir Edward Hyde East, Chief Justice of the Supreme Court who called a meeting of 'European and Hindu Gentlemen' in his house in May 1816. The purpose of the meeting was to "discuss the proposal to establish an institution for giving a liberal education to the children of the members of the Hindu Community". The proposal was received with unanimous approbation and a donation of over Rs. 100, 000 was promised for the setting up of the new college. Raja Ram Mohan Roy showed full sympathy for the scheme but chose not to come out in support of the proposal publicly for fear of "alarming the prejudices of his orthodox countrymen and thus marring the whole idea".

The College was formally opened on Monday, January 20, 1817 with 20 'scholars'. The foundation committee of the college, which oversaw its establishment, was headed by Raja Rammohan

Roy. The control of the institution was vested in a body of two Governors and four Directors. The first Governors of the college were Maharaja Tejchandra Bahadur of Burdwan and Babu Gopee Mohan Thakoor. The first Directors were Babu Gopeemohan Deb of Sobhabazar, Babu Joykissen Sinha, Babu Radha Madhab Banerjee and Babu Gunganarain Doss. Babu Buddinath Mukherjee was appointed as the first Secretary of the college. The newly established college mostly admitted Hindu students from affluent and progressive families, but also admitted non-Hindu students such as Muslims, Jews, Christians and Buddhists.

At first the classes were held in a house belonging to Gorachand Bysack of Garanhatta (later renamed 304, Chitpore Road), which was rented by the college. In January 1818 the college moved to 'Feringhi Kamal Bose's house' which was located nearby in Chitpore. From Chitpore, the college moved to Bowbazar and later to the building that now houses the Sanskrit College on College Street.

Early 19th Century

The increasing realization of the value of western education made the college a coveted destination for scholars from all over the subcontinent. Pupils came from Behar, especially Patna, Vizagapatnam and Assam. By 1828 enrolment of students steeply rose to 400. The obvious question, that then arose, was whether it would not be wiser for the Government of Bengal to establish a new 'English College' open to all classes and community of students. The Committee of Managers of Hindu College had soon after the inception of the college become dependent on government subsidy, due to serious shortage of funds. The government had began to play a greater role in the administration of the College.

By the middle of the nineteenth century the college had outgrown the plans made by its founders. Not only did it attract an ever-increasing number of scholars from the province and the rest of the Bengal Presidency, but it had also introduced courses in Law, Drawing, and Engineering, which catered to the needs of all classes of students-Hindus as well as non-Hindus. The government had also to consider whether this growing institution, spending a good deal of public money, could be retained as a non-governmental institution, particularly when Calcutta had no general college managed exclusively by the Council of Education.

When other towns in Bengal had government colleges, it was felt in official and non-official circles that Calcutta should also have one.

From Hindu College to Presidency College

The proposal to set up a new college called the Calcutta College, or the Metropolitan College, open to students from all communities had already been mooted, but this would have meant greater financial liability for the government, which would also have to provide it with a competent faculty. A viable alternative seemed to be the conversion of Hindu College into a general institution open to all communities, managed by the government. On 21 October, 1853, Lord Dalhousie, the Governor of Bengal, suggested that

> *"a new general college should be established at Calcutta by the government and designated "The Presidency College".. the College should be open to all youths of every caste, class or creed."*

The new name, 'Presidency', referred to the Bengal Presidency, which was the local administrative unit of British India. Accordingly, the Committee of Management for Hindu College met for the last time on 11 January, 1854. The Court of Directors renamed the College as Presidency College. The College started functioning on 15 June, 1855. The 'scholars' of the College Department of Hindu College were transferred to Presidency College and 101 new students were freshly admitted. Of these 101 pupils, two were Muslims, while the rest were Hindus.

Initially, the Civil Engineering College and Medical College, that were located nearby, were associated with Presidency College. But with the formation of the University of Calcutta, also located close by, the Council of Education shelved plans for allowing the expansion of the these three premier institutions into a full fledged university. The college was formally placed under the control of the University of Calcutta in 1857.

Expansion of Presidency

The college continued to grow rapidly after its renaming and relocation. In 1856, it had 132 students on its rolls. 94 students were in the General Branch and 38 students were in the Legal Branch. Of them, 82 students had paid tuition fees, 43 were scholarship holders, and 7 enjoyed free studentships. The Legal Branch was given a measure of autonomy: its students were subject to examination by held by the branch itself. Two years later Bankimchandra Chattopadhyay, a student of the Law Department earned the distinction of being one of the first two graduates in Arts of the University of Calcutta. The college became an institution preparing candidates for the BA examination under the aegis of Calcutta University. At the first Entrance Examination, held in 1857, it sent 23 students. The MA degree was conferred for the first time on six students of this college in 1863.

The College authorities were faced with space shortage even after the expansion of the Sanskrit College building. The process for acquisition of land for building a separate building and grounds started in September 1865 and in 1870 the principal of the college submitted a plan for the construction of a new building on the premises where it is presently located. The new building was opened on March 31, 1874 by the then Lieutenant–Governor Sir George Campbell in the presence of His Excellency, the Viceroy of India. The finishing touch was given by Babu Nuffer Chandra Pal Chaudhuri, who provided it with a turret clock, at a cost of nearly Rs. 5000 soon after the new building's inauguration. Professor J. Sutcliffe was the principal of the college when the new building was opened.

The First Arts or F.A. Examination was introduced in 1861. The first candidate to qualify in this examination from the college was Gooroodas Banerji, who later became the first Indian Vice-Chancellor of Calcutta University. The ever-increasing rolls of the college demonstrated the keen interest shown by students from all over the Bengal Presidency. The prestigious award of Gilchrist Scholarship for pursuance of further studies in England went to students of this college for four successive years since its introduction in 1868. Between 1868 and 1900, 25 students of the college were awarded the Premchand Roychand studentship, the highest honour for academic excellence awarded by Calcutta University. The college soon expanded its premises and the present edifice was officially opened by the Lieutenant Governor on 31 March, 1874 in the presence of the Viceroy.

The construction of the new building was beneficial for the science departments which now had adequate space for holding classes and carrying out laboratory work. The chemistry department introduced practical classes in the new building in 1875. Engineering classes, until then held at the college, were discontinued in 1880 when the Shibpur Engineering College was set up. In order to augment the Faculty of Science, a professorship in Geology was instituted in 1892. The Department of Biology was founded eight years later and Subodh Chandra Mahalanabish was made a professor there. The last two decades of the nineteenth century saw the appointment of distinguished scholars to teaching positions in the college. For instance, H.M.Percival joined in 1880, Bipinvihary Gupta in 1883, Jagadish Chandra Bose in 1885, Prafulla Chandra Ray in 1889, and Manmohan Ghosh in 1896.

In 1897 the colleges admitted female students for the first time.

The Baker Laboratory, named after Edward Norman Baker, the then Lieutenant Governor of Bengal, was formally opened on 20 January, 1913 and the Departments of Physics, Physiology, Botany and Geology were transferred to the new establishment. One of the biggest rooms in the Baker Laboratory accommodated the science library (the Peake Library, named after Professor C.W. Peake). Commerce classes were started in 1903.

Meanwhile in 1902, Dr. P.K.Roy became the first Indian to take over as principal (*offtg.*) of the college. He served two more terms as the principal (again in officiating capacity) in 1903 and from 1905-6. Bhupatimohan Sen became the first Indian full-time principal of the college from 1934-6.

The outbreak of World War I in 1914 interrupted plans for the building of an additional hostel and other facilities but the college continued to cross important milestones in the advancement of teaching and higher learning. New dimensions were added to the college with the reorganisation of the college library in 1908 and the introduction of a College Union in 1914. The 1920s continued to see eminent teachers such as Professor Wordsworth, Professor Sterling, Professor Home and Dr. Harrison increase the reputation of the college.

Presidency During the Indian Freedom Struggle

During the Non-Cooperation Movement and the Civil Disobedience Movement J.R.Barrow was the principal of the college. He set the highest standards of discipline and academic excellence, but also meted out punitive action to students participating in the National Movement. His objective, of increasing the academic standards of the college and its reputation, however, was never in doubt, and he earned the deep respect and appreciation of teachers as well as students. This was the period when the Oaten Affair, in which Subhas Chandra Bose, then a student of the college, insulted by Professor Oaten, happened. Bose, responding angrily to a racial insult made by Oaten, had pushed the professor down the main building's staircase.

From the early 1930s, Indian principals headed the college, though the Education Department formally retained the services of British officers until 1947. From the 1920s to the end of the 1940s the college remained a centre of nationalist activities. Throughout this period the college continued to enjoy great deal of popularity and prestige in *bhadralok* society. Phani Bhushan Chakrabarty, a former student of the college who later became the first Indian Chief Justice of the Calcutta High Court wrote a short verse in later years explaining the awe with which the college was held by the educated middle classes in Bengal: *Prathom jakhon collegey elam/Bollam bahabaharey/Aschi hotey Hindu Hare/Koriney care kaharey* (When I first came to college,/I said, "Oh! Wow,/Have come from Hindu-Hare,/Don't care for the high-brow).

Presidency after Independence

The college's continued presence in Bengal's higher education was evident in its predominance as an undergraduate and postgraduate institution even at the time of India's independence. Before 1947 and soon after, especially in the 1950s the college was still the *numero uno* of Indian education. Anybody who was somebody in India *had* to be a student of this college. In 1956 the centenary celebrations of the college were organised. The building in which the economics, political science and sociology departments as well as the Derozio Hall are presently located was built during the centenary celebrations under the stewardship of the then principal, Professor J.C. Sengupta.

In the 1950s, 1960s and 1970s the college became a centre of leftist and then far-left politics. Through the 1970s and 1980s the college fought off repeated attempts to control it from outside, especially by the government as well as dominant political parties. In 1972 an unsigned article was released by members of the college's faculty suggesting that the college should be given full university status. In 2007 the college was granted partial autonomy by the state government. On 16 December 2009 the state government tabled a Bill, entitled the Presidency University Act, 2009, in the West Bengal Legislative Assembly which will grant the college full university status. Once the college becomes a full university it will be renamed Presidency University.

Other changes that were brought to the college in this period includes the appointment of Mamata Roy as the first woman principal of the college in 2005.

Presidency in Film and Fiction

The college has been depicted in both Bengali fiction and films. Sunil Gangopadhyay's novel *Shei Samaye* (*Those Days*) mentions this college in the context of nineteenth century Bengali society. The Bollywood blockbuster *Yuva* starring Ajay Devgan, Abhishek Bachchan and Rani Mukherjee shows this college. It is the college where Devgan, called Michael in the movie, is a student leader.

Department of Economics

It is one the most illustrious departments of the college. A student when he/she joins this department is "Welcomed into a Brotherhood", one no less strong than "Blood Ties". Many former students and teachers of this department are legendary. Some of them are: Abhijit Banerjee, Amartya Sen, Amit Bhaduri, Amitava Bose, Amiya Kumar Bagchi, Anindya Sen, Anup K. Sinha, Ashok Lahiri, Asim Dasgupta, Avirup Sarkar, Badal Mukherjee, Basubeb Biswas, Bhabotosh Dutta, Bhaskar Dutta, Bibek Debroy, Bimal Jalan, Debraj Ray, Dhiresh Bhattacharya, Dilip Mukherjee, Dipankar Dasgupta, Dipak Banerjee, Kalyan Chaterjee, Kalyan Sanyal, Kunal Sengupta, Maitreesh Ghatak, Mihir Rakshit, Mukul Majumdar, Prabal Roychowdhuri, Pranab Bardhan, Ratan Lal Basu, Sanjit Bose, Soumen Sikdar, Subhasis Gangopadhyay, Sugata Marjit, Sukhamoy Chakravarty, Sujoy Mookerjee, Tapan Mitra, Tapas Majumdar, Udayan Mukherjee. The Department has been organising "Professor Dipak Banerjee Memorial Lecture" since 2007.

Department of English

It is one of the most popular and well known departments of the college. It boasts of students and teachers such as Peary Charan

Sarkar, Taraknath Sen, Subodh Chandra Sengupta and Amal Bhattacharya, all of whom studied and taught here from the first half to the middle of the twentieth century. Other equally popular and erudite students and teachers of this department in the second half of the twentieth century include Arun Kumar Dasgupta, Sukanta Chaudhuri, Supriya Chaudhuri, Kajal Sengupta and Pralay Kumar Deb.

Department of History

This is one of the most notable departments of the college. Some of its eminent students and teachers in the first half of the twentieth century include Hem Chandra Raychaudhuri, Kiran Shankar Ray, Kuruvilla Zachariah, Susobhan Sarkar, Hirendranath Mukherjee, Amalesh Tripathi, Pratap Chandra Chunder, Pratap Chandra Sen and Tapan Raychaudhuri. Eminent students and teachers of the department in the second half of the twentieth century include Mohit Sen, Sipra Sarkar, Ashin Dasgupta, Hirendranath Chakrabarty, Parthasarathi Gupta, Benoy Bhushan Chaudhuri, Barun De, Nitish Sengupta, Sumit Sarkar, Rajat Kanta Ray and Tanika Sarkar. The department has a Seminar Library of its own with a seminar secretary and a seminar librarian elected by the students of the department from amongst themselves. In 1990, a lecture series entitled P.C. Sen Memorial Lecture, named after Pratap Chandra Sen, another former student of the department, was started with an endowment given by the members of his family. In 2004, Gopal Krishna Gandhi, who had just become the Governor of West Bengal, attended a class taken by Rajat Kanta Ray.

Department of Law

The college until the beginning of the twentieth century had a separate Department of Law. This was not one of its original departments, but as mentioned above it had been started soon after the inception of Hindu College. Two of its more prominent students were Bankim Chandra Chatterjee and HH Maharaja Nripendra Narayan Bhup Bahadur of Coochbehar.

Department of Physics

This department is one of the most well known departments of the college. The department has had as students or as teachers several eminent people, including Sir Jagadish Chandr Bose,

Satyendra Nath Bose, Meghnad Saha, Amal Kumar Raychaudhuri, Bikash Sinha, Prasad Ranjan Ray and Ashoke Sen. The Baker Laboratory and the Physics Lecture Theatre, in the majestic new building built in 1913 are two of the most famous features of the college. Since 2004 the department started an autonomous post-graduate course in physics recognised by Calcutta University. Earlier, the department's course in post graduate studies was carried out at the University College of Science and Technology of Calcutta University in Rajabazar. On 27 February, 2009, the department organized a one-day symposium on the 150th birth anniversary of Sir J.C. Bose.

Department of Physiology

This department was founded in 1900. The first phase of the development of this department which coincided with the founding of physiology as a discipline in India took place between 1900 and 1913. Subodh Chandra Mahalanobis returned to India from England in 1900 and joined the Bengal Education Service. He was posted at Presidency College as the Head of the Department of Biology, which was at that time composed of Human Physiology and Botany, in the same year. In 1902, study of Human Physiology started as a separate course at this college, which was officially recognized in 1903 by the University of Calcutta. On the Founders' Day, i.e. 20 January, in 1913, the new building for science subjects, later named as Baker Laboratories, was formally inaugurated and the Department of Human Physiology was shifted to the second floor of the new building.

In 1915, the Calcutta University started the M.Sc. in Human Physiology in this department. In 1923, during the tenure of Dr. N.M.Basu as Head of the Department, E. H. Sterling visited this department. In 1939, Dr. Syama Prasad Mookerjee, as Vice-Chancellor of Calcutta University, convened a historic meeting and passed two important resolutions in favour of this department: (a) PG teaching in Physiology at Presidency College should continue as before; and (b) the university should not open Honours course in Physiology as this was running at its best at Presidency College. In 1944, Sir A.V. Hill visited the department. From 1947 to 1959, the department was guided under the able stewardship of Prof. Sachchidananda Banerjee, the first D.Sc. in Physiology from Calcutta University.

In 1960, Dr. Achintya Kumar Mukherjee joined as Professor and Head of Department. Dr. Haripada Chattopadhyay worked as an interim Head of Department from 1984-1987. In 1988, Dr. Chandan Mitra joined as Professor and Head of Department. In 2001, the department celebrated 100 years of UG teaching. The Centenary Postgraduate Wing was inaugurated during that celebration and in the same year the department was affiliated for independent postgraduate teaching by Calcutta University. In 2004, the department was given full academic autonomy for postgraduate teaching. The department organized The XVIII Annual Conference of the Physiological Society of India between 8-10 December, 2006.

Department of Political Science

This department emerged out of the Department of Economics and is in the early twenty-first century one of the finest departments of Political Science in India. A creation of the second half of the twentieth century, it already boasts of an alumus which is world famous. Among its ex-students are Partha Chatterjee and Sudipta Kaviraj, both extremely well known in Indian political studies. Yet another student was Amal Mukhopadhyaya, who was a Professor and Head of this department and also one of the better known Principals of the college at the time of its 175th birth anniversary.

Department of Statistics

Although the Department of Statistics is small in size and relatively young it was at one time the premier statistics department in the country & is still very well known. Originally it was started as a Statistical Laboratory by Prasanta Chandra Mahalanobis. Later, it housed the ISI before the that institute moved to Baranagar. Through the second half of the twentieth century, the department grew in stature under the tutelage of Professor Bhattacharya and Professor Atindra Mohan Gun. Some of its famous alumni include Jayanta K. Ghosh, Pranab K. Sen, Malay Ghosh, and Bani Kumar Mallick, among others.

Department of Zoology

It is one of the best departments in the college with a rich museum and well equipped laboratories. It has both postgraduate and undergraduate courses. Research fellows are also recruited through various examinations. The department was built by Sivatosh Mookerjee. The present Head of Department is Trilochan

Midya. The department has a good teacher-student ratio. Well-equipped laboratories, rich faculties and educational excellence are the three main characteristics of this department. It has a Central Computer Room with ultra-modern servers, a rich-with-books Seminar Library and an state of the art laboratory for modern researches. All forms of modern biochemical and biotechnological researches can be done in these laboratories.

Institutions that were Started in Presidency

This college, being the oldest educational institution in the country, boasts of a number of prestigious institutions of primary, secondary and higher learning that were started under its aegis. The Hindu School was the college's school when it was established, although it is now independent.

The Hare School has been from the middle of the nineteenth century located inside the premises of the college and has been traditionally associated with the college. Its students used to complete their higher education in the college in the nineteenth and early twentieth centuries. The Bengal Engineering and Science University, Shibpur was founded in this college and was a department of the college frm 1865 to 1879. The Indian Statistical Institute, Calcutta was founded in the Statistical Laboratory of this college in 1931.

Administration

The college is administered on a daily basis by a principal, a burser, a deputy controller of examinations and the respective heads of departments. It offers several scholarships to meritorious students, such as B.C.Law Free Studentship (185), Book Prizes (50), Cash Prizes (33), FAEA Scholarships (5), Hindi Scholarship (6), Hostel Stipend (14), Lump Grant (9), Medals (19), National Scholarship (14), Presidency College Graduate Scholarships (6), T.S.Sterling Onetime Grant (17), T.S.Sterling Scholarships (16).

Hostel Facilities

The college has two halls of residence, one each for boys and girls. The boys hostel is the famous Eden Hindu Hostel, which was started in 1886. It stands on Peary Charan Sarkar Street, which separates the college's premises to the south from the hostel, which is next to the central premises of the University of Calcutta, called the Ashutosh Shiksha Prangan, that includes the Ashutosh

Building and Darbhanga Building. After 1990, the college administration also built a girls' hostel in Salt Lake in Calcutta.

Extra-Curricular Activities

Students' Union: The Students' Union room is located behind the main building. The Union has been active since the first half of the twentieth century. It is run by a President and a General Secretary. It plays a constructive role in the day-to-day running of the students' affairs. It is pertinent to note that the Union has always been controlled by elected students' groups that seek to challenge and question policies framed and actions taken by the establishment, both inside and outside the college, especially at the state level. In the first decade after independence, when the college was starting off as a centre of excellence, wholly managed by Indians, and more specifically by Bengalis, the Union was firmly in the hands of forces not always friendly towards the Students Federation (SF). From the sixties until the end of the eighties, the Union was controlled by the Marxist-Leninists. After a brief period of students' apathy and indifference towards politics in the late eighties, the Union, in 1989, came under the control of a loosely formed group called the Independent Consolidation (IC), covertly formed by an assortment of progressive democratic elements, owing allegiance to left-of-centre and Marxist-Leninist parties which are hostile to the Students Federation of India (SFI). Barring a brief spell of a few years at the end of the last century and the beginning of this century, the IC has kept control of the student body. The Union is now under the control of the SFI, which returned to power in 2009.

Sports

The college has a long history of excellence in sports, especially in cricket and lawn tennis. Until date it has a strong cricket team. Until the mid-1950s the college used to have a lawn tennis court to the west of the premises, which was later replaced by the new building housing the economics, political science and sociology departments as well the college's auditorium, Derozio Hall. Until the mid-twentieth century the college's sporting facilties were managed and maintained by a Sports Secretary elected from the student body. There is a table tennis board in the Junior Common Room of the college on the ground floor and a badminton court in a room close to the Student's Union Room.

The college has a long association with Mohan Bagan AC, the first Bengali football club, whose history is closely linked to the rise of the Indian national movement. One of the preliminary matches played by Mohan Bagan was against Eden Hindu Hostel's team. Some students of the college who had joined this club earlier invited Professor F.J. Row, a grammatologist, to visit the club ground, then at Mohan Bagan Villa, on the day it was founded, i.e. 15 August 1889. At this occasion Row suggested that the Club could be called 'Athletic', due to its excellent infrustructural facilities.

Cultural Events

Presidency has an annual festival organised by the students union called the 'Milieu' which hosts events in which students of all other colleges and universities of West Bengal participate. The events of the festival comprise of a wide variety of activities such as outdoor sports and literary events including debates and quizzes. The college always had a great tradition of debates. Amartya Sen's first lecture entitled 'Bigyaponer Arthoniti' ('The Economics of Advertisement') was delivered at a debate organised by the Student's Union soon after he joined the college in 1951.

Canteen

The college also has a students' canteen situated at the back of the main building, beyond the Students' Union room and next to the badminton Court. In the 1940s the college's canteen was called "Ray Babur Canteen". A decade later in the 1950s the students of the college frequently visited the neighbouring Coffee House, on the lane that is now called Bankim Chatterjee Street, which soon became a hub of both academic and political activities and discussions and is now famous for its debates.

Several eminent academics of the second half of the twentieth century, many of whom joined the government and/or have or still are teaching in the finest world universities were regulars at the Coffee House. Later, in the last quarter of the twentieth century, the students of the college began to return to the college's canteen, which has been run by Pramodda since the 1980s and is now called "Pramoddar Canteen". The canteen remains the most popular meeting place for the students of the college. The Coffee House retains its popularity amongst Presidencians.

Building and Grounds

The main building, housing the English, History, Geography, Bengali and Philosophy Departments of the college, which also has a clock tower, was built in the nineteenth century and is representative of the architecture of the middle of that century. It has a quadrangle in the middle, next to the central library of the college which is located on the ground floor. The science building, which has the Physics Lecture Theatre in it, is situated to the south of the college premises and opens out on to Peary Charan Sarkar Street. It was built in 1913. The new building housing the Economics, Political Science and Sociology Departments and the Derozio Hall was built in 1956, while the newest building built to the west of the main building for the holding of post-graduate classes, was built in 1990.

Alumni Association

The college has an active Alumni Association. It works from within the main building of the college. Some of the eminent past Presidents of the Association were Radhabinod Pal and Pratap Chandra Chunder. Dr. Shyamaprasad Mookherjee was a past Vice President of the Association. The Association publishes an yearly journal entitled the 'Autumn Annual'. Professor Subodh Chandra Sengupta was the longest serving editor-in-chief of the journal.

Notable Alumni

The former students of this college are still the best and the brightest in India and abroad. Until the middle of the twentieth century this college was widely considered to be the very best in higher education in the country. In the second half of the twentieth century it can still claim to be among the top five colleges in the country and is clearly still the most famous of all the Indian colleges. That the college continues to be the alma mater of eminent professionals, including senior politicians and industrialists, who are still working gives evidence of its relevance today and also shows that it is still at the height of its powers. Students of this college have continued to be awarded all the major scholarships, such as the Rhodes Scholarship, the Commonwealth Scholarship, Inlaks Scholarship, Radhakrishnan Scholarship and Government of India and State Scholarship to study in either Oxford or Cambridge.

The college started with the expressed objective of encouraging boys of landed and aristocratic families of the Bengal Presidency to join it, but has also traditionally attracted extremely meritorious students from district schools and colleges to it since the nineteenth century. It has the distinction of being the college where Academy Award winner Satyajit Ray and the Nobel Laureate Professor Amartya Sen studied. Rabindranath Tagore was admitted into the college, but spent only one day there.

In politics, it has amongst its students, some of the biggest names of the Indian national movement, such as five Presidents of the Indian National Congress, including Surendranath Banerjea, Romesh Chandra Dutt, Bhupendra Nath Bose, Lord Satyendra Prasanno Sinha and Netaji Subhas Chandra Bose. The first President of India, Dr. Rajendra Prasad studied in this college. The Speaker of the Indian Lok Sabha, Somnath Chatterjee was a student of this college. The first President of Bangladesh, Abu Sayeed Chowdhury was also a student of this college. It has had one Governor of an Indian state, Sir Chandeshwar Prasad Narayan Singh, as its student also. Since elections were first held in Indian provinces in 1937, and after independence, it has had three Prime Ministers, one each of Pakistan, Bengal and Assam, five Chief Ministers of West Bengal and one Chief Minister of Assam as its former students. They are the first Prime Minister of Pakistan, Mohammad Ali Bogra, first Prime Minister of Bengal, A.K. Fazlul Huq, the first Prime Minister of Assam, Sir Saiyid Mohammed Saadullah, the first and second Chief Ministers of West Bengal, Prafulla Chandra Ghosh and Dr. Bidhan Chandra Ray, later Chief Ministers of the same state, Shri Siddhartha Shankar Ray, Shri Jyoti Basu and Shri Buddhadeb Bhattacharya and the sixth Chief Minister of Assam, Shri Bishnu Ram Medhi. The first Deputy Chief Minister of Bihar, Anugrah Narayan Sinha was a student of this college. The college has had as its students a host of other politicians including central and state level ministers.

Scions of former Indian Princely States and substantial landholding families also studied in this college, such as the former Maharaja of Coochbehar, HH Maharaja Sir Nripendra Narayan Bhup Bahadur. Other Princely and zamindari families from where boys came to study in this college included Burdwan, Susanga, Cossimbazar, Jhargram, and Teota in Bengal and Sonepur and Jarasingha in Orissa.

There are several senior judges, such as the first Indian judge of the High Court of Calcutta, Sir Gooroodas Banerjee and a Chief Justice of India, Sabyasachi Mukherjee who were students of this college. Several senior civilians, such as the first Indian member of the ICS, Satyendranath Tagore and first Chief Election Commissioner of India, Sukumar Sen studied in this college.

This college has also performed equally well in industry. Sir Rajen Mookerjee was its student and Shri Rama Prasad Goenka also studied in this college.

In academics too, eminent intellectuals and vice chancellors, such as the scientist, Sir Jagadish Chandra Bose, the pre-eminent vice chancellor of Calcutta University, Sir Ashutosh Mukherjee, the doyen of Indian history, Sir Jadunath Sarkar, and India's first planner, Professor Prasanta Chandra Mahalanobis, have been students of this college. In literature, it has amongst its students, Michael Madhusudan Dutt, Bankim Chandra Chatterjee, Sukumar Ray and Jibanananda Das. Amongst journalists, Avik Sarkar, M. J. Akbar and Pritish Nandy studied here.

In the entertainment industry, this college can boast of such legendary names as Satyajit Ray, Pramathesh Barua, Ashok Kumar, and Aparna Sen among other equally gifted and well known film and theatre personalities. Vece Paes, a member of India's hockey team was also a student of this college.

University of Calcutta

The University of Calcutta (also known as Calcutta University) is a public university located in the city of Kolkata (previously Calcutta), India, founded on 24 January 1857. It was the first modern university in the Indian subcontinent. It is a state-government administered urban-based affiliating and research university. It has its central campus in College Street (called Ashutosh Shiksha Prangan). Its other campuses are in Rajabazar (called Rashbehari Shiksha Prangan), Ballygunge (called Taraknath Palit Shiksha Prangan), Alipore (called Sahid Khudiram Siksha Prangan), Hazra and South Sinthi.

History

Vice Chancellors:

- James William Colvile, 1857-1859

- William Ritchie, 1859-1862
- Claudius James Erskine, 1862-1863
- Henry Sumner Maine, 1863-1867
- W. S. Seton-Karr, 1867-1869
- Edward Clive Bayley, 1869-1875
- Arthur Hobhouse, 1875-1877
- William Markby, 1877-1878
- Alexander Arbuthnot, 1878-1880
- Arthur Wilson, 1880-1883
- H. J. Reynolds, 1883-1886
- C. P. Ilbert, 1886-1886
- W. W. Hunter, 1886-1887
- William Comer Petheram, 1887-1889
- Gooroodass Banerjee, 1890-1892
- Jones Quain Pigot, 1893-1893
- Alfred Croft, 1893-1896
- E. J. Trevelyan, 1897-1898
- Francis William Maclean, 1898-1900
- Thomas Raleigh, 1900-1904
- Alexander Pedler, 1904-1906
- Asutosh Mookerjee, 1906-1914
- Deva Prosad Sarbadhicary, 1914-1918
- Lancelot Sanderson, 1918-1919
- Nilratan Sircar, 1919-1921
- Asutosh Mookerjee, 1921-1923
- Bhupendra Nath Bose, 1923-1924
- William Ewart Greaves, 1924-1926
- Jadunath Sarkar, 1926-1928
- W. S. Urquhart, 1928-1930
- Huseyn Shaheed Suhrawardy, 1930-1934
- Syama Prasad Mookerjee, 1934-1938
- Mohammad Azizul Huque, 1938-1942
- Bidhan Chandra Roy, 1942-1944
- Radhabinod Pal, 1944-1946

- Pramathanath Banerjee, 1946-1949
- Charuchandra Biswas, 1949-1950
- Sambhunath Banerjee, 1950-1954
- Jnanchandra Ghosh, 1954-1955
- Nirmalkumar Sidhanta, 1955-1960
- Subodh Mitra, 1960-1961
- Surajit Chandra Lahiri, 1962-1962
- Bidhubhushan Malik, 1962-1968
- S. N. Sen, 1968-1976
- Sushil Kumar Mukherjee, 1976-1983
- Ramendra Kumar Podder, 1979-1983
- Santosh Bhattacharya, 1983-1987
- Bhaskarananda Ray Chaudhuri, 1987-1991
- Rathindra Narayan Basu, 1991-1999
- Asis Kumar Banerjee, 1999-2008
- Suranjan Das, 2008-present.

The University of Calcutta is the oldest of the modern universities in India. It has so far produced 4 Nobelists, more than any other Indian university: Ronald Ross, Rabindra Nath Tagore, C. V. Raman and Amartya Sen. It was founded in 1857 during the administration of Lord Canning, the Governor General of India. Dr Fredrick John, the education secretary to the then British Government in India, first tendered a proposal to the British Government in London for the establishment of a university in Calcutta, similar to London University, to create an educated class that would help them rule India; at that time the plan failed to obtain the necessary approval. However, a proposal to establish two universities, one in Calcutta and the other in Bombay was later accepted in 1854 and the necessary authority was given. The Calcutta University Act came into force on 24 January 1857 and a 41-member Senate was formed as the policy making body of the university. When the university was first established it had a catchment area covering the area from Lahore to Rangoon (now in Myanmar), and Ceylon, the largest of any Indian university.

The first Chancellor and Vice-Chancellor of the Calcutta University were Governor General Lord Canning and Chief Justice of the Supreme Court, Sir James William Colvile, respectively. In

1858, Joddu Nath Bose and Bankim Chandra Chattopadhyay became the first graduates of the university. On 30 January 1858, the Syndicate of the Calcutta University started functioning. The first meeting of the Senate was held in the Council room of the Calcutta Medical College. A temporary office of the university was started in a few rented rooms in Camac Street. For several years afterwards the meetings of the Senate and Syndicate were held in a room of the Writers' building. 244 candidates appeared for the first entrance examination of the university, held in March 1857 in the town hall of Calcutta. In 1862, a decision was taken by the Senate to construct for the university a building of its own. Accordingly, the historical Senate Hall was constructed at a cost of Rs. 2,52,221/-and inaugurated on 12 March 1873 by holding the convocation of the university.

In 1857 Nawab Jassa Singh Ahluwalia Government College in Kapurthala, Punjab province of British India became one of the first colleges to be affiliated with University of Calcutta. Later many institutions came under its jurisdiction. Kadambini Ganguly and Chandramukhi Basu became the first female graduates of the country in 1882. The Honourable Justice Gooroodas Banerjee became the first Indian Vice-Chancellor of University of Calcutta in the year 1890. Sir Ashutosh Mukherjee was the Vice-Chancellor for four consecutive two-year terms (1906–1914) and a fifth two-year term (1921–23).

Campus

The university has several campuses spread over the city of Kolkata and its suburbs. The university also has many affiliated colleges spread over southern West Bengal. The main campus of the university, located on College Street, is spread over a small area of 2.7 acres (0.011 km^2). The main campus is also known as the *Asutosh Siksha Prangan,* and contains Darbhanga Building, Asutosh Building, Hardinge Building, and the Centenary Building. The *Rashbihari Siksha Prangan* (also known as University College of Science and Technology or popularly Rajabazar Science College), located on Acharya Prafulla Chandra Road, houses several scientific and technological departments, e.g., pure and applied chemistry, pure and applied physics, applied mathematics, psychology, physiology, biophysics and molecular biology, to name but a few. *Taraknath Siksha Prangan* (also known as University College of

Science or Ballygunge | accessdate = 2007-04-11 Science College) on Ballygunge Circular Road in the southern part of the city houses the departments of agriculture, anthropology, biochemistry, botany and genetics among others. Sahid Khudiram Siksha Prangan at Alipore houses the department of Archeology, Business Management, Political Science, Sociology and others. Other campuses are Hazra Road Campus, University Press And Book Depot, B. T. Road Campus, Viharilal College of Home Science Campus, University Health Service, Haringhata Campus, Dhakuria Lakes (University Rowing Club) and University Ground and Tent at Maidan. The university has a plan to create a "Techno Campus", to bring together the engineering and technical departments under one roof, in Salt Lake.

Visva-Bharati University

Visva Bharati University, Santiniketan is a Central University for research and teaching in India, located in the twin town of Santiniketan and Sriniketan Indian state of West Bengal. It was founded by Rabindranath Tagore who called it *Visva Bharati*, which means the communion of the world with India. In its initial years Tagore expressed his dissatisfaction with the word 'university', since university translates to *Vishva-Vidyalaya*, which is smaller in scope than *Visva Bharati*. Until independence it was a college. Soon after independence, in 1951 the institution was given the status of a university, and was renamed *Visva Bharati University*.

History

The origins of the university date back to 1863 when Maharshi Debendranath Tagore, himself the *zamindar* of Silaidaha in East Bengal, bought a tract of land from the *zamindar* of Raipur, which was a neighbouring village not too far from present day Santiniketan and set up an *ashram* at the spot that has now come to be called *chatim tala* at the heart of the town. The *ashram* was initially called *Brahmacharya Ashram*, which was later renamed *Brahmacharya Vidyalaya*. It was established with a view to encourage people from all walks of life to come to the spot and meditate. In 1901 his youngest son Rabindranath Tagore established a co-educational school inside the premises of the *ashram*.

From 1901 onwards, Tagore used the *ashram* to organise the *Hindu Mela*, which soon became a centre of nationalist activity.

Through the early twentieth century the former *zamindars* of Surul, another neighbouring village, a few minutes by cycle from the Uttarayan Complex, continued to accede their lands and other properties to the *ashram* and the college that was being built on this spot. On 23 December 1921 Tagore formally started the college with proceeds from the prize money of the Nobel Prize he received in 1913 for the publication of his book of poems entitled *Gitanjali*. The college also became a centre of Brahmo learning in this period. It was granted full university status in May 1951 by the Government of independent India. The poet's eldest son, Rathindranath Tagore, became the first *upacharya* of the newly founded university. Another member of the Tagore family who performed the role of *upacharya* of the university was Indira Devi Chaudhurani, a niece of the poet.

Upacharyas:

- Rathindranath Tagore, 1951-1953
- Kshitimohan Sen, 1953-1954
- Probodhchandra Bagchi, 1954-1956
- Indiradevi Chaudhurani, 1956-1956 (acting)
- Satyendranath Bose, 1956-1958
- Kshitishchandra Chaudhuri, 1958-1959 (acting)
- Sudhi Ranjan Das, 1959-1965
- Kalidas Bhattacharya, 1966-1970
- Pratul Chandra Gupta, 1970-1975
- Surajit Chandra Sinha, 1975-1980
- Amlan Dutta, 1980-1984
- Nemai Sadhan Bosu, 1984-1989
- Ajit Kumar Chakrabarty, 1989-1990 (performed the duty of upacharya)
- Ashin Dasgupta, 1990-1991
- Sisir Mukhopadhyaya, 1991-1991 (performed the duty of upacharya)
- Sabyasachi Bhattacharya, 1991-1995
- Sisir Mukhopadhyay, 1995-1995 (performed the duty of upacharya)
- R.R.Rao, 1995-1995 (performed the duty of upacharya)
- Dilip K.Sinha, 1995-2001

- Sujit Basu, 2001-2006
- Rajat Kanta Ray, 2006-present.

Administration

The high officials of the university include the *Paridarshaka* (Visitor), *Acharya* (Chancellor), and the *Upacharya* (Vice Chancellor). The *Paridarshaka* of this university is the President of India, while the *Acharya* is the Prime Minister of India. The university is run by its *Karma Samity* (Executive Council) which is chaired by the *Acharya*. The institutes and departments are located in both Santiniketan and Sriniketan.

Academics

The university is divided in to institutes, centres, departments and schools. The respective departments are included in the institutes. The university's various programmes dealing with its rich cultural heritage as well as art and dance education are funded by the Department of Science and Technology (DST), Government of India.

Institutes and Museums

- *Cheena Bhavana* (Institute of Chinese Language and Culture): It was founded in April 1937 with the great vision of Tagore. Tagore invited Prof. Tan Yunshan to serve as the first chairperson of *Cheena Bhavana*. International scholars such as Sylvain Levi and Jan Yun-hua worked at the Cheena-Bhavana on topics ranging from Sino-Indian studies, Buddhism and Chinese philosophy. Chiang Kai-shek and Zhou Enlai donated a large number of Chinese books to *Cheena Bhavan*, making it one of the most important libraries for classical Chinese studies in India.
- *Darshan Bhavana* (Institute of Philosophy): This department is also well-known for its research and teaching. Professor Jiten Mohanty has been associated with the work of this department.
- *Kala Bhavana* (Institute of Fine Arts): Arguably one of the most well known of all the departments of the university, it boasts of an extremely well known faculty and students' body. It is most well known for the spread of Bengal

School of Art. Abanindranath Tagore, one of India's most eminent artists was one of its founders and chief patrons. Luminaries such as Abanindranath Tagore, Gaganendranath Tagore, Nandalal Bose, Binode Bihari Mukherjee, Ramkinkar Baij, Dinkar Kaushik, K.G. Subramanyan and Ghulam Mohammed Sheikh have either taught or been students here.

- *Palli Charcha Kendra* (Sriniketan):
- *Palli-Samgathana Vibhaga* (PSV) (Institute of Rural Reconstruction) (Sriniketan):
- *Palli Siksha Bhavana* (Institute of Agricultural Science) (Sriniketan):
- *Rabindra Bhavana* (Institute of Tagore Studies and Research) (Uttarayan complex): Dr. Swapan Chakrabarty is the present Director of this institution.
- *Sangeet Bhavana* (Institute of Dance, Drama & Music): The eminent Rabindrasangeet singer, Kanika Bandopadhyay was a Principal of *Sangeet Bhavana.*
- *Siksha Bhavana* (Institute of Science): This department houses the Centre for Biotechnolology, Physics, Chemistry, Mathematics, Statistics, Computer Science, Botany, Zoology
- *Silpa Sadan* (Sriniketan):
- Rural Extension Centre (Sriniketan):
- *Vidya-Bhavana* (Institute of Humanities & Social Sciences): This institute includes the humanities and social science departments, such as the Department of History and the Department of Economics.
- *Vinaya Bhavana* (Institute of Education):

Associated Institutes

- Bengal Institute of technology and Management (BITM, Santiniketan)
- IIIT, Kolkata.

Both these institutes are now affiliated with the WBUT (West Bengal University of Technology), which was formed to bring all engineering education under different universities in West Bengal under a single umbrella. IIIT Kolkata (International Institute of

Information Technology) was renamed to IERCEM Institute of Information Technology after its affiliation with the WBUT.

Schools

- *Patha Bhavana*: It is not only the oldest school of the university, but also the oldest institution on which the university was subsequently built. It is the university school of Santiniketan. Initially called *Ashram Vidyalaya* it was also later called *Santiniketan Vidyalaya*. It was started by Tagore in 1901. The distinctive features of this co-educational school include its open air classrooms and emphasis upon oriental learning. The school, being the nucleus of the university and the town is within the *Santiniketan Ashram*. The first four students of the school included Tagore's son Rathindranath Tagore, the first *Upacharya* of the university and Sudhi Ranjan Das, a Chief Justice of India. The future Nobel Laureate in economics, Amartya Sen completed his school education from this school. So did one of the first Indian Rhodes Scholars, Asim Datta. Supriyo Tagore, a great grandson of Satyendranath Tagore, the eldest brother of the poet, was one of its longest serving and most well known Principals. The eminent historians, Tapan Raychaudhuri and Ashin Dasgupta have periodically taken classes here.
- *Mrinalini Ananda Pathsala*: Founded in 1954 it was named after Rabindranath Tagore's wife Mrinalini Devi. It is a preparatory school for *Patha Bhavana*. It is housed in the *Notun Bari* and *Dehali*.
- *Santosh Pathsala*: Founded in 1988 it is kindergarten school named after Santosh Chandra Majumdar. It is a preparatory school for *Shiksha Shastra*.
- *Shiksha Shatra*: It was founded in 1924. It was later shifted to Sriniketan in 1927. The students of this school are from the neighbouring villages.
- *Uttar Shiksha Sadana*: This school was started in 1976.

Ram Mohan Roy

Raja Ram Mohan Roy (May 22, 1772-September 27, 1833) was a founder (with Dwarkanath Tagore and other Bengali Brahmins) of the *Brahma Sabha* in 1828 which engendered the Brahmo Samaj, an influential Indian socio-religious reform movement. His influence was apparent in the fields of politics, public administration and education as well as religion. He is best known for his efforts to abolish the practice of sati, the Hindu funeral practice in which the widow was compelled to sacrifice herself on her husband's funeral pyre. It was he who first introduced the word "Hinduism" into the English language in 1816. For his diverse contributions to society, Raja Ram Mohan Roy is regarded as one of the most important figures in the Bengal Renaissance. His efforts to protect Hinduism and Indian rights by participating in British government earned him the title "The Father of the Bengal Renaissance" or "The Father of the Indian Nation."

Early Life and Education (1774-1796)

Roy was born in Radhanagari, Bengal, in 1774 (some sources suggest 1772). His family background displayed religious diversity-his father Ramkanta was a Vaishnavite, while his mother Tarinidevi was from a Shivaite family. This was unusual for Vaishanavites did not commonly marry Shaivites at the time.

"Thus one parent prepared him for the occupation of a scholar, the *sastrin*, the other secured for him all the worldly advantage needed to launch a career in the *laukik* or worldly sphere of public administration. Torn between these two parental ideals from early childhood, Rammohan vacillated the rest of his life, moving from one to the other and back.

Ram Mohan Roy was married three times by the time he was ten years old, which fell in the strict framework of his polygamous and caste customs. His first wife died early in his childhood. He conceived two sons, Radhaprasad in 1800 and Ramaprasad in 1812 with his second wife, who died in 1824. Roy's third wife outlived him.

Roy's early education was controversial. The common version is Rammohan started his formal education in the village *pathshala* where he learned Bengali and some Sanskrit and Persian. Later he is said to have studied Persian and Arabic in a *madrasa* in Patna and after that he was sent to Benares (Kashi) for learning the intricacies of Sanskrit and Hindu scripture, including the Vedas and Upanishads.

The dates of his sojourn in both these places is uncertain. However, we will go by the commonly held belief that he was sent to Patna when he was nine years old and two years later to Benares."

His faithful contemporary biographer writes,

"Rammohan with his new found *madrasa* knowledge of Arabic also tasted the fruit forbidden to Brahmins of *Quran* and was converted to its strict monotheism. Rammohan's mother Tarini Devi was scandalised and packed her son off to Benares (to study Sanskrit and Vedas) before he could take the irrevocable step. In Benares, Rammohan's rebellion continued and he persisted in interpreting the Upanishads through the Holy Quran's monotheist strictures especially against idolatry. Benares, the spiritual seat of traditional Hinduism, was awash with temples to the billion gods of Hindu pantheon, and Rammohan would not complete his formal Vedantic education there. He instead travelled widely (not much is known of where he went, but he is said to have extensively studied Buddhism at this time) to eventually return to his family around 1794 when a search party sent by his father tracked him down to Benares in the company of some Buddhists with similar notions. Between 1794 and 1795 Rammohan stayed with his family attending the family zamindari holdings. There was considerable friction in the family between Rammohan and his father, who died in about 1796 leaving some property to be divided amongst his sons.

Impact

Ram Mohan Roy's impact on modern Indian history was a revival of the pure and ethical principles of the Vedanta school of philosophy as found in the Upanishads. He preached the unity of God, made early translations of Vedic scriptures into English, co-founded the Calcutta Unitarian Society and founded the Brahma Samaj.

The Brahma Samaj played a major role in reforming and modernising the Indian society. He successfully campaigned against sati, the practice of burning widows. He sought to integrate Western culture with the best features of his own country's traditions. He established a number of schools to popularize a modern system of education in India. He promoted a rational, ethical, non-authoritarian, this-worldly, and social-reform Hinduism. His writings also sparked interest among British and American Unitarians.

Christianity and the Early Rule of the East India Company (1795-1828)

During these overlapping periods, Ram Mohan Roy acted as a political agitator and agent, representing Christian missionaries whilst employed by the East India Company and simultaneously pursuing his vocation as a Pandit. To understand fully this complex period in his life leading up to his eventual Brahmoism needs reference to his peers.

In 1792 the British Baptist shoemaker William Carey published his influential missionary tract *"An Enquiry of the obligations of Christians to use means for the conversion of heathens.*

In 1793 William Carey landed in India to settle. His objective was to translate, publish and distribute the Bible in Indian languages and propagate Christianity to the Indian peoples. He realized the "mobile" (i.e. service classes) Brahmins and Pundits were most able to help him in this endeavour, and he began gathering them. He learnt the Buddhist and Jain religious works to better argue the case for Christianity in the cultural context.

In 1795 Carey made contact with a Sanskrit scholar-the Tantric Hariharananda Vidyabagish-who later introduced him to Ram Mohan Roy who wished to learn English.

Between 1796 and 1797 the trio of Carey, Vidyavagish and Roy fabricated a spurious religious work known as the "Maha Nirvana Tantra" (or "Book of the Great Liberation") and pass it off as an ancient religious text to "the One True God" actually the Holy Spirit of Christianity masquerading as Brahma. Carey's involvement is not recorded in his very detailed records and he reports only learning to read Sanscrit in 1796 and only completed a grammar in 1797, the same year he translated from Joshua to Job, itself a massive task. (The explanation later given by Ram Mohan Roy to his family concerning his whereabouts during this period is that he went to "Tibet" –then as far away as "Timbuktoo"). For the next two decades this document was regularly added to. Its judicial sections are used in the law courts of the English Settlement in Bengal as Hindu Law for adjudicating upon property disputes of the zamindari. However a few British magistrates and collectors begin to suspect it as a forgery and its usage (as well as the reliance on pundits as sources of Hindu Law) was quickly deprecated. Vidyavagish has a brief falling out with Carey and separated from the group but maintained ties to Ram Mohan Roy. (The Maha Nirvana Tantra's significance for Brahmoism lay in the wealth that accumulated to Rammohan Roy and Dwarkanath Tagore by its judicial use, and not due to any religious wisdom within,–although it does contain an entire chapter devoted to "the One True God" and his worship).

In 1797, Rammohan reached Calcutta and became a "banian" (i.e. moneylender) mainly to impoverished Englishmen of the Company living beyond their means. Rammohan also continued his vocation as pundit in the English courts and started to make a living for himself. He began learning Greek and Latin.

In 1799, Carey was joined by missionary Joshua Marshman and the printer William Ward at the Danish settlement of Serampore.

From 1803 till 1815, Rammohan served the East India Company's "Writing Service" commencing as private clerk "munshi" to Thomas Woodforde, Registrar of the Appellate Court at Murshidabad (whose distant nephew-also a Magistrate-later made a rich living off the spurious Maha Nirvana Tantra under the pseudonym Arthur Avalon).

Roy resigned from Woodforde's service due to allegations of corruption. Later he secured employment with John Digby a company collector and Rammohan spent many years at Rangpur and elsewhere with Digby, where he renewed his contacts with Hariharananda. William Carey had by this time settled at Serampore and the old trio renewed their profitable association. William Carey was also aligned now with the English Company, then headquartered at Fort William, and his religious and political ambitions were increasingly intertwined.

The East India Company was draining money from India at a rate of three million pounds a year in 1838. Ram Mohan Roy was one of the first to try to estimate how much money was being driven out of India and where it was disappearing. He estimated that around one-half of all total revenue collected in India was sent out to England, leaving India, with a considerably larger population, to use the remaining money to maintain social wellbeing. Ram Mohan Roy saw this and believed that the unrestricted settlement of Europeans in India governing under free trade would help ease the economic drain crisis.

At the turn of the 19th century the Muslims, although considerably vanquished after the battles of Plassey and Buxar, still posed a formidable political threat to the Company. Rammohan was now chosen by Carey to be the agitator among them.

Under Carey's secret tutelage in the next two decades, Rammohan launched his attack against the bastions of Hinduism of Bengal, namely his own Kulin Brahmin priestly clan (then in control of the many temples of Bengal) and their priestly excesses. The social and theological issues Carey chose for Rammohan were calculated to weaken the hold of the dominant Kulin class (especially their younger disinherited sons forced into service who constituted the mobile gentry or "bhadralok" of Bengal) from the Mughal zamindari system and align them to their new overlords of Company. The Kulin excesses targeted include-sati (the concremation of widows), polygamy, idolatory, child marriage, dowry. All causes equally dear to Carey's ideals.

Roy's contemporary biographer records:

"In 1805 Rammohan published Tuhfat-ul-Muwahhidin (A Gift to Monotheists)-an essay written in Persian with an introduction in Arabic in which he rationalised the unity of God. Being published in Persian, it antagonised sections of the Muslim community and for the next decade Rammohan travelled to serve with John Digby of the East India Company as munshi and then as Diwan. His English and knowledge of England's Baptist Christianity increased tremendously. He also cultivated friendship in a Jain community to better understand their approach to Hinduism-rejecting priesthood (which for long in Bengal demanded bloody ritual sacrifices) and God itself.

In 1815 after amassing large wealth, enough to leave the Company, Rammohan resettled in Calcutta and started an Atmiya Sabha-as a philosophical discussion circle to debate monotheistic Hindu Vedantism and like subjects. Rammohan's mother, however, had not forgiven him and ironically from 1817 a series of lawsuits were filed accusing Rammohan of apostasy with the object of severing him from the family zamindari. Rammohan countered denouncing his family's practice of sati where widows were burned on their husband's pyres so that they laid no claim to property via the British courts. 1817 was also the year when Rammohan was alienated from Hindu zamindars in an incident concerning the

Hindu (later Presidency) College involving David Hare. Hindu public outrage in 1819 also followed Rammohan's triumph in a public debate over idolatry with Subramanya Shastri, a Tamil Brahmin. The victory, however, also exposed chinks in Rammohan's command over Brahmanical scripture and Vedanta whose study he had somewhat neglected. The trusted younger brother of Hariharanda, a Brahmin of great intellect Ram Chunder Vidyabagish was brought in to repair the breech and would be increasingly identified as Rammohan's alter-ego in matters theological for the rest of Rammohan's life especially in matters of Bengali concern and language. By now it was suspected (but never established) that Carey and Marshman were behind Rammohan's English works, a charge repeatedly made by the Hindu zamindars. From time to time Dwarkanath Tagore a young Hindu Zamindar had been attending Sabha meetings and he privately persuaded Rammohan (financially reduced by lawsuits and in constant danger from Hindu assassins) to disband the Atmiya Sabha in 1819 and instead be political agent for him."

From 1819, Rammohan's battery now increasingly turns against Carey and the Serampore missionaries. With Dwarkanath's munificence he launches a series of attacks against Baptist "Trinitarian" Christianity and is now considerably assisted in his theological debates by the Unitarian faction of Christianity."

Middle "Brahmo" Period (1820-1830)

This was Rammohan's most controversial period. Sivanath Shastri commenting on his published works alone writes:-

"The period between 1820 and 1830 was also eventful from a literary point of view, as will be manifest from the following list of his publications during that period

- Second Appeal to the Christian Public, Brahmanical Magazine^ Parts I, II and III, with Bengali translation and a new Bengali newspaper called Sambad Kaumudi in 1821;
- A Persian paper called *Mirat-ul-Akbar* contained a tract entitled Brief Remarks on Ancient Female Rights and a book in Bengali called Answers to Four Questions in 1822;
- Third and final appeal to the Christian public, a memorial to the King of England on the subject of the liberty of the press, Ramdoss papers relating to Christian controversy,

Brahmanical Magazine, No. IV, letter to Lord Arnherst on the subject of English education, a tract called "Humble Suggestions" and a book in Bengali called "Pathyapradan or Medicine for the Sick," all in 1823;

- A letter to Rev. H. Ware on the " Prospects of Christianity in India" and an "Appeal for famine-smitten natives in Southern India " in 1824;
- A tract on the different modes of worship, in 1825;
- A Bengali tract on the qualifications of a God loving householder, a tract in Bengali on a controversy with a Kayastha, and a Grammar of the Bengali language in English, in 1826;
- A Sanskrit tract on " Divine worship by Gayatri " with an English translation of the same, the edition of a Sanskrit treatise against caste, and the previously noticed tract called " Answer of a Hindu to the question &c.," in 1827;
- A form of Divine worship and a collection of hymns composed by him and his friends, in 1828;
- "Religious Instructions founded on Sacred Authorities" in English and Sanskrit, a Bengali tract called "Anusthan," and a petition against Suttee, in 1829;
- A Bengali tract, a grammar of the Bengali language in Bengali, the Trust Deed of the Brahmo Samaj, an address to Lord William Bentinck, congratulating him for the abolition of Suttee, an abstract 'in English of the arguments regarding the burning of widows, and a tract in English on the disposal of ancestral property by Hindus, in 1830.

Life in England (1831-1833)

In 1831 Ram Mohan Roy travelled to the United Kingdom as an ambassador of the Mughal Empire to ensure that the Lord Bentick's regulation banning the practice of Sati was not overturned. He also visited France.

He died at Stapleton then a village to the north east of Bristol (now a suburb) on the 27th September 1833 of meningitis and is buried in Arnos Vale Cemetery in southern Bristol.

Reformer

Religious reforms of Rammohan:

- He believed in one Supreme Being-"Author and Preserver of Existence".
- He denounced idolatry and vowed to erase it from India.
- He denounced rituals, which he deemed meaningless and giving rise to superstitions.

Social Reforms of Rammohan:

- Crusaded against social evils like sati, polygamy and child marriage etc.
- Demanded property inheritance rights for women.
- In 1828, he set up the *Brahmo Sabha* a movement of reformist Bengali Brahmins to fight against social evils.

While Ram Mohan Roy worked to create social reform for the Indian people, his status as a member of the new class of English-educated landholders gave him a connection to British interests. Because this new class of elites profited from the presence of the British, they could not completely disregard British interests. Roy's efforts to these ends conflicted with his interest in aiding the Indian populace. For example, in 1829 Roy advocated the unrestricted immigration of British indigo planters. "As to the indigo planters, I beg to observe that I have travelled through several districts in Bengal and Bihar, and I have found the natives residing in the neighbourhood(*sic*) of indigo plantations evidently better-clothed and better conditioned than those who live at a distance from such stations." However, Indian opponents of British indigo planters made the claim that the plantations had an opposite effect. They saw the British plantation owners as exploiting the Indian workers: forcibly taking their land and keeping them in a condition akin to slavery.

Roy's political background fit influenced his social and religious to reforms of Hinduism. He writes,

"The present system of Hindoos is not well calculated to promote their political interests.... It is necessary that some change should take place in their religion, at least for the sake of their political advantage and social comfort."

Rammohan Roy's experience working with the British government taught him that Hindu traditions were often not credible or respected by western standards and this no doubt affected his religious reforms. He wanted to legitimize Hindu traditions to his European acquaintances by proving that "superstitious practices which deform the Hindu religion have nothing to do with the pure spirit of its dictates!"

The "superstitious practices" Rammohan Roy objected included sati, caste rigidity, polygamy and child marriages. These practices were often the reasons British officials claimed moral superiority over the Indian nation.

Rammohan Roy's ideas of religion actively sought to create a fair and just society by implementing humanitarian practices similar to Christian ideals and thus legitimize Hinduism in the modern world.

Educationist:

- Roy believed education to be an implement for social reform.
- In 1817, in collaboration with David Hare, he set up the Hindu College at Calcutta.
- In 1822, Roy founded the Anglo-Hindu school, followed four years later (1826) by the Vendanta College; where he insisted that his teachingings of monotheistic doctrines be incorporated with "modern, western curriculum.".
- In 1830, he helped Alexander Duff in establishing the General Assembly's Institution, by providing him the venue vacated by *Brahma Sabha* and getting the first batch of students.
- He supported induction of western learning into Indian education.
- He also set up the Vedanta College, offering courses as a synthesis of Western and Indian learning.

Journalist:

- Roy published journals in English, Hindi, Persian Bengali,
- His most popular journal was the *Sambad Kaumudi.* It covered topics like freedom of press, induction of Indians into high ranks of service, and separation of the executive and judiciary.
- When the English Company muzzled the press, Rammohan composed two memorials against this in 1829 and 1830 respectively.

Tomb

The tomb built in 1843, located in the Arnos Vale Cemetery on the outskirts of Bristol, is in need of restoration and repair. It was built by Dwarkanath Tagore in 1843, 10 years after Rammohan Roy's death (due to meningitis) in Bristol on Sep 27, 1833.

In September 2006 representatives from the Indian High Commission came to Bristol to mark the anniversary of Ram Mohan Roy's death. During the ceremony Hindu, Muslim and Sikh women sang Sanskrit prayers of thanks. Following on from this visit the Mayor of Kolkata, Bikash Ranjan Bhattacharya (who was amongst the representatives from the India High Commission) decided to raise funds to restore the tomb.

In June 2007 businessman Aditya Poddar donated £50,000 towards the restoration of his grave after being approached by the Mayor of Calcutta for funding.

His tomb contains the following Epitaph: "To great natural talents, he united through mastery of many languages and distinguished himself as one of the greatest scholars of his day. His unwearied labour to promote the social, moral and physical condition of the people of India, his earnest endeavours to suppress idolatry and the rite of sati and his constant zealous advocacy of whatever tended to advance the glory of God and the welfare of man live in the grateful remembrance of his countrymen."

Sati (Practice)

Satî is a funeral practice among some Hindu communities in which a recently widowed woman would either voluntarily or by use of force and coercion immolate herself on her husband's funeral pyre. This practice is now rare and outlawed in modern India.

The term is derived from the original name of the goddess Sati, also known as Dakshayani, who self-immolated because she was unable to bear her father Daksha's humiliation of her (living) husband Shiva. The term may also be used to refer to the widow herself. The term *sati* is now sometimes interpreted as "chaste woman."

Origin

Few reliable records exist of the practice before the time of the Gupta empire, approximately 400 AD. After about this time, instances of *sati* began to be marked by inscribed memorial stones. The earliest of these are found in Sagar, Madhya Pradesh, though the largest collections date from several centuries later, and are found in Rajasthan. These stones, called *devli*, or sati-stones, became shrines to the dead woman, who was treated as an object of reverence and worship. They are most common in western India.

By about the 10th century *sati*, as understood today, was known across much of the subcontinent. It continued to occur, usually at a low frequency and with regional variations, until the early 19th century.

Some instances of voluntary self-immolation by both women and men that may be regarded as at least partly historical accounts are included in the Mahabharata and other works. However, large portions of these works are relatively late interpolations into an original story, rendering difficult their use for reliable dating. Also, neither immolation nor the desire for self-immolation are regarded as a custom in the Mahabharata. Use of the term 'sati' to describe the custom of self-immolation never occurs in the Mahabarata, unlike other customs such as the Rajasuya yagna. Rather, the self-immolations are viewed as an expression of extreme grief at the loss of a beloved one.

The ritual has prehistoric roots, and many parallels from other cultures are known. Compare for example the ship burial of the Rus' described by Ibn Fadlan, where a female slave is burned with her master.

Aristobulus of Cassandreia, a Greek historian who travelled to India with the expedition of Alexander the Great, recorded the practice of *sati* at the city of Taxila. A later instance of voluntary co-cremation appears in an account of an Indian soldier in the army of Eumenes of Cardia, whose two wives vied to die on his funeral pyre, in 316 BC. The Greeks believed that the practice had been instituted to discourage wives from poisoning their husbands.

Voluntary death at funerals has been described in northern India before the Gupta empire. The original practices were called *anumarana*, and were uncommon. Anumarana was not comparable to later understandings of *sati*, since the practices were not restricted to widows — rather, anyone, male or female, with personal loyalty to the deceased could commit suicide at a loved one's funeral. These included the deceased's relatives, servants, followers, or friends. Sometimes these deaths stemmed from vows of loyalty, and bear a slight resemblance to the later tradition of *seppuku* in Japan.

Practice

The Commission of Sati (Prevention) Act of 1987 Part I, Section 2(c) defines *Sati* as:

The burning or burying alive of – (i) any widow along with the body of her deceased husband or any other relative or with any article, object or thing associated with the husband or such relative; or (ii) any woman along with the body of any of her relatives, irrespective of whether such burning or burying is claimed to be voluntary on the part of the widow or the women or otherwise The act of *sati* is said to exist voluntarily; from the existing accounts, many of these acts did indeed occur voluntarily. The act may have been expected of widows in some communities, and the extent to which social pressures or expectations constitute compulsion has been much debated in modern times. However, there were also instances where the wish of the widow to commit *sati* was not welcomed by others, and where efforts were made to prevent the death.

Traditionally, a person's funeral would have occurred within a day of the death, requiring decisions about *sati* to be made by that time. When the husband died elsewhere, the widow might still die by immolation at a later date.

Sati often emphasized the marriage between the widow and her deceased husband. For instance, rather than mourning clothes, the to-be *sati* was often dressed in marriage robes or other finery. In the preliminaries of the related act of Jauhar, both the husbands and wives have been known to dress in their marriage clothes and re-enact their wedding ritual, before going to their separate deaths.

Accounts describe numerous variants in the sati ritual. The majority of accounts describe the woman seated or lying down on the funeral pyre beside her dead husband. Many other accounts describe women walking or jumping into the flames after the fire had been lit, and some describe women seating themselves on the funeral pyre and then lighting it themselves.

Some written instructions for the ritual exist. For instance, the *Yallajeeyam* provides detailed instructions about who may commit sati, cleansing for the sati, positioning, attire, and other ritual aspects.

Compulsion

Sati was supposed to be voluntary, but it is known that it has often been forced. Setting aside the issue of social pressures, many accounts exist of women being physically forced to their deaths. Pictorial and narrative accounts often describe the widow being seated on the unlit pyre, and then tied or otherwise restrained to keep her from fleeing after the fire was lit. Some accounts state that the woman was drugged. One account describes men using long poles to prevent a woman from fleeing the flames.

Royal Funerals

Royal funerals sometimes have included the deaths of many wives and concubines. A number of examples of these occur in the history of Rajasthan. Maharani Raj Rajeshwari Devi of Nepal became regent in 1799 in the name of her son, after the abdication of her husband, who became a sanyasi. Her husband returned and took power again in 1804. In 1806 he was assassinated by his brother, and ten days later on 5 May 1806, his widow was forced to commit sati.

Symbolic Sati

There have been accounts of symbolic *sati* in some Hindu communities. A widow lies down next to her dead husband, and certain parts of both the marriage ceremony and the funeral ceremonies are enacted, but without her death.

Jauhar

The Rajput practice of Jauhar, known from Rajasthan and Madhya Pradesh was the collective suicide of a community facing certain defeat in war. It consisted of the mass immolation of women, children, the elderly and the sick, at the same time that their fighting men died in battle.

Burials

In some Hindu communities, it is conventional to bury the dead. Deaths of widows have been known to occur in these communities, with the widow being buried alive beside her husband, in ceremonies that are largely the same as those performed in an immolation.

Prevalence

Records of *sati* exist across most of the subcontinent. However, there seem to have been major differences historically, in different regions, and among different communities.

Numbers

There are no reliable figures for the numbers who died by *sati* across the country. A local indication of the numbers is given in the records kept by the Bengal Presidency of the British East India Company. The total figure of known occurrences for the period 1813 to 1828 is 8,135; another source gives a comparable number of 7,941 from 1815 to 1828, thus giving an average of about 507 to 567 documented incidents per year in that period. Raja Ram Mohan Roy estimated that there were ten times as many cases of Sati in Bengal compared to the rest of the country. Bentinck, in his 1829 report, states that 420 occurrences took place in one (unspecified) year in the 'Lower Provinces' of Bengal, Bihar and Orissa, and 44 in the 'Upper Provinces' (the upper Gangetic plain).

Communities

It is said by some authorities that the practice was more common among the higher castes, and among those who considered themselves to be rising in social status. It was little known or unknown in most of the population of India and the tribal groups, and little known or unknown in the lowest castes. According to at least one source, it was very rare for anyone in the later Mughal empire except royal wives to be burnt. However, it has been said elsewhere that it was unusual in higher caste women in the south.

Regional Variations

It was known in Rajasthan from the earliest (6th century) to the present. About half the known *sati* stones in India are in Rajasthan. However, the extent to which individual instances of deaths resulted in veneration (glorification) implies that was not very common.

It is known to have occurred in the south from the 9th century through the period of the Vijayanagara empire. Madhavacharya, who is probably the best known of those historical figures who justified the practice, was originally a minister of the court of this empire. The practice continued to occur after the collapse of the empire, though apparently at a fairly low frequency. In one instance more than fifty women committed Sati in Hampi after the war of Talikot. In the North-Western Karnataka about fifteen sati stones brought from Vijayanagara can be found. The actual immolation of widows might have taken place elsewhere. The relatives of Sati when they migrated took Sati stones along with them and resurrected at their new abodes. A record exists of a minister of the kingdom of Mysore giving permission for a widow to commit *sati* in 1805.

In the Upper Gangetic plain, while it occurred, there is no indication that it was especially widespread. The earliest known attempt by a government to stop the practice took place here, that of Muhammad Tughlaq, in the Sultanate of Delhi in the 14th century.

In the Lower Gangetic plain, the practice may have reached a high level fairly late in history. According to available evidence and the existing reports of the occurrences of it, the greatest incidence of *sati* in any region and period, in terms of total numbers, occurred in Bengal and Bihar in the late 18th and early 19th centuries. This was during the earlier period of British rule, and before its formal abolition. The Bengal Presidency kept records from 1813 to 1829. The frequency increased in periods of hardship and famine. Ram Mohan Roy suggested that it was more prevalent in Bengal than in the rest of the subcontinent. An unusually large number of the surviving reports for this period are from Bengal, also suggesting that it was most common there.

In modern times, *sati* has been largely confined to Rajasthan, mostly in or near Shekhawati, with a few instances in the Gangetic plain.

Current Incidence

Sati still occurs, albeit rarely, in the rural areas. A well documented case from 1987 was that of 18-year old Roop Kanwar. In response to this incident, some more recent legislation against the practice was passed, first by the state government of Rajasthan, then by the central government of India.

On 18 May 2006, Vidyawati, a 35-year-old woman allegedly committed sati by jumping into the blazing funeral pyre of her husband in Rari-Bujurg Village, Fatehpur district in the State of Uttar Pradesh. On 21 August 2006, Janakrani, a 40-year-old woman, burnt to death on the funeral pyre of her husband Prem Narayan in Sagar district. On October 11, 2008, a 75-year-old woman committed 'sati' by jumping into her 80-year-old husband's funeral pyre at Checher in the Kasdol block of Chhattisgarh's Raipur district.

Justifications and Criticisms

Brahmin scholars of the second millennium justified the practice, and gave reasonings as to how the scriptures could be said to justify them. Among them were Vijnanesvara, of the Chalukya court, and later Madhavacharya, theologian and minister of the court of the Vijayanagara empire, according to Shastri, who quotes their reasoning. It was lauded by them as required conduct in righteous women, and it was explained that this was considered not to be suicide (suicide was otherwise variously banned or discouraged in the scriptures). It was deemed an act of peerless piety, and was said to purge the couple of all accumulated sin, guarantee their salvation and ensure their reunion in the afterlife.

Law Books

These are relatively late works. Justifications for the practice are given in the Vishnu Smriti.

Now the duties of a woman (are)... After the death of her husband, to preserve her chastity, or to ascend the pile after him.

There is also justification in the later work of the Brihaspati Smriti (25-11). Both this and the Vishnu Smriti date from the first millennium.

The Manu Smriti is often regarded as the culmination of classical Hindu law, and hence its position is important. It does not mention or sanction *sati* though it does prescribe life-long asceticism for most widows.

Scriptures

Although the myth of the goddess Sati is that of a wife who dies by her own volition on a fire, this is not a case of the practice of *sati*. The goddess was not widowed, and the myth is quite unconnected with the justifications for the practice.

The Puranas have examples of women who commit *sati* and there are suggestions in them that this was considered desirable or praiseworthy: *A wife who dies in the company of her husband shall remain in heaven as many years as there are hairs on his person.* (Garuda Purana 1.107.29) According to 2.4.93 she stays with her husband in heaven during the rule of 14 Indras, i.e. a kalpa.

In the Ramayana, Tara, in her grief at the death of husband Vali, wished to commit *sati*. Hanuman, Rama, and the dying Vali dissuade her and she finally does not immolate herself. However, Sulochana wife of Indrajit (Meghanath) became Sati on his funeral pyre. In the Mahabharata, Madri, the second wife of Pandu, immolates herself. She holds herself responsible for the death of her husband, who had been cursed with death if he ever had intercourse. He died while performing the forbidden act with Madri, who blamed herself for not having rejected his advances, although she was well aware of the curse. However it must be noted that this may be a much later addition to the Mahabharata as the entire epic as it exists now was not written and modified over millennia. Passages in the Atharva Veda, including 13.3.1, offer advice to the widow on mourning and her life after widowhood, including her remarriage.

Argument that the Rig Veda Sanctions Sati

It is often claimed that this most ancient text sanctions or prescribes sati. This is based on verse 10.18.7, part of the verses to be used at funerals. Whether they even describe *sati* or something else entirely, is disputed, The hymn is about funeral by burial, and not by cremation. There are differing translations of the passage. The translation below is one of those said to prescribe it.

Let these women, whose husbands are worthy and are living, enter the house with ghee (applied) as collyrium (to their eyes). Let these wives first step into the pyre, tearless without any affliction and well adorned.

The text does not mention widowhood, and other translations differ in their translation of the word here rendered as 'pyre' (*yoni*, literally "seat, abode"; Griffith has "first let the dames go up to where he lieth"). In addition, the following verse, which is unambiguously about widows, then contradicts any suggestion of the woman's death; it explicitly states that the widow should return to her house.

Rise, come unto the world of life, O woman — come, he is lifeless by whose side thou liest. Wifehood with this thy husband was thy portion, who took thy hand and wooed thee as a lover.

A reason given for the discrepancy in translation and interpretation of verse 10.18.7, is that one consonant in a word that meant house, *yonim agree* "foremost to the *yoni*", was deliberately changed by those who wished claim scriptural justification, to a word that meant fire, *yomiagne*.

Counter-Arguments within Hinduism

No early descriptions or criticisms of the practice within Hinduism, (or in the other native religions of Buddhism or Jainism), are known before the Gupta period, as the practice was little known at that time.

Explicit criticisms later in the first millennium, included that of Medhatithi, a commentator on various theological works. He considered it suicide, which was forbidden by the Vedas

One shall not die before the span of one's life is run out,

Another critic was Bana, who wrote during the reign of Harsha. Bana condemned it both as suicide, and as a pointless and futile act.

Reform and bhakti movements within Hinduism tended to be anti-caste, favoured egalitarian societies, and in line with the tenor of these beliefs, they generally condemned the practice, sometimes explicitly. The Alvars condemned sati, in the 8th century. The Virashaiva movement in the 12th and 13th centuries, also condemned it.

In the early 19th century, Ram Mohan Roy wrote and disseminated arguments that the practice was not part of Hinduism, as part of his campaign to ban the practice.

Non-Hindu Views and Criticisms

The Sikh religion explicitly proscribed the practice since Sikhism's origin.

The principal early foreign visitors to the subcontinent who left records of the practice, were from Western Asia, mostly Muslim, and later on, Europeans. Both groups were fascinated by the practice, and they sometimes described it as horrific, but they also often described it as an incomparable act of devotion. Ibn Battuta described an instance, but said that he collapsed or fainted and had to be carried away from the scene. European artists in the eighteenth century produced many images for their own native markets, showing the widows as heroic women, and moral exemplars.

As Islam established itself in the subcontinent, opinions about sati changed and it was increasingly regarded as a barbaric practice. The earliest known governmental efforts to halt the practice were undertaken by Muslim rulers, including Muhammad Tughlaq.

Europeans also showed a change in their attitudes regarding local customs as their home countries became dominant local powers. The earliest Europeans to establish themselves were the Portuguese in Goa. They tried early on to override local customs and practices, including *sati*, as they attempted to spread Christianity throughout the territories in their control. The British entered India as a trading body, and in the earlier periods of their rule, they were largely indifferent to local practices. The practice of *sati*, and its later legal abolition by the British (along with the suppression of the thuggee) went on to become one of the standard justifications for British rule. British attitudes in their later history in India are usually given in the following much repeated quote, usually ascribed to General Napier-

You say that it is your custom to burn widows. Very well. We also have a custom: when men burn a woman alive, we tie a rope around their necks and we hang them. Build your funeral pyre; beside it, my carpenters will build a gallows. You may follow your custom. And then we will follow ours.

In her article "Can the Subaltern Speak?", Gayatri Spivak, then an English professor at Columbia University, discusses whether sati can be a form of self-expression by women who cannot demonstrate their independence in any other manner.

Suppression

Mughal Period

Humayun issued a royal fiat against sati, which he later withdrew.

Akbar required that permission be granted by his officials, and these officials were instructed to delay the woman's decision for as long as possible. The reasoning was that she was less likely to choose to die once the emotions of the moment had passed. In the reign of Shah Jahan, widows with children were not allowed to burn under any circumstances. In other cases, governors did not readily give permission, but could be bribed to do so. Later on in the Mughal period, pensions, gifts and rehabilitative help were offered to the potential sati to wean her away from committing the act. Children were strictly forbidden from following the practice. The later Mughal rulers continued to put obstacles in the way but the practice still persisted in areas outside their capitals.

Guru Nanak, the first Guru of the Sikhs spoke out against the practice of sati.

The strongest attempts to control it were made by Aurangzeb. In 1663, he "issued an order that in all lands under Mughal control, never again should the officials allow a woman to be burnt". Despite such attempts however, the practice continued, especially during periods of war and upheaval.

British and other European Territories

By the end of the 18th century, the practice had been banned in territories held by some European powers. The Portuguese banned the practice in Goa by about 1515, though it is not believed to have been especially prevalent there. The Dutch and the French also banned it in Chinsurah and Pondicherry. The British who by then ruled much of the subcontinent, and the Danes, who held the small territories of Tranquebar and Serampore, permitted it until the 19th century.

Attempts to limit or ban the practice had been made by individual British officers in the 18th century, but without the backing of the British East India Company. The first formal British ban was imposed in 1798, in the city of Calcutta only. The practice continued in surrounding regions. Toward the end of the 18th century, the evangelical church in Britain, and its members in India, started campaigns against *sati*. Leaders of these campaigns included William Carey and William Wilberforce, and both appeared to be motivated partly by a desire to convert Indians to Christianity. These movements put pressure on the company to ban the act, and the Bengal Presidency started collecting figures on the practice in 1813.

From about 1812, the Bengali reformer Raja Rammohan Roy started his own campaign against the practice. He was motivated by the experience of seeing his own sister-in-law being forced to commit *sati*. Among his actions, he visited Calcutta cremation grounds to persuade widows not to so die, formed watch groups to do the same, and wrote and disseminated articles to show that it was not required by scripture.

On 4 December 1829, the practice was formally banned in the Bengal Presidency lands, by the then governor, Lord William Bentinck. The ban was challenged in the courts, and the matter went to the Privy Council in London, but was upheld in 1832. Other company territories also banned it shortly after. Although the original ban in Bengal was fairly uncompromising, later in the century British laws include provisions that provided mitigation for murder when "the person whose death is caused, being above the age of 18 years, suffers death or takes the risk of death with his own consent".

Sati remained legal in some princely states for a time after it had been abolished in lands under British control. Jaipur, banned the practice in 1846. [6] Nepal continued to practice Sati well into the 20th century. On the Indonesian island of Bali, *sati* was practised by the aristocracy as late as 1905, until Dutch colonial rule pushed for its termination.

3

Central Sati Act-An Analysis

Maja Daruwala traces the history of sati legislation in India and analyses the Central Sati Prevention Act in this context

Four months after the Roop Kanwar incident at Deorala, the focus of attention shifted to the need for central legislation to stamp out the oppressive practice of Sati. Two rallies in Delhi, Rajasthan women activists, MP's in the State and at the Centre all called for stringent legislation against Sati. By 1 October, the Rajasthan Legislature had already promulgated an ordinance against Sati which is now a State Act passed by assembly and upheld by the Rajasthan High Court. By the new year, the Commission of Sati (Prevention), Act had passed through both houses with a minimum of debate or amendment.

The particular barbarism of consigning a vibrant life to the flames of a funeral pyre has always provoked the rulers of India to prevent this horror, despite the spurious sanctity that has come to be attached to the practice.

Historically, efforts to prevent Sati by formal means were extent even before the Mughal rulers came to power. Under the Delhi Sultanates (circa 1325) permission had to be sought prior to any Sati. In time this check against compulsion became a mere formality. In any case Hindu women from royal families continued to burn unchecked. Humayun tried, but withdrew a royal fiat against Sati. Akbar insisted that no woman could commit Sati without the specific permission of his Kotwals. They were instructed to delay the woman's decision for as long as possible. Pensions, gifts and rehabilitative help was offered to the potential Sati to wean her away from committing the Act. Children were strictly forbidden from the practice. The later Moghuls continued to put obstacles in the way but the practice carried on in the areas outside Agra. In their own sphere of influence the Portuguese, Dutch and French banned Sati but efforts to stamp out Sati were formalised only under Lord William Bentinck after 1829.

British Regulation

The British were by no means certain of their approach to the custom no matter how abhorrent they found it. Following Mughal example, for a while they tried to regulate it by requiring that it be carried out in the presence of their officials and strictly according to custom.

Perhaps Bentinck was spurred on to Legislation by the unacceptable rise in Satis in his province, Bengal. In the 10 years between 1815 and 1825, the figure had doubled to 639 deaths by burning. He was certainly egged on by the constant entreaties of the missionaries and encouraged to action by the sea change being wrought amongst an influential section of Hindus led by Raja Ram Mohan Roy's Brahmo Samaj.

Despite this, Bentinck approached the question with caution. He sent circulars to 58 of his administrators to discover whether the army would revolt, whether legislation was advisable and whether Hindu resistance could be contained. The consensus of opinion was that the army would pose no problem.

Finally, within 18 months of having assumed the governorship of Bengal, Lord William Bentinck passed the Sati Regulation, XVII of 1827 on 4 December. The regulation was clear, concise and unequivocal in its condemnation of Sati, declaring it illegal and punishable by the criminal courts. It made zamindars, petty land owners, local agents and officers in charge of revenue collection especially accountable for immediate communication to the officers of their nearest police station of any intended sacrifice of the nature described. In case of willful neglect the responsible officer was liable to a fine of Rs.200 or 6 months in jail for default.

Immediately on receiving intelligence that a sacrifice was to take place, the police daroga accompanied by others was to go to the spot and declare the gathering illegal, prevail upon the crowd to disperse, explain that any persistence was likely to make them all liable to a crime and if necessary prevent the Sati from taking place or go and inform the nearest magistrate of the names and addresses of all those present. If the sacrifice was over, a full and immediate inquiry had to be undertaken in the same way as for any unnatural death.

Most significantly the regulation eschewed any debate about voluntariness which has so much in the forefront of the Sati debate in 1987. Aiding and abetting a sacrifice whether voluntary or not was to deemed culpable homicide. Punishment was at the discretion of the court according to the nature and circumstances of the case. No justification was to be made that the victim desired to sacrificed. The death penalty was specially spelled out for any violence or compulsion or helping or assisting in burning of a widow while she laboured under a state of intoxication or stupefaction or because any other cause impeded her free will. In such cases the court was instructed to show no mercy.

Fundamental Opposition

Even before the regulation was out, some three hundred orthodox Hindus petitioned Lord Bentinck to stop the abolition. They pleaded that the practise of "self immolation", was not merely a sacred duty but a "privilege" of believers. Bentinck however would not relent.

The sequence of events that followed are and eerie precursor to the events after Roop Kanwars Sati in 1987. Orthodox Bengali Brahmins formed themselves into the Dharma Sabha, just as today we have the Dharam Raksha Samiti in Rajasthan. In all they collected more than Rs.30,000/-a huge sum in those days, to fight the Regulation all the way upto the highest court. By contrast Raja Ram Mohan Roy was given Rs.5000/-to assist the Government in their representations before the Privy Council in England. Both sides gathered petitions and pamphleteered extensively.

In 1832 the appeal was heard by the Privy Council. The petitioners argued that it went against the basic assurance given in George III Statute 37 whereby the Hindus were assured complete noninterference with their religion. The abolitionists argued that there was really no freedom of religion that could go beyond what was "compatible with the paramount claims of humanity and justice." Of 7 privy councillors, three finally voted against Bentinck's regulation but finally it was it was upheld.

With the last hurdle cleared, Madras and then Bombay followed suit with their own legislation banning Sati. Slowly local rulers who came under the yoke of the British also conceded legislation against Sati in conformity with the British regulations. The rulers of Jaipur banned it in 1846.

Indian Penal Code

The 1833 Charter to the East India Company empowered the government to make laws for British India with due respect for native custom and usage. T.B. Macaulay, brilliant academician and lawyer was given the brief of formulating a comprehensive criminal code of universal application through the entire subcontinent. He had no doubt in his mind that Sati was a barbarous practice which could brook no justification. But the administration of 1860 and the Law Commissioners who revised the first draft, were unnecessarily alive to the sensitivities of high caste brahmanical feeling and watered down the murder provisions in their relation to Sati by enacting exception 5 of section 300. Under this, a mitigation was provided for murder when "the person whose death is caused, being above the age of 18 years, suffers death or takes the risk of death with his own consent." Despite this concession under the IPC, taking of life is absolutely prohibited to everyone in every circumstance. But Punishment varies depending on the nature and circumstances of the offense.

If on the facts, the ritualistic public burning or burying alive of a woman is shown to be involuntary, it is murder plain and simple (Section 300 IPC 1860). In the unlikely even that the woman was a willing participant, her death still amounts to culpable homicide (Section 299 or via exception 5 of Section 300) or at the very least to abetment to suicide (Section 306). Even where a Sati is deemed to be a suicide i.e. voluntary self-killing, the presence of any intoxicant or anything which in fact inhibits free will makes the abettor as culpable as if he had helped murder the victim (section 305 IPC). The punishment for this is exactly the same as for murder.

Where the Sati is incomplete, a person helping to achieve it is caught by the attempt sections of the IPC. Depending again on the circumstances, the crime may be attempt to murder (section 307); attempt to culpable homicide not amounting to murder (Section 308); or abetment to suicide punishable with one year's imprisonment and attempt to commit suicide which is an offence for the woman as well.

Under the present IPC no one who abets a Sati should escape the consequences of his acts. Abetment can take the form of instigation, conspiracy to do an act or make an illegal omission, intentional aiding, or willful misrepresentation or willful concealment (Section 107). Again depending on the facts, the aider could be abeting murder, culpable homicide. Form all the above it is clear that there are enough and more laws on the statute books to punish those guilty of making any human sacrifice including widow burning.

Fresh Sati Legislation

Despite this, the Central government has passed the Commission of Sati Prevention Act of 1987. Womens groups had been asked for suggestions. Had the Central government taken time to consider and passed judicious amendments to the present laws which are compatible and in consonance with the general jurisprudence of the country, the anomalies that have now arisen would not have come about.

While an entirely new act has the advantage of bringing under one, enactment scattered offenses so as to form a ready code, it also fuels the belief that there was no law against Sati in the first place. A special law again Sati related offenders also has the disadvantage of elevating a run of the mill criminal to the status of a conscientious offender. Specific legislation also provides a rallying point for pro-Sati lobbyists and a ready made cause in the name of religion and identity. Though the High Court at Rajasthan has already upheld the constitutionality of the State legislation which the Central law copies, both acts undoubtedly suffer from all the ills of hastily drafted and ill-considered legislation.

Burden of Proof

The least attractive feature of the new law is Section 16, which reverses the burden of proof on to the accused. Under the philosophy or criminal law adopted in India and used uniformly throughout the Penal Code, each accused is innocent until proven guilty. In every case the prosecution must prove its case positively beyond reasonable doubt. The only argument for shifting the burden of proof sometimes put forward is that the prosecution is so extremely disadvantaged in some circumstances that there would be absolutely minimal chance of catching the culprit. In statutory minimal chance of catching the culprit. In statutory cases where burden of proof is shifted, the offenses are relatively minor and the accused has a generally easy time proving his innocence.

In the public, even tamasha atmosphere of a sati, witnesses are available; independent, corroborative evidence is there for the authorities to gather and there is no justification for reversing the burden of proof for a mere abettor to sati when a brutal sadistic or psychotic murderer in any other circumstances has the full protection of the law requiring the prosecution to prove its case in each and every particular.

If the new law had been in the form of an amendment in the homicide sections of the IPC, declaring that henceforth all Satis (or any ritual killings) shall be presumed to be as murder unless otherwise established by the defence, the problem of women killers getting off lightly for merely abetting to suicide would have been solved.

The woman herself in this case would have always been the victim. But under the new act a woman who attempts Sati is herself liable to punishment for 6 months jail.

Abetting Sati

Without the principal there can be no abettor so the new act in its muddled way has to treat the woman as an offender in order to catch all those who take part in the commission of a Sati.

Justice requires that the punishment fit the crime. The Penal Code while absolutely forbidding all killing carefully differentiates between degrees of moral opprobrium society attaches to a crime. This is reflected in the punishments handed out for different types of killing.

The new Sati Act throws these fine and necessary distinctions to the winds.

Section 4 first of all obfuscates the difference between abetment to a crime and the principle offender. It lumps together all sorts into a single section entitled 'Abatement of Sati'. It punishes both the person who actually prevents or obstructs a widow from saving herself from being burnt or buried alive in the same measure as a person who participates "in any procession in connection with the commission of Sati".

Yet the degree of guilt is totally varied. In fact the man who intoxicates a woman or prevents her getting out of the fire is not an abettor at all but a murderer and should be treated as such. The bystander may be deemed an abettor and should be punished accordingly. The does not mean that an abettor to the attempt would go free. Abetment to Sati can cover a wide variety of activities, such as standing around shouting 'sati mata ki jai' and attending a ceremonial killing. The degree of culpability should matter but under the new law the latter person is as liable to the death sentence as the person who actually holds down the widow and prevents her from escaping from the pyre.

The bystander at a Sati ceremony is now certainly more disadvantaged than the gruesome murderer or his aide is under the ordinary law. In their case at least the prosecution must prove the case beyond reasonable doubt.

Under the Indian Penal Code what is worrisome is the willingness of the authorities to treat cases of widow burning as suicide rather than murder or culpable homicide, because by its very definition a classic Sati is self immolation. The result is that abettors are let off comparatively lightly and escape the ignominy and moral opprobrium that attaches to these. Of course a great deal depends on the willingness of the police to pursue inquiries and lodge an appropriate FIR. Even in the Roop Kanwar case, one cannot help but feel that but for the hue and cry raised, the matter would not have been taken up and under the murder sections of the IPC.

Glorification

The new Sati Act forbids any glorification of sati, makes it punishable with upto 7 years imprisonment and a possible fine of Rs.30,000/-(Section 5). Glorification" in relation to the practice of Sati includes, among other things, "the observance of any ceremony or the taking out of a procession in connection with the Sati or the creation of a trust or the collection of funds for the construction of the temple with a view to perpetuating the honour of, or to preserve the memory of the person committing Sati."

Under the IPC 'glorification' before an act of Sati could be dealt with under the incitement to crime and violence sections. But 'glorification' after an act of Sati is not covered.

In a democracy legislation has always to try to maintain the fine balance between freedom of speech and its abuse. The naked opportunism seen after the Deorala incident has undoubtedly provoked this part of the legislation, as well as Section 19 which disqualifies people' representative from elections if convicted under the Act. It also tries to prevent unscrupulous candidates from using the Sati issue to make their political fortunes. The danger of preventing the lunatic fringe from airing their views lies in their ability to go underground with them and also clouds the limits of democratic debate.

The commercialisation aspect of Sati has been directly dealt with. But even today donation received by the perpetrators of a crime can be confiscated under the general rule that no man may benefit from the fruit of his crime. Donations at the Sati sthal are liable for confiscation if it is thought they will be used for an illegal purpose, like building a temple against the public policy. Such donations when they are in the hands of a committee can also be diverted away from their illegal purpose under Section 92 of the Civil Procedure Code. This allows the court to direct how trust monies may be used if the purpose for which they have been collect fails for intervening illegality. At the behest of the Advocate-general or any person interested, the money can be diverted for purposes such as widow rehabilitation.

There is still room for more specific legislation to discourage the commercial success of tamashas like Sati. An amendment to the Income Tax Act removing exemption from charitable donations made to temples which commemorate or have come up as a consequence of an ancient or recent Sati, will at least discourage large donors. Specifically excluding Sati temples from benefits given to charitable institutions will also discourage them.

The tremendous attention and debate that a single events at Deorala generated is evidence of the ability of the womens movement to bring about positive changes through sustained agitation. But even at the height of lobbying for some kind of legislation it was never anyones case that liberation for women from years of oppression could be brought only through essentially illiberal legislation, by robbing others of their legitimate rights. If the old law under the IPC were but enforced no new jumbled legislation would be necessary.

Hopefully there will never be another Sati and the entire discussion here will be academic. But recent experiences both of the lack of political will to implement existing legislation and the determination of the Rajputs to defy the law suggest that whatever Central laws may be enacted, may end up honoured more in the breach than in the letter.

Brahmo Samaj

Brahmo Samaj is the societal component of Brahmoism. It has without doubt proved to be the most influential religious movement of the nineteenth century. It was conceived as reformation of the prevailing Bengal of the time and began the Bengal Renaissance of the 19th century pioneering all religious, social and educational advance of the Hindu community in the 19th century. From the *Brahmo Samaj* springs Brahmoism, the most recent of legally recognised religions in India and Bangladesh, reflecting its non-syncretic "foundation of Rammohan Roy's reformed spiritual Hinduism (contained in the 1830 Banian deed) and scientifically invigorated by inclusion of root Hebraic-Islamic creed and practice."

Meaning of Names

The *Brahmo Samaj* is a community of people assembled for orderly public meeting, discussion or worship of the Eternal, Immutable Supreme Being, Author and Preserver of the Universe, "but not under or by any other name designation or title peculiarly used for and applied, to any particular being or beings by any man or set of men whatsoever".

"The *Brahmo Samaj*, represents a body of men who are struggling, in India, to establish the worship of the Supreme Being in spirit as opposed to the prevailing idolatry of the land."

Brahmo literally means "one who worships Brahman", and *Samaj* mean "community of men".

History and Timeline

Raja Ram Mohan Roy

Brahmo Sabha

On 20 August 1828 the first assembly of the *Brahmo Sabha* (progenitor of the Brahmo Samaj) was held at the North Calcutta house of *Feringhee* Kamal Bose. This day is celebrated by Brahmos as *Bhadrotsab*. This *Sabha* was convened at Calcutta by religious reformer Raja Rammohan Roy for his family and friends settled there. The *Sabha* regularly gathered on Saturday between seven o'clock to nine o'clock. These were essentially informal meetings of Bengali Brahmins (the "twice born"), accompanied by Upanishadic recitations in Sanskrit followed by Bengali translations of the Sanskrit recitation and singing of Brahmo hymns composed by Rammohan. These meetings were open to all Brahmins and there was no formal organisation or theology as such.

On 8 January 1830 influential progressive members of the closely related Kulin Brahmin clan (scurrilously described as Pirali Brahmin *i.e.* ostracised for service in the Mughal *Nizaamat* of Bengal) of Tagore (*Thakur*) and Roy (*Vandopadhyaya*) *zumeendar* family mutually executed the Trust deed of Brahmo Sabha for the first Adi Brahmo Samaj (place of worship) on Chitpore Road (now Rabindra Sarani), Kolkata, India with Ram Chandra Vidyabagish as first resident superintendent.

On 23 January 1830 or 11th *Magh*, the *Adi Brahmo* premises were publicly inaugurated (with about 500 Brahmins and 1 Englishman present). This day is celebrated by Brahmos as *Maghotsab*.

In November 1830 Rammohan Roy left for England.

Decline of Brahmo Sabha

With Rammohan's departure for England in 1830, the affairs of Sabha were effectively managed by Trustees Dwarkanath Tagore and Pandit Ram Chandra Vidyabagish, with Dwarkanath instructing his *diwan* to manage affairs. Weekly service were held consonant with the Trust directive, consisting of three successive parts: recitation of the Vedas by Telegu Brahmins in the closed apartment exclusively before the Brahmin members of the congregation, reading and exposition of the Upanishads for the general audience, and singing of religious hymns. The reading of the Vedas was done exclusively before the Brahmin participants as the orthodox Telugu Brahmin community and its members could not be persuaded to recite the Vedas before Brahmins and non-Brahmins alike.

By the time of Rammohan's death in 1833 near Bristol (UK), attendance at the *Sabha* dwindled and the Telugu Brahmins revived idolatry. The *zumeendars*, being preoccupied in business, had little time for affairs of *Sabha*, and flame of *Sabha* was almost extinguished.

Tattwabodhini Period

On 6 October 1839 Debendranath Tagore, son of (Prince) Dwarkanath Tagore, established *Tattvaranjini Sabha* which was shortly thereafter renamed the Tattwabodhini (*Truth-seekers*) Sabha. Initially confined to immediate members of the Tagore family, in 2 years it mustered over 500 members. In 1840 Debendranath published a Bangla translation of *Katha Upanishad*. Contemporary researchers describe the Sabha's philosophy as *modern middle-class (bourgeois) Vedanta.*

Foundation of Samaj

On 7th Pous 1765 Shaka (1843) Debendranath Tagore and twenty other Tattwabodhini stalwarts were formally invited by Pt. Vidyabagish into the Trust of Brahmo Sabha. The Pous Mela at Santiniketan starts on this day which is considered as foundation of the 'Adi' (First) *Brahmo Samaj* which was named the Calcutta *Brahmo Samaj*. The other Brahmins who took the First Covenant are:-

- Shridhar Bhattacharya
- Shyamacharan Bhattacharya
- Brajendranath Tagore
- Girindranath Tagore, brother of Debendranath Tagore & father of Ganendranath Tagore
- Anandachandra Bhattacharya
- Taraknath Bhattacharya
- Haradev Chattopadhyay
- Shyamacharan Mukhopadhyaya
- Ramnarayan Chattopadhyay
- Sashibhushan Mukhopadhyaya.

First Schism

The admittance of Keshub Chandra Sen (a non-Brahmin) into the Calcutta Brahmo Samaj in 1857 while Debendranath was away in Simla caused considerable stress in the movement, with many old Tattvabodhini Brahmin members leaving the Samaj and institutions due to his high-handed ways. These events took place intermittently from 1859, coming to a head publicly between the period of 1 August 1865 till November 1866 with many tiny splinter groups styling themselves as *Brahmo*. The most notable of these groups styled itself "Brahmo Samaj of India". This period is referred to in the histories of these secessionists as the "First Schism".

Spread of Influence

Although the *Brahmo Samaj* movement was born in Kolkata, the idea soon spread to the rest of India. That happened to be the period when the railways were expanding and communication was becoming easier. Outside Bengal presidency some of the prominent centres of Brahmo activity were: Punjab, Sindh, and Bombay and Madras presidencies. Even to this day, there are several active branches outside West Bengal. Bangladesh Brahmo Samaj at Dhaka keeps the lamp burning.

Social & Religious Reform

In all fields of social reform, including abolition of the caste system and of the dowry system, emancipation of women, and improving the educational system, the *Brahmo Samaj* reflected the ideologies of the Bengal Renaissance. Brahmoism, as a means of discussing the dowry system, was a central theme of Sarat Chandra Chattopadhyay's noted 1914 Bengali language novella, *Parineeta*.

Debendranath Tagore

Debendranath Tagore (*Debendronath Ṭhakur*) (15 May 1817 – 19 January 1905) was the founder in 1848 of the Brahmo Religion which today is synonymous with Brahmoism the youngest religion of India and Bangladesh.

A Bengali, he was born in Calcutta, India. His father, was the fabulous "Prince" Dwarkanath Tagore.

Debendranath was a deeply religious man. His movement the Brahmo Samaj was formed in 1843 by merging his Tattwabodhini Sabha with the Brahmo Sabha, ten years after the death of the latter's founder, Raja Ram Mohan Roy. The Brahmo Sabha had fallen away from its original practices put forth in its Trust deed of Brahmo Sabha, however, Tagore revived the importance of this deed.

Debendranath's spiritual prowess was of the highest order, even while he maintained his worldly affairs – not renouncing his material possessions as some Hindu traditions prescribed but rather continuing to enjoy them in a spirit of detachment. His considerable material property included several estates spread over the districts of Bengal; most famously, the later acquisition Santiniketan estate near Bolpur in the Birbhum district where his eldest son Dwijendranath Tagore set up his school.

Debendranath was a master of the Upanishads and played no small role in the education and cultivation of faculties of his sons.

Children

Dwijendranath (1840–1926) was an accomplished scholar, poet and music composer. He initiated shorthand and musical notations in Bengali. He wrote extensively and translated Kalidas's Meghdoot into Bengali.

Satyendranath (1842–1923) was the first Indian to join the Indian Civil Service. At the same time he was a great scholar with a large reservoir of creative talents.

Hemendranath (1844–1884) was the scientist and organiser of the family. He was a spiritual seer and Yogi of the highest order and he was responsible for development of the modern Brahmoism which is now the Adi Dharm religion. He was a "doer" of his Tagore generation and worthy successor to his grandfather Dwarkanath and father. He sided with his "conservative" siblings Dwijendranath and Birendranath in the family disputes against "modern" Satyendranath, Jyotindranath and Rabindranath.

Jyotirindranath (1849–1925) was a scholar, artist, music composer and theatre personality.

Rabindranath (1861–1941) was his youngest son. His other sons were Birendranath (1845–1915) and Somendranath.

His daughters were Soudamini, Sukumari, Saratkumari, Swarnakumari (1855–1932) and Barnakumari. Soudamini was one of the first students of Bethune School and a gifted writer. Swarnakumari was a gifted writer, editor, song-composer and social worker. All of them were famous for their beauty and education. His part in creating the legacy of Thakurbari – the House of Tagore – in the cultural heritage of Bengal, centred in Kolkata, was not negligible. It was largely through the influence of the Tagore family, following that of the writer Bankim Chandra Chatterjee, that Bengal took a leading role on the cultural front as well as on the nationalistic one, in the Renaissance in India during the nineteenth century.

Thakur Bari (House of Tagores)

The house of the Tagore family in Jorasanko, popular as Jorasanko Thakur Bari in North-western Kolkata, was later converted into a campus of the Rabindra Bharati University.

Religion

As son of Dwarkanath, a close friend of Ram Mohan Roy, Debendranath came early into the influence of Brahmoism through the Brahmo Sabha, a reformist movement in Hinduism formulating as Adi Dharma (Original Dharma) what it considered as the original pristine principles of Hinduism corrupted over time.

But even earlier, deeply affected in childhood by the death of his grandmother to whom he was greatly attached, Debendranath was drawn to religion and began contemplating the meaning and nature of life. He commenced a deep study of religious literature, particularly the Upanishads. In 1839, with tutelage from Pandit Ram Chandra Vidyabageesh, a leader of the Brahmo Sabha, he formed his own active Tattwabodhini Sabha (Truthseekers' Association) to spread his new experiences and knowledge.

In 1843, Debendranath started the Tattwabodhini Patrika as mouthpiece of the Tattwabodhini Sabha. In the same year, he revived the Brahma Sabha, fallen in vigour and following since the death of Rammohan in 1833. The Brahmo Sabha was formally absorbed into the Tattwabodhini Sabha and renamed as Calcutta Brahma Samaj. The day Pous 7 of the Bengali calendar is commemorated as the foundation day of the Samaj. The Patrika became the organ of the Samaj and continued publication till 1883.

In 1848, Debendranath codified the Adi Dharma Doctrine as Brahmo Dharma Beej (Seed of the Brahmo Dharma). In 1950, he published a book titled Brahmo Dharma enshrining the fundamental principles. These principles emphasise monotheism, rationality and reject scriptural infallibility, the necessity of mediation between man and God, caste distinctions and idolatry.

With the influence of Brahmoism under Debendranath spreading far and wide throughout India, he gathered reputation as a person of particular spiritual accomplishment and came to be known as Maharshi. His spiritual stature was confirmed by Sri Ramakrishna, the great Hindu sage of the 19th century who paid Debendranath a visit. Debendranath's roles in the Indian renaissance and the reform and rejuvenation of Hindu religion are indubitable.

An influence of Hasidism over Brahmoism has been claimed.

Ishwar Chandra Vidyasagar

The country, whose male population is unkind unreligious and unaware of the distinction between the good and the evil and don't care about justice and fairness and where abiding the rituals is the chief preoccupation of religion, should not give birth to girls!

[His god-like kindness expressed in the 2nd volume of publication on Remarriage of Widows.]

The materialistic world of the West looks down on India as a poor nation. That assessment is and remains empirically valid, no doubt, even at the end of the twentieth century.

But a society, nation or country that is ever endowed with a great man with a personality, grace and kind soul like Ishwar Chandra Vidyasagar can be impoverished but hardly poor! Popularly known as Vidyasagar (meaning 'sea of knowledge'), Ishwar Chandra himself was the seat of learning. A gift of God his life was a glittering gem of morality, an exposition of the bliss of modest living, a blue sky of compassion, an everest of unfaltering dedication, a fountain of inspiration, a river of love and indeed an ocean of kindness.

Watch closely how this man lived his life, how he shared his time between his family, his friends, his community and his nation, how he spent his endless energy for awakening awareness of his countrymen and for the emancipation of his nation, how he gave away every comfort of life for the sake of others and your heart will warm up to the message of this man's life. And your life will never be the same again! His graceful gift of love and affection will enrich your existence and humble your thoughts for ever.

Born on Monday the 26th of September 1820 (12 Aswin BY1227) in a village called Veerasingha of the then Hoogley (now part of Midnapore) district of West Bengal Vidysagar spent his childhood in extreme poverty. But poverty did not touch his soul, nor could it deter him from his chosen path of achieving his life's goals.

Ishwar commenced primary education at the village pathshaala-an indigenous Indian school where language, grammar, arithmatic and other shastras were taught to younsters. In the pathshaala he was a fond student of Pundit Kalikanta Chatterjee for his dedication to learning, modest manners, supreme honesty and great respect. Following his grandfather's death, he accompanied his father to Calcutta. At the time his father was employed as accounts receivable clerk with a metal goods importers store at Barobazar. Ishwar joined a pathshaala in neigbouring Jorashanko. His father's wish was for him to be educated as a Sanskrit scholar so that he would go back to his village and start a Chuspahathi (a Sanskrit school) thus maintaining the family tradition in teaching Sanskrit. But one family relative-Madhusudan Bachaspati who was then studying at the Sanscrit College-convinced his father to send Ishwar to that college arguing that this course of education will allow the youngman to gain access to both Sanskrit and English streams of education.

It is not clear as to what role Ishwar played in this decision but with the possibility of enhanced job opportunities in the future his father relented. Within a short while Ishwar was admitted to the Sanscrit College in grammar class III. As it turned out, this decision was a small turning point in the life of one man, but a giant leap in the history of Bengal. Young Ishwar applied himself to learning with full discipline, diligence and perseverence-often in the most arduous of circumstances. He passed successive annual examinations with exemplary brilliance. His meritorious performance in every field of study rewarded him with prizes and scholarships which were a welcome relief in his impoverished financial condition. It is here he came in close contact with half a dozen Sanskrit scholars who would a leave an indelible mark on the young impressionable mind of Ishwar.

In 1839 he graduated in law examination conducted by the Hindu Law Committee. His well rounded education at Sanscrit College saw him amassing considerable knowledge and mastery in a number of shastras or disciplines-*kabya (poetry), alonkar (rhetorics), vedanta (vedic literature and anthology), smriti (philosophy of law), nyaya (logic, science and jurisprudence), and jyotish (astronomy).* It is here at a tender age the title Vidyasagar was endowed to him. He lived up to that expectation and offered to his society far more than that... In a thousand years that would follow, Bengali people and indeed the world at large, would not be able to rid itself of the debt owed to this man.

On 29th December in 1841 Vidyasagar joined Fort William College (FWC) as a Principal Lecturer (or Pundit). G. T. Marshall who was the Secretary of the College at the time acted as the catalyst for gaining this prestigious position for him at the age of 21. Marshall had been thoroughly impressed by Ishwar's scholastic achievements! After a five year stint with the FWC Vidyasagar joined the Sanscrit College as Assistant Secretary. In the first year of service with Sanscrit College, he brought out a report to the authorities outlining and recommending a number of changes to the curricula and the education system. This report attracted criticisms from the College Secretary Rashamoy Dutta (who was jealous of his youthful and energetic Assistant) but it generated keen interest of authorites and a tremendous amount of favourable comments and praises from the Education department-particularly from G. T. Marshall. Because of irreconcilable differences with Dutta on this subject-Vidyasagar resigned and took up the temporary head clerical position at FWC (again on Marshall's advice FWC employed him so he is not lost to the Education system) until a teaching position could be made available.

Ishwar Chandra's principles, determination and courage were unparallel in every detail. He never deviated from his goals in the face of all advarsities. He knew not how to compromise on any matter of substance neither in fear nor for favour. Fear was not in his dictionary. He resigned from the college, after the skirmish with Dutta. His well wishers tried in vain to prevent him saying "what will you do? how will you survive?". His reply was "I will sell vegetables, open a grocery shop, I will find something to survive on".

Another example was cited by Tagore. When Vidyasagar went to visit the Principal of the Hindu College, he was offended by Mr. Kerr's rude manners as the latter sat in his chair in a posture resting his booted feet on the desk in a complete disregard for showing any courtesy to his native visitor. Mr. Kerr was reported to have been very displeased when this same courtesy was reciprocated to him on his visit to Sanscrit College at a later date. Tit for tat!

In 1950 Vidyasagar came back to Sanscrit College as Lecturer in Literature. Satisfied with his hard work and his substantive contribution to the betterment of the education system, his remuneration was doubled. Soon afterwards he was appointed

Principal of Sanscrit College. His well documented protestations against Education department officials of the day testify to the degree of intensity with which he pursued the course of education reform. He favoured English and Bengali as a medium of learning alongside Sanskrit and wanted to offer to students a wider range of subjects and thus broaden their horizons in examining European and Indian concepts and practices side by side so they could apply their own judgement in discovering the truth for themselves. He was not afraid of discarding erroneous beliefs of Indian shastras and in preferring European science in its place where appropriate. By the same token he did not accept everything that Europe had to offer. His mind was open and was open only to discovering the truth and reality. In these matters his determination was unmistakable and his resolve unshakable. Here is a sample paragraph of one of his letters to F. J. Mouat, Secretary to the Council of Education:

Leave me to teach Sanskrit for the leading purpose of thoroughly mastering the Vernacular and let me superadd to it the acquisition of sound knowledge through the medium of English and you may rest assured that before a few years are over I shall be enabled if supported and encouraged by the Council to furnish with you a body of young men who will be better qualified by their writings and teachings to disseminate widely among the people sound information than it has hitherto been possible to accomplish through the instrumentality of the Educated clever of any of your Colleges whether English or oriental.

To enable me to carry out this great, this darling object of my wishes I must (excuse the strong word) to a considerable extent be left unfettered, so far as I can approve of Dr. Ballantyne's abtracts and treatises such for instance as his excellent Edition of the Novum Organan in English. I will avail myself of them most readily and cheerfully.

But if compelled to adopt all his compilations without any reference to my own humble judgement as to their utility and value or to their adaptation to the peculiar wants of the Institution over which I have the honour to preside, my occupation is gone-such a system would break in upon and interrupt my own plan of instruction and in spite of my sense of duty as a servant of the Council the responsibility which I now keenly feel will be assuredly weakened if not destroyed.

In addition to his responsibilities as the Principal of Sanscrit College, he travelled around Bengal in the capacity of Inspector of Schools. This latter role gave him the opportunity to witness the pervading darkness and superstitions in which people of Bengal lived in the absence of education. This caused him great distress. He hurriedly established 20 Model schools in only two months. He also realised that unless women of the land could be educated it was impossible to emancipate and liberate them from the terrible burden of inequalities and injustice imposed on them by the cruel society of the day. He worked day and night and opened thirty girls schools.

In 1854 FWC was closed and a Board of Exeminers was created instead. Vidyasagar was an active member of that Board. He resigned from Sanscrit College after a disagreement with the young new head of the Education department in 1958. It was not in his blood to work under a regime that did not pay full respect to his unquestionable ability to manage the affairs of his institution independently and without any undue outside interference.

There is not a single living Bengali soul on this planet today who has not heard of Vidyasagar or has not commenced the process of education with his first book of alphabet (Part I and Part II) called Varna Porichoy first published in 1855. His pioneering works-in Bengali education, in laying the base foundation stone of Bengali prose (even though his writing style was considered at the time as conservative since it was aligned closely with Sanskrit lexicon and grammatical traditions) and in translation of the Sanskrit masterpieces to Bengali-shall remain as the fitting monument of human endeavour in the quest for and spread of knowledge.

Vidyasagar's heart was gold-full of mercy and kindness! It always cried out in distress of the poor, in sufferings of the sick and for injustice to humanity. Even when he was a student at Sanscrit College, he would spend part of his scholarship proceeds and cooked mishtanno (rice pudding) to feed the poor and buy medicine for the sick. Later on, he paid fixed sums of monthly allowances to each member of his joint family, to family servants, to needy neighbours, to villagers who needed help and to the village surgery and school. This he continued without break even when he was unemployed and had to borrow substantially from time to time. Once he borrowed Rs.7,500 from Maharani

Swarnamayee. In his will he kept all those regular names as beneficiary who received his monthly allowance and he added more names to that list. Then he had also added a blanket category 'who needed help'.

Vidyasagar did not believe that his responsibility to the suffering humanity ended with his financial donation. He opened the doors of Sanscrit College to lower caste students (previously it was exclusive to the Brahmins), nursed sick cholera patients, went to crematorium to bury unclaimed deadbodies, dined with the untouchables, walked miles in darkness to take urgent messages to people who would benefit from them. The list goes on! Even a thousand Nobel prizes wouldn't go close to recognise this man's contribution to the suffering humanity, such gold was Vidyasagar's heart! Vidyasagar was a social reformer. His soft heart melted at the pain and suffering imposed by the society, often in the name of religion, on Indian women. Polygamy, ban on widows from remarrying, child marriage, inequalities, keeping them away from the light of education, depriving them from property rights etc. All of this distressed him immensely. Pleading the case for the remarriage of widows he lamented:

Oh poor India!...you think the woman whose husband dies immediately turns into a stone; she does not have sorrow anymore, cannot feel pain any more and all her senses of passions and sensualities diasappear without trace suddenly! But you well know that such notions are based on false pretences as evidence to the contrary abounds. Just think how these erroneous notions are poisoning this world. How sad! The country, whose male population is unkind, unreligious and unaware of the distinction between the good and the evil and don't care about justice and fairness and where abiding the rituals is the chief preoccupation of religion, should not give birth to girls!

He took up his pen, called discussion meetings, ran seminars and saw Government officials. All of these efforts were directed to wipe out the evil traditions of the nation. But his call fell on deaf ears. On every instance, dictates from Hindu shastras were forwarded by the clergy as an excuse! So Vidyasagar set out to prove them wrong! He conducted extensive reseach into Hindu scriptures and puranas and tried to explain that there was nothing against widows marrying a second time and why polygamy was an evil and hence unacceptable. He published two separate volumes on remarriage of widows and another two volumes on polygamy citing quotes from scriptures and explaning the validity of his arguments.

To prove that his compassion for widows was not empty rhetoric as some might have assumed, he married his own son off to a widow. He compiled a list of 'distinguished' polygamous Calcuttans and another for surrounding districts. It is unthinkable that a considerable number on those lists married up to 80 times often under-age girls and yet were unable to control their boundless thirst for lust.

For his stand he was virulently attacked by conservative vested interest groups and the shastrakars (cleric) of the day. He often received threats of physical violence and death. But nothing stopped Vidyasagar from what he set out to do! His iron-will prevailed in the end. On 26th July 1856 widow marriage was legalised by the then Government.

Although Vidyasagar cannot be judged as one of the best pure literary figures of Bengal, for he mostly devoted his time writing reformist literature and text books, his pioneering work in Bengali prose certainly deserves the very best of appreciation. His simplification of idiomatic expressions and clarification of the writing style provided the sound base on which latter Bengali writers like Tekchand Thakur, Pyarichand Mitra and Bankim Chandra Chatterjee built their literary superstructures. Indeed, Tagore revered him as 'the father of modern Bengali prose'. Vidysagar's other contribution in this area was to translate the best of Sanskrit works to Bengali so that the ordinary person, who were not sufficiently versed with that language, could appreciate the immortal contribution by literary greats of India. He wrote biographical notes on numerous noteworthy personalities in the history of the world so the the young generation could be inspired by the great examples of their edurance, hard work, honesty, patience, perseverence, courage, determination and, above all, philosophy of life.

Betal Panchavinsati (The Bytal-Pancheesee-the twenty-five tales of the Demon) published in 1847-a translation from the Sanskrit *Kathasaritsagara,* is probably the most popular work of Vidysagar. In its Preface he wrote: The Bytal Pancheesee is a collection of legendary stories relating to that clelebrated character in Hindu

Annals, Raja Vikramaditya. The work contains no traces of art or genius in its composition, but on the contrary exhibits those clumsy attempts at the wonderful, sometimes bordering on childishness, which are so general in legends of a dark age. It is, however, very popular among the great mass of the people of this country and expresses accurately their ideas and feelings on many subjects".

Other notable literary contributions by him include Banglaar Itihaas (1848), Jivancharita (1849), Shakuntala (1854), Mahabharata (1860), Seetar Vanavas (1860), Bhrantivilaas (1869), Oti Alpa Hoilo (1873), Aabaar Oti Alpa Hoilo (1873), Brajavilaas (1884) and Ratnopariksha (1886). But the most far-reaching and controversial of his social reform monologues are:

- Bidhobabivah (whether widows should remarry) the first exposure (1855)
- Bidhobabivah-the Second Book (1855)
- Bahubivah-(whether polygamy should be banned) the first exposure (1871)
- Bahubivah-the Second Book (1873)
- Balyabivah (flaws of child marriage)-publication date not known.

Its not his literary prowess, but his act of kindness, his fierce determination and courage, his education and social reform programmes made Vidyasagar immortal. Tagore was hard pressed to find a comparable personality in the West and according to him, the closest that he found who could come to resemble him was Samuel Johnson.

He lived as a modest man but his work of charity was that of a king. Even his friend Lieutenant Governor Halliday could not get him to dress up properly when he used to visit him. He preferred plain dress made from home spun cotton-as his mother used to make his dresses when she was alive.

Vidyasagar was a lonely tall tree in the bush around him. He was not happy and his health deteriorated badly in the latter part of his life. Disaffected with petty-mindedness and confronted with selfish behaviour he severed connection with his family and lived with a tribal people in the last years of his life. He died on 29th July 1891 (13th Shrabon BY 1298).

4

The Young Bengal Movement

Young Bengal a socio-intellectual label that was given by the contemporary Calcutta society to the students of HINDU COLLEGE who followed their teacher Henry Louis Vivian DEROZIO, a free thinker and rationalist, when he was a teacher there from 1826 to 1831.

Derozio taught his students to have critical outlook about life and societal processes. He taught them how social institutions take root and develop and how people become attached to dead and fossilised ideas and institutions. Drawing examples from world history and philosophy, Derozio tried to persuade his students to love knowledge and abandon the habit of believing groundlessly. To his students his repeated sermon was 'to live and die for truth'.

The most favourite students of Derozio were a band of brilliant students of the Hindu College like Krishnamohan Bndyopadhyay, Rashik Krishna Mallik, Dakhinaranjan Mukhopadhyay, Ramgopal Ghose, Madhab Chandra Mallik, ramtanu lahiri, Maheshchandra Ghose, Sibchandra Deb, Harachandra Ghose, Radhanath Sikder, Govindachandra Basak, Amritalal Mitra and others. They were inspired and excited by a spirit of free thought and revolt against the existing social and religious structure of the Hindu society.

As a mark of emancipation from old and decaying traditions they exulted in taking beef and drinking wine, which they regarded as a yardstick to measure their freedom from all religious superstition and prejudice and a notable effort to break social fetters. Many of Derozio's students found logic and substance in the arguments of the christian missionaries against many superstitious and cruel beliefs of the Hindus. Quite a number of them like Dakhinaranjan Mukhopadhyay and Krishnamohan Bandopadhyay even left Hinduism and embraced Christianity.

In 1828 Derozio founded with his students the 'Academic Association' which organised debates on various subjects. The meetings of the Academic Association were well attended and a number of distinguished men were often present. Derozio's students made an intense study of the writings of Voltaire, Hume, Locke, Tom Paine etc. and quoted them freely in their debates. Another organisation of these students was the 'Society for the Acquisition of General Knowledge' founded in 1838. Tarachand Chakravarty was the president of the society and secretaries were Pearychand Mitra and Ramtanu Lahiri.

Quite a few journals were run by the Derozians between 1828 and 1843 to give wider currency to their views and principles. Among these were the *Parthenon, Hesperus, Jnananvesan, Enquirer, Hindu Pioneer, Quill* and the *Bengal Spectator*. Only one issue of the *Parthenon* came out in 1830 and then it discontinued. Encouraged by the missionaries, the Young Bengal group published the *Jnananvesan* (Quest for Knowledge) for propagating their views. It had a longer life; starting in 1831, it continued up to 1844. Organised by Rashik Krishna Mallik, it was a bilingual journal aimed at educating the people in the science of government and jurisprudence. Krishnamohan started the *Enquirer* in 1831 and vehemently criticised the orthodox community that had mobilised its forces against the young redicals. Many of the groups were faced with social excommunication and all kinds of pressure were brought to compel them give up radical trend. The articles written by members of Young Bengal group and published in the *Hindu Pioneer* (started in 1838) clearly showed the growth of political consciousness among them. The *Quill*, run by Tarachand Chakravarty, also was critical of the government. In their writings the Young Bengal expressed frustration about the unequal political status of the natives and Europeans. The *Bengal Spectator,* a progressive publication, was perhaps the last of the Young Bengal journals. Starting in 1842, this monthly published articles on social, political and economic problems of the period and discussed such subjects as female education and remarriage of Hindu widows. It ultimately became a daily.

Besides their attacks on Hinduism, the Young Bengal supported most vocally the westernisation processes initiated by the colonial state. The Young Bengal movement is one of the most controversial phases of the bengal renaissance in the nineteenth century. They earned both unstinted praise and outright condemnation. They were connected with the efforts made for the introduction of western medical education in the country, which ultimately led to the foundation of the Calcutta medical college in 1835. They also encouraged the students of the Medical College to overcome the prevailing prejudice against dissecting dead bodies and thus removed an obstacle. Some scholars assert that the Young Bengal activists were the pioneers of the Bengal Renaissance. There is no doubt that they contributed much to the awakening of Bengal in the early nineteenth century and appreciated the introduction of English as official language of the state and establishment of several public libraries in Calcutta.

The greatest folly on the part of the Young Bengal, however, was that they found perfection in everything western. Oriental ways of life appeared to them superstitious. Their aversion to native practices led them to adopt western habits and manners, though unsuccessfully, which made them hateful in the eyes of the natives in general and their guardians in particular.

The Young Bengals were too immature to grasp and evaluate the significance of freethinking and disinterested questioning. Their half-baked knowledge about western civilization and their ignorance of the oriental culture made them highly audacious to the extent of downgrading Bengal culture and tradition as a whole. Consequently, in spite of their eloquent arguments against many aspects of contemporary life and institutions, they failed to enlist support from the Bengal literati and sustain their ideology. The Young Bengal spirit proved to be ephemeral and shallow and faded away as quickly as it appeared. In the later part of the nineteenth century Young Bengal turned into a social gossip.

Krishna Mohan Banerjee

Krishna Mohan Banerjee (1813-1885) (also referred to as Rev. Krishnamohan Bandopadhyay) was a prominent member of Henry Louis Vivian Derozio's (1808-1831) Young Bengal group, educationist, linguist and Christian missionary.

Early Life

Son of Jibon Krishna Banerjee, he was born on 28 May 1813

in the house of his maternal grand father at Shyampukur, Kolkata. His maternal grand father was Ramjay Vidyabhusan, court-pundit of Santiram Singha of Jorasanko.

Around 1819, Krishna Mohan joined the School Society institution opened by David Hare at Kalitala. Impressed by his talents, Hare took him to his school at Pataldanga, later famous as Hare School in 1822.

He joined the newly founded Hindu College with a scholarship. He was profoundly influenced by Derozio and that changed the course of his life. He used to live in his maternal grandfather's house, which he used as a meeting place for Derozians. One day, when he was absent, they consumed hand-made bread and meat prepared by Muslims, an unthinkable act for upper-caste Hindus in those days, threw the leftover bones into neighbours' houses, and started shouting, "Cow-meat! Cow-meat!" In the commotion that followed, Ramjay Vidyabhusan, his maternal grandfather, was forced to turn him out of the house. He found a place for a short while in the house of a Christian friend.

In 1831, he started publishing the *Inquirer*. In the same year his *The Persecuted* fell like a bomb shell among his contemporaries. It described in vivid colours the characters of reformers, conformists and the orthodox sections of society. It tore asunder the veil of respectability which had concealed the secret debaucheries of the leaders of society and thoroughly exposed the greed, the insincerity and the trickery of those particular Brahmins.

While at college, he used to attend lectures of Dr. Alexander Duff, who had come in 1830 from Scotland to preach Christianity. They also went to the houses of Duff and Dealtry for serious discussions. His father died of cholera in 1828. In spite of his diverse activities and self-support in manual work, he continued to excel in his examinations.

Conversion to Christianity

On completion of his studies in 1829, he joined the Pataldanga school as an assistant teacher. In 1832, he converted to Christianity, under the influence of Duff. As a result of his conversion, he lost his job in David Hare's school.

His conversion to Christianity raised a storm in Hindu society. The journals of the day became full of angry tirades against the activities of the Christian missionaries. He himself was too independent a man to remain silent. He declared his determination to pursue with steadfastness his course of action and endure with patience all opposition. The campaign against Hindu College led to the dismissal of Derozio.

When the missionary society was later established he became the first Bengali priest. In 1833, he was convicted of forcibly converting a young boy to Christianity. That did not daunt him. He converted his wife, his brother Kali Mohan, and Ganendra Mohan Tagore, the son of Prasanna Coomar Tagore. Subsequently, Ganendra Mohan married his daughter Kamalmani and became the first Indian to qualify as a barrister. He was also instrumental in the conversion of Michael Madhusudan Dutt. He became a deacon of the Anglican Church in 1836 and was superintendent of the Mirzapur School of Christ Church. He used to preach and deliver sermons in Bengali.

Later Life

In 1852, he was made a professor of Bishop's College at Shibpore. In 1864, he was elected to be a member of the Royal Asiatic Society along with Ishwar Chandra Vidyasagar. In 1876, the University of Calcutta honoured him with a doctorate degree. Subsequently the citizens of Kolkata honoured him.

He was a pioneer in developing the encyclopaedia in Bengali and published a 13-volume English-Bengali encyclopaedia *Vidyakalpadrum.* He knew Bengali, English, Sanskrit, Greek, Latin and Hebrew, and was author of such books as *The Aryan Witness, Dialogues on the Hindu Philosophy,* and *Upadeshkatha.*

He died on 11 May 1885.

Sib Chandra Deb

Sib Chandra Deb (also spelt Shib Chandra Deb, Shibchandra Deb, Shib Chander Deb) (20 July, 1811-12 November, 1890) was one of the leading Derozians, virtually the first generation of English-knowing Indians. He had joined Hindu College in 1825 and was subsequently drawn towards Derozio. Sivanath Shastri recalls that even in his old age he fondly recalled in detail what Derozio used to say. A brilliant student he won a scholarship while studying at Hindu College. As a student, he occasionally attended the meetings of the Brahmo Sabha established by Raja Rammohan

Roy. Initially, he joined the survey department as he had acquired proficiency in higher mathematics but changed over to general administration to become a deputy collector in 1838. The English allowed Indians to be promoted/posted as deputy collectors in 1833. He was one of the early English-knowing Indian officials in government service.

Brahmo Samaj

He joined the Brahmo Samaj in 1843, around the same time as Debendranath Tagore, and rose to be one of its prominent leaders by the 1850s. He established the Medinipur Brahmo Samaj in 1846 and the Konnagar Brahmo Samaj in 1863. At the time of founding of the Brahmo Samaj of India, he was with the progressives and assisted the movement in many ways. At the time of establishment of the Sadharan Brahmo Samaj, his sympathies were with the protesting party. He was one of the leaders of the Sadharan Brahmo Samaj, along with Sivanath Shastri, Ananda Mohan Bose, Umesh Chandra Dutta and Durga Mohan Das, when it was established in 1878 and was its first president and subsequently for many years.

After the second break-up of the Brahmo movement, his house at Konnagar became a place of pilgrimage to the members of the new samaj. They would often flock there so that his example of earnest piety, inborn humility, wide range of knowledge, methodical performance of the smallest duties of life, moderation in speech and conduct and constant attention to the good of others could inspire them. Indeed, he was the living embodiment of an ideal Brahmo life. He was one of strongest proponents of women's education because he was convinced that society could not progress unless women were educated. He admitted his daughters into Bethune School. In 1860, he opened a girls' school in his own house. It later shifted to a building of its own. He wrote a book *Sishupalan* (child care) for use by women.

Posted for sometime in 24 Parganas, he participated actively in the social life of Kolkata during the period. He contributed considerably to the development of Konnagar, including the inauguration of Konnagar railway station in 1856 and a post office in 1858. He was commissioner of Serampore municipality from 1865 to 1878. His father Braja Kishore Deb was in government service and was considered to be a moneyed man.

Brahmo Marriage Consternation

Satyapriya Deb, son of Sib Chandra Deb, was married, in 1876, to Saratkumari, daughter of Kalinath Bose, a close friend and devotee of Keshub Chunder Sen. Trouble started with a notice in the *Indian Mirror* about performance of the marriage as per the reformed ceremonies of the Brahmo Samaj. It was to be organised without the presence of Brahmin priests and without any salagram shila (family stone deity) or the traditional hom or fire witnessing (agni sakhyi). Many considered it a challenge to traditional Hindu society and systems. There was considerable public consternation about the marriage and the possibility of large-scale demonstrations against the proposed marriage rites loomed large over the occasion. The danger of people coming and physically disrupting the marriage ceremony was a distinct possibility.

Kalinath Bose rushed to Keshub Chunder Sen. He took personal interest to find a suitable alternative place of wedding on Circular Road. Almost everything had to be organised afresh. The groom's party came by boat under police guard. There was a distinct fear that somebody could attack the groom en route. The marriage took place under extremely difficult circumstances. Many of those who came to attend the wedding were jeered.

Sivanath Shastri mentions this marriage as one of the notable social incidents of that period in his book *Ramtanu Lahiri O Tatkalin Banga Samaj*. Saratkumari Deb has given vivid details of the wedding ceremony in her book *Amar Sansar*.

Hara Chandra Ghosh

Hara Chandra Ghosh (archaic Hurro Chunder Ghose) was one of the prominent leaders of the Young Bengal group (a group of radical Bengali free thinkers emerging from Hindu College, Calcutta of British India in the early 19th century). He was the first Bengali to be a judge of the Calcutta Small Causes Court from 1854 to 1868. H.E.A. Cotton says, "In his youth, he was a favourite pupil, as the Rev. K.M.Banerjee had been of David Hare and Derozio: but unlike others he maintained his Hinduism." He earned fame as a judge and was not involved in religion and social reform.

Formative Years

The family of Hara Chandra Ghosh hailed from Sarsuna in South 24 Parganas. In those days, it was a custom to learn Persian, but Ghosh was not satisfied with learning Persian only. He was keen to learn English also. As a result of his own efforts, he joined the newly founded Hindu College and later became a favourite student of Derozio. He was one of the students actively involved in the Academic Association, where he used to deliver speeches.

Career

As a youngster, he attracted attention of Lord William Bentinck, who wanted to appoint him on his personal staff and take Ghosh with him but the latter could not accept the offer because of opposition from his mother. However, in 1832, when the position of *munsif* was created for the Indians, Bentinck appointed him *munsif* of Bankura. Within a few days of his arrival in Bankura the situation started changing. The court started working from ten to five. When there was shortage of staff, Ghosh himself took down notes and wrote out judgments. His honesty and devotion enhanced the respect for the judiciary in the eyes of the public.

After successfully working in Bankura for six years, he was transferred to Hooghly in 1838, and in 1844, he became principal *sadar amin* of 24 Parganas. After serving for twenty years as a member of the subordinate Civil Judiciary in Bengal, he was gazetted as junior police magistrate of Kolkata (then known as Calcutta) in 1852, on the unanimous recommendation of the judges of the *Sadar Diwani Adalat*. In 1854, he was transferred to the Small Causes Court, where he remained till his death. He was associated with John Elliot Drinkwater Bethune in the formation of the Bethune School and was a member of the school committee. He joined the other Derozians for the construction of a memorial statue for David Hare.

Honours

He enjoyed the confidence of Lord William Bentinck, Lord Auckland and Lord Dalhousie. He was made a *Rai Bahadur* (a title of honour issued in British India to individuals who have performed a deed of great service to the nation). A memorial meeting was held in the Town Hall, on 4 January 1869, where Chief Justice Norman, mentioned Ghosh as 'the very model of what a native gentleman should be.' A marble bust of Hara Chandra Ghosh was unveiled in the main entrance to the Small Causes Court by Sir Arthur Macpherson, then a judge of Calcutta High Court on 8 March 1876.

Ramgopal Ghosh

Ramgopal Ghosh was one of the leaders of the Young Bengal group, a successful businessman, a brilliant orator and a social reformer. He was called the Indian Demosthenes. Ghosh was one of the persons who helped John Elliot Drinkwater Bethune to establish his girls school.

Early Life

The family hailed from Bagati, near Mogra in Hooghly District. His father, Gobinda Chandra Ghosh had a small shop in Kolkata's China Bazar. His maternal grandfather, Dewan Ramprasad Singha, used to work in the office of King Hamilton & Co. in Kolkata. Ghosh was born in his maternal grandfather's house.

There are two opinions about his childhood. The first says that he initially joined Sherburne's School and started learning English. At that time Hara Chandra Ghosh, then a student of Hindu College and later one of the leading Derozians, married a relative of his. Observing the keenness of young Ramgopal, Hara Chandra pestered the former's father to get him admitted in Hindu College. His father did not have the means to pay for his education at Hindu College.

However, one Mr. Rogers of King Hamilton & Co. agreed to pay the fees and he was admitted to Hindu College. The second opinion is that Mr. Rogers got him admitted in Hindu College right from the beginning.

Ghosh did not have to continue that way for long. His brilliance attracted the attention of David Hare and soon he was on the latter's free student list. In time he joined the class of Derozio. He became friendly with Ramtanu Lahiri and the other Derozians. His dedication attracted Derozio's attention and he used to coach him in English philosophy and poetry outside class hours.

When Derozio established the Academic Association, Ghosh became one of its leading members. It was in the meeting of the Association that Ghosh learnt to express himself fluently in English. The meetings of the Academic Association were attended by such people as Sir Edward Ryan, who was a judge of the Supreme Court and W.W.Bird, who later became lieutenant governor of Bengal. They warmly appreciated Ghosh's talent and openly encouraged him.

Business Activities

Ghosh had to leave his studies unfinished and get on in working life. On the recommendation of David Hare, he started working with a Jewish businessman named Joseph. Later, another businessman name Kelsall joined the firm, Ghosh served them as a middle-man. When the two fell out, Ghosh formed a jointly owned firm Kelsall, Ghose & Co., and still later, around 1848, he floated his own firm, R.G.Ghosh & Co. In the process he accumulated fabulous wealth.

One of the great qualities of Ghosh was that he never forgot his old friends. Even as he went up the financial and social ladder he kept close contact with them and helped them whenever they were in need. There were occasions when he helped his old friends such as Ramtanu Lahiri and Rasik Krishna Mallick.

When his grand father died, there was a hue and cry in society that he was opposed to Hindu religion and there was possibility of his being ostracised. His father appealed to him to declare publicly his faith in Hindu religion but he turned to his father and said, "I am ever willing to obey you and bear any pains for that but I cannot tell a lie." When this spread around, he gained in the esteem in society. On another occasion his business had nosedived and there was possibility of his becoming bankrupt. His friends advised him to transfer his assets to others but he refused to follow an illegal path. His personal integrity has been acknowledged even by more recent historians.

Oration and Social Reforms

His speeches on the Black Acts (1850), which aimed at bringing disputes between Europeans and Asians under the jurisdiction of the Company's courts and those criticising the European protests against a well-intentioned government move to bring Europeans on par with the natives in judicial treatment were a landmark. He was the first, as early as 1853, to demand the eligibility of Indians in the civil service examinations. In 1854, he was the first Indian to propose the establishment of universities in India. He supported the move of Dwarkanath Tagore to send four students to England for higher medical studies.

Ghosh not only delivered fiery speeches but also wrote effectively. His publication of a booklet *A Few Remarks on Certain Draft Acts, Commonly Called Black Acts* so angered the English that he was forced out of his position as vice-president of the Agri-Horticultural Society. He was closely associated with the publications of the time, such as *Jnananwesan* and *Bengal Spectator*. He took an active part in the establishment of the British Indian Association and was a member of its committee.

He not only indulged in politics but also other causes. It was at his initiative that a decision was taken to erect a statue of David Hare. He was the first to offer one month's income for the purpose; others followed and the statue stands to this day in the compound of Presidency College.

In his last days, he wrote off loans totalling Rs. 40,000 given to his friends.

Ramtanu Lahiri

Ramtanu Lahiri (1813-1898) was a leading Derozian, a renowned teacher and a social reformer. Peary Chand Mitra wrote about him, "There are few persons in whom the milk of kindness flows so abundantly. He was never wanting in appreciation of what was right, and in his sympathy with the advanced principles." Sivanath Shastri's *Ramtanu Lahiri O Tatkalin Bangasamaj*, published in 1903, was not only his biography but also an overview of Bengali society of the era, "a remarkable social document on the period of the Bengal Renaissance." It is still widely read and used as reference material for the period. An English version *A History of Renaissance in Bengal-Ramtanu Lahiri: Brahman and Reformer*, edited by Sir Roper Lethbridge, was published in London in 1907.

Early Life

Ramtanu Lahiri was son of Ramakrishna Lahiri. They belonged to a deeply religious family attached to the dewans of the Nadia Raj. Some of them were also employed as dewans or occupied other high positions in the Raj. At that time, Krishnanagar was amongst the more enlightened towns of Bengal, and Kolkata had just started growing. His father, Ramakrishna Lahiri, was a person of limited means, earning a living in the service of the landed aristocracy and from some property he owned.

As per the traditions of the age, Ramtanu Lahiri attended the local pathsala and tol and learnt Arabic, Persian and some English. The environment of song, dance and drinks, in the palace, was not considered ideal for a child to grow up. His elder brother, Keshab

Chandra Lahiri, took him to Kolkata at the age of 12. He taught him at home but desired to place the young boy in David Hare's school.

In those days, there was such a mad rush for learning English and the opportunities were so limited that young boys used to run alongside David Hare's palanquin, pleading "Me poor boy, have pity on me, me take in your school." The number of aspirants were so many that David Hare could hardly do anything much.

Keshab Chandra Lahiri managed to line up Gour Mohan Vidyalankar, a person close to David Hare, to plead with him for the admission of Ramtanu Lahiri. He did accordingly and took the young boy to David Hare, but he refused to oblige. Then, Vidyalankar advised Ramtanu to run along David Hare's palanquin, along with the other boys. The youngster did so for around two months, sometimes even without having any food in the morning. Ultimately, he won over David Hare with his determination. Ramtanu Lahiri was admitted as a free student in the school established by the School Society. The school later became famous as Hare School, and was known as Colutola Branch School for some time.

Young Ramtanu did not have a place to stay in Kolkata. His elder brother mostly lived in Krishnanagar. He crowded in with other boys in Vidyalankar's house for some time and later found a place in a relative's house. In 1828, Ramtanu Lahiri passed Entrance with flying colours, winning a grand scholarship of Rs. 14 per month, good enough in those days to manage a living in Kolkata. He joined Hindu College.

College Days

The most renowned name of Ramtanu Lahiri's college days was Derozio. He used to publish poems and essays in Dr. Grant's *India Gazette*. Then aged only nineteen years, he joined Hindu College as a teacher in 1828. Within a short period, Derozio became immensely popular amongst the students. They mobbed him in college and he invited them to their home. On one occasion, Ramtanu Lahiri went with some others to Derozio's house. They were offered tea but Ramtanu Lahiri would not have it. It was against the traditions of the day to have food or drinks in the house of an alien. Not only Derozio's erudition and scholarship, but his liberal ways also had an immense impact on the students.

For the first time, they were learning to question things. When Ramtanu Lahiri was in the third class (second year, as per today's concept), the followers of Derozio published a monthly magazine named *Athenium*. One of the students, Madhab Chandra Mallick, wrote in it, "If there is anything we hate from the bottom of our heart, it is Hinduism." Madhab Chandra Mallick was a friend of Ramtanu Lahiri and was later posted as a deputy collector in Krishnanagar.

The student-society was overwhelmed by Derozio. Sivanath Shastri quotes extensively from his biographer, Thomas Edwards:

"Derozio acquired such an ascendancy over the minds of his pupils that they would not move even in their private concerns without his counsel and advice. On the other hand, he fostered their taste in literature; taught the evil effects of idolatry and superstition and so far formed their moral conceptions and feelings, as to place them completely above the antiquated ideas and aspirations of the age. Such was the force of his instructions, that the conduct of the students outside the College was most exemplary and gained them the applause of the outside world, not only in literary or a scientific point of view, but what was of still greater importance, they were all considered men of truth."

In third class, Ramtanu Lahiri won a scholarship of Rs. 16 per month. He brought two of his brothers for education in Kolkata. That was not enough money for three persons to survive on. They had two square meals only and skipped refreshments in between. They went to school bare foot and did the cooking and all household work on their own.

Once when Ramtanu Lahiri was ill, David Hare came and treated him in his house in a dingy lane. Hare used to keep track of all his students. Those were also the days when Kolkata society was in turbulence about the formation of the Brahma Sabha by Raja Rammohan Roy in 1828. It was an age of change. The practice of suttee was banned in 1829. That led to enormous debates and petitions for and against it. In 1831, Derozio was forced to resign from Hindu College and he died soon afterwards at the tender age of only 22 years, but what a brilliant array of students he left behind: Krishna Mohan Banerjee, Ram Gopal Ghosh, Rasik Krishna Mallick, Sib Chandra Deb, Hara Chandra Ghosh, Peary Chand Mitra, Radhanath Sikdar and Ramtanu Lahiri, to name a few, all fired with the zeal to serve and change the county. In 1832, Krishna Mohan Banerjee, one of the Derozians converted to Christianity. From 1833 onwards, Indians were allowed to be deputy collectors and deputy magistrates, and some of the Derozians benefitted because of the relaxation.

First Job

Ramtanu Lahiri passed out in 1833 and joined Hindu College as a teacher. It may be recalled that the system of graduation had not been introduced till then. With a salary of Rs. 30 per month. He started living a life surrounded by relatives, many of whom came to Kolkata for education or other work. Ramtanu Lahiri had already come under the influence of David Hare and Henry Vivian Derozio. Now it was his turn to be influenced by Thomas Babington Macaulay. Initially the English had sponsored classical education in India, based on Arabic, Persian and Sanskrit, but as new ideas came from England, it was felt essential to introduce Indians to western education, particularly the sciences. There were strong protagonists on both sides. Indeed, the setting up of Hindu College in 1817 was a big step forward in the direction of western education.

Former students of Hindu College were strongly in favour of Thomas Babington Macaulay's move for western education. They even went to the extent of supporting his theory, expounded in 1835, "I am quite ready to take oriental learning at the valuation of orientalists themselves. I have never found one among them, who could deny that that a single shelf of a good European library was worth the whole native literature of India and Arabia." That was an age when India's past was still to be fully realised.

Entire society was then in turmoil and Ramtanu Lahiri was going through all that. However, certain events in his personal life affected him seriously. First was the death of two of his brothers, one younger and the other elder. His elder brother had by then risen to the position of a sheristadar, a remarkable achievement in those days. The death of his elder brother brought on the entire responsibility of the family on to his shoulders. Second, two of his wives had died and he married a third time. Third, the death of David Hare in 1842. It was a tremendous shock for Ramtanu Lahiri. He revered him as his own father. Throughout his life, he never failed to gather his friends and pay respect to him at his grave on his death anniversary every year.

Outside Kolkata

Krishnanagar College was opened in 1846. Capt. D.L.Richardson was appointed principal and Ramtanu Lahiri was appointed the second teacher on a monthly salary of Rs. 100. As a teacher, Ramtanu Lahiri had picked up the qualities of Derozio. He could light up within his students the urge to acquire knowledge. While teaching he was always engrossed in the subject, trying to explain things in the widest possible manner. He used to mix freely with the students beyond the classroom and often took part in games with them.

In 1844, Maharaja Srish Chandra Roy had initiated steps for setting up a Brahmo Samaj at Krishnanagar. By the time, Ramtanu Lahiri went to Krishnanagar, it had already attracted both converts and strong opponents in the orthodox community. At that time a great debate was raging in the Brahmo Samaj as to whether to accept the infallibility of the Vedas or not. Tattwabodhini Patrika had also engaged in a bitter debate with the Christian missionaries and had launched a tirade against Christianity. While Ramtanu Lahiri was in general agreement with the Brahmo principles, he had some strong reservations on certain points.

In a letter to Rajnarayan Basu he wrote-

"I cannot think much of the Vedantic movements here or elsewhere. The followers of Vedanta temporize. They do not believe that the religion is from God, but will not say so to their countrymen, who believe otherwise. Now, in my humble opinion, we should never preach doctrines as true, in which we have no faith ourselves. I know that the subversion of idolatry is a consummation devoutly to be wished for, but I do not desire it by employing wrong means. I do not allow the principle that means justify the end. Let us follow the right path assured that it will ultimately promote the welfare of mankind. It will never do otherwise.

I wish to request the secretary of the Tottobodhini Sabha to discontinue sending me the Society's paper (Patrika), as a person cannot subscribe to it, who is not a member of the Society… I fear also that there is a spirit of hostility entertained by the Society against Christianity which is not creditable. Our desire should be to see truth triumph. Let the votaries of all religions appeal to the reason of their fellow-creatures and let him who has truth on his side prevail."

He did not join the Brahmo Samaj then but inspired the youth of Krishnanagar along the path of modernity. Some of his students later emerged as leaders of the new movement. One of them was Dinanath Mazumdar, a renowned Brahmo preacher. It was only when things improved in the Brahmo Samaj that Ramtanu Lahiri joined it.

Ramtanu Lahiri was possibly the first person in that society to discard his sacred thread. He is believed to have done it at Bardhaman in 1851. This daring act of his led to a huge uproar in orthodox society and he was socially boycotted for a long time. That, however, did not daunt him. Another movement that rocked society of the time was the debate for re-marriage of widows first raised by Ramgopal Ghosh and other Derozians in the *Bengal Spectator* from 1842 onwards, but it was possible that Pandit Ishwar Chandra Vidyasagar was behind the scene.

While Ramtanu Lahiri was moving from one place to another on transfer-Bardhaman, Uttarpara, Baraset, Rasapagla, Barisal-new developments were taking place in Kolkata. John Elliot Drinkwater Bethune established his girls' school in 1849. Ramtanu Lahiri and other Derozians extended warm support to the enlightened journalism of Harish Chandra Mukherjee.

Retired Life

Ramtanu Lahiri returned to Krishnanagar College before retirement. Alfred Smith, principal of Krisnanagar College, wrote on his application for pension, "In parting with Baboo Ram Tanoo Lahiri I may be allowed to say that Government will lose the services of an educational officer, than whom no officer has discharged his public duties with greater fidelity, zeal and devotion, or has laboured more assiduously and successfully for the moral elevation of his pupils." On retirement, Ramtanu Lahiri settled down in Krishnanagar but it could not be for long. He lived in Gobardanga for some time as guardian of the zemindar's sons. When Keshub Chunder Sen established the Bharat Ashram in 1872, he moved in along with his family. He presided over the first day meeting of the All-India National Conference in Kolkata in 1883.

With several deaths in the family, Ramtanu Lahiri was somewhat heart broken. When he died, people of Kolkata gathered in large numbers to bid farewell to a saintly man.

A few lines from Max Muller will summarise his achievements: "The Brahminical thread which was retained by the members of the Brahma Samaj as late as 1861, was openly discarded by him as early as 1851. And we must remember that in those days such open apostasy was almost a question of life and death, and that Rammohan Roy was in danger of assassination in the very streets of Calcutta. It is true that European officials respected and supported Ramtonoo, but among his own countrymen he was despised and shunned. However, he continued his career, undisturbed by friend and foe... Later in life he was attracted to the new Brahmo Samaj and became a close friend of Keshub Chunder Sen... While cultivating his little garden he was found lost in devotion at the sight of full-blown rose and while singing a hymn in adoration of God, his whole countenance seemed to beam with heavenly light... When his end approached, his old friend Debendranath Tagore went to take leave of him, and when he left, he cried, 'Now that the gates of heaven are open to you, and the Gods are waiting with their outstretched arms to receive you to the glorious region.'"

Addendum

One of the direct descendants of Ramtanu Lahiri, Sanat Lahiri, was the first Asian to be president of the International Public Relations Association in 1979. Public Relations Society of India periodically organises the Sanat Lahiri memorial lecture in his honour.

Rasik Krishna Mallick

Rasik Krishna Mallick (1810-8 January 1858) was one of the brilliant students of Hindu College, Kolkata, a leading Derozian and journalist, who shocked the court in British India in the 1820s with the statement that he did not believe in the sacredness of the Ganges.

Early Life

Son of Naba Kishore Mallick, he was born in 1810 at Sinduriapatti in Kolkata. His father was engaged in thread trading and was linked to the Seths, the original residents of Govindapur, which was one the villages that developed into the city of Kolkata. The family had a great standing in society. After initial education at home with some grounding in English, Rasik Krishna Mallick joined Hindu College and turned out to be a highly successful student, one of the flowers of the institution. He greatly admired the activities of Raja Rammohan Roy, who was then active in Kolkata and was greatly influenced by his thinking. In 1828, when Derozio joined Hindu College, he became one of his disciples.

While still a student, Rasik Krishna Mallick appeared as witness in some case in the supreme court at Kolkata. In those days, the system was that the Hindu witnesses had to take oath touching a copper vessel containing Ganges water and tulsi (holy basil) leaf. An Oriya Brahmin came with these things to every witness. When the process was repeated with Rasik Krishna Mallick, he refused to comply. When his Bengali statement was translated in court as, "I do not believe in the sacredness of the Ganges," there was a hush, every one put their hands to their ears and thought, "How can a boy from the Mallick family say this?" The Ganges has always been considered to be sacred by the Hindus.

The result was that his family drugged him and wanted to take him forcibly to Varanasi for penance and reformation. However, Rasik Krishna Mallick recovered and ran away. His family turned him out of the house. He worked in Hare School for some time. When Indians were allowed for the first time to be appointed or promoted as deputy collectors Rasik Krishna Mallick was one of the beneficiaries and was posted to Bardhaman. While he was in Bardhaman, his old friend Ramtanu Lahiri, then posted in the same town, created a sensation by discarding his sacred thread. He became religious-minded and carried out his duties fearlessly. He spurned all efforts to bribe him and established a great reputation for honesty.

Achievements

He was editor of the magazine *Jnananwesan* and was one of the sponsors of *Parthenon,* the first English magazine to be edited and published by Indians in 1830. He was editor of *Jnantarangasindhu.* He was vocal on many issues of the day and enlightened public opinion on many matters.

He was actively involved in the social reforms launched by the organisation named Suhrid Samiti of Kishori Chand Mitra, brother of his friend Peary Chand Mitra. In 1831, he established a free Hindu school for the spread of education. He also tried for the spread of education though Calcutta Public Library of Rasamay

Dutta. He was a strong advocate of the use of the mother tongue as the medium of education without ignoring the learning of English. He campaigned strongly for the replacement of Persian in courts by Bengali and was partly successful in the matter.

Citing specific examples of political thinking by Derozians, Nitish Sengupta writes, "In 1833 Rasik-Krishna Mallik criticised police corruption, attributed the lack of protection of the peasantry to the Permanent Settlement, and advocated the abolition of the political power of the merchant company.

Still in the prime of his life, he died of illness on 8 January 1858.

Notes

On page 73 of *Ramtanu Lahiri O Tatkalin Banga Samaj* Sivanath Shastri mentions that prior to this Indians were not allowed to occupy positions above that of sheristadar. Even Raja Rammohan Roy had risen only to that position. During his visit to England, the Raja had taken up the matter with the British government and when the charter of the company was renewed in 1833, Indians were allowed to be promoted or appointed as deputy collectors and deputy magistrates for the first time.

Peary Chand Mitra

Peary Chand Mitra (1814-1883), a member of Derozio's Young Bengal group, author and journalist, played a leading role in the Bengal renaissance with the introduction of simple Bengali prose. His *Alaler Gharer Dulal* pioneered the novel in the Bengali language, leading to a tradition taken up by Bankim Chandra Chatterjee and others.

Early Life

Son of Ramnarayan Mitra, he was born at Kolkata on 22 July 1814. As per the custom of the day, he started learning Persian at a young age and in 1829 joined the Hindu College, where he started learning English. While still a student he started a school in his own home in order to teach others in his locality what he learnt. At some point in time his friends Rasik Krishna Mallick, Radhanath Sikdar and Sib Chandra Deb joined him to bolster his efforts. David Hare and Derozio helped him. A brilliant student, he passed with rewards and prizes, and joined the 'Public Library' as deputy librarian in 1835. The Public Library was established the same year in the residence of an Englishman named Strong in the Esplanade. It was later shifted to the Fort William College and when the Metcalfe Hall was constructed to pay respect to the memory of Charles Metcalfe, the library was moved to the hall in 1844. Peary Chand Mitra rapidly rose up the ladder as librarian, secretary and finally curator, a position he held till his retirement.

Family

He had one daughter named Uma Shashi Mitra who was married to Bengali Lawyer Shri B N Das of sambalpur Orissa.

'The Dickens of Bengal'

While working in the library, Peary Chand Mitra used his tenure there extensively to enhance his knowledge. He used to write widely in magazines then being published-*Bengal Spectator, Bengal Harkara, Englishman, Hindu Patriot, Calcutta Review*. Along with his Derozian friend Rasik Krishna Mallick, he edited the *Jnananeswan*. Another Derozian, Ram Gopal Ghosh, was associated with it.

That was the age when Ishwar Chandra Vidyasagar was writing Bengali heavily loaded with Sanskrit words and Akshay Kumar Datta was experimenting with the language in Tattwabodhini Patrika. Both were masters of Sanskrit and used all the ornamentation of that rich language. Bengali prose was in its infancy. Learned people used to poke fun at it and ridiculed the language, and a newspaper such as Ishwar Chandra Gupta's *Sambad Prabhakar* published all that.

In 1857, Peary Chand Mitra and Radhanath Sikdar started a small magazine, *Masik Patrika,* which used simple spoken Bengali prose everybody could understand.

It was a major breakthrough in the use of Bengali, and the magazine instantly became popular. His novel *Alaler Gharer Dulal,* written under the pseudonym Tek Chand Thakur, used simple Bengali prose, closer to the spoken speech of the day, and was serialised in the magazine. It was one of the earliest Bengali novels and became an instant success. So great was its popularity that the language style came to be known as 'Alali'. That set the trend for Bengali prose then. In 1864, Bankim Chandra Chattopadhyay published his first novel *Durgeshnandini* to finally lay down the standard for Bengali prose. *Alaler Ghare Dulal* was translated into English. Rev. James Long, who was a keen observer of the literary scene in Bengal, and was imprisoned and fined for the English translation of the controversial play *Nil Darpan,* used to call him 'the Dickens of Bengal'. Peary Chand Mitra wrote a number of books-*Abhedi, Jatkinchit, Bamatoshini, Ramaranjika, Adhyatika, Mad Khaoa Baro Daey*. He wrote a biographical sketch of David Hare in English.

Other Activities

In later life, he was a successful businessman. Along with his Derozian friend Tarachand Chakraborty, he was involved in export-import business. He was associated with a variety of social welfare activities of his day. He was a member of the Calcutta University Senate, the society for prevention of cruelty to animals, and Bethune Society. He was secretary of the British India Society (later Association). He was a Justice of the Peace.

He had great interest in the development of agriculture in the country. His criticism of the permanent settlement, *The Zemindar and Ryots*, created a sensation. While a member of the Agricultural Society, he started an organisation for the translation of books on agriculture from English to Bengali.

In 1881, when Madame Blavatsky and Col Olcott visited India, he became involved with the Theosophical Society. He died on 23 November 1883 at Kolkata.

Dakshinaranjan Mukherjee

Raja Dakshinaranjan Mukherjee Taluqdar of the formerly confiscated taluq of Shankarpur in the United Provinces (1814-15 July 1898) was one of the leaders of the Young Bengal group in 19th-century India, an orator, editor of several periodicals, and a social reformer who had donated land for the Bethune School and assisted David Hare in his social works.

Early Life

Dakshinaranjan Mukherjee's father Jaganmohan Mukherjee, who belonged to Bhatpara, had married into the Pathuriaghata branch of the Tagore family and agreed to be a 'ghar-jamai' (a groom who remains back with his in-laws as part of their family). Dakshinaranjan studied at Hare School and Hindu College. While a student of Hindu College, he was influenced by Henry Louis Vivian Derozio, the main person behind the Young Bengal movement. When his friend Krishna Mohan Banerjee was turned out of his house for converting to Christianity, Mukherjee provided him protection and support.

Activities at Kolkata

In 1838 was established the Society for Acquisition of General Knowledge which had 200 members in 1843. On 8 February 1843, Dakshinaranjan Mukherjee read in a meeting of the society his well known essay on *Present Conditions of the East India Company's Courts of Judicature and Police under the Bengal Presidency.*

"The delivery of the essay," observed the *Bengal Harkaru* on 2 March 1843, "was interrupted, as our readers will recollect, by the Principal of the Hindu College, on the ground of its seditious and treasonable tendency. The attempts made to throw ridicule upon the intelligent natives of their country, for their laudable efforts to acquire knowledge of the government under which they live, and to aid in the removal of its abuses, appear to us as most ungenerous and illiberal." —Sengupta, Nitish

While a student Mukherjee published the magazine *Jnananneswan* in 1831. The next year it became a bilingual magazine. He spoke against suppression of newspapers by the government. He was one of main initiators for the establishment of the British Indian Association and contributed regularly to the *Bengal Spectator*. He practiced as a lawyer and was the first Indian to be appointed as a collector of Calcutta Municipality. Later he also worked in the court of the Nawab at Murshidabad.

He had once given a loan of Rs. 60,000 to David Hare. As Hare was unable to pay back the loan, he gave Mukherjee some land in lieu of it. Mukherjee, in turn, donated that land in 1849 to John Elliot Drinkwater Bethune for the establishment of Kolkata's first secular school for girls.

Marriage

After the death of Maharaja Tej Chandra Ray of Bardhaman in 1832 Mukherjee visited the family home in connection with some legal disputes. He met Tej Chandra's young widow, Basanta Kumari, the maharaja's 8th wife, whom Mukherjee later married by registration. The episode created quite a sensation in Calcutta, since Mukherjee and Basanta Kumari, chose to elope and get married, but were later caught by the girl's father, Pran Chand Kapoor.

Later Life at Lucknow

Mukherjee prospered in Lucknow. For helping the British during the Sepoy Mutiny, he was rewarded with the Shankarpur taluk in 1859. He was made honorary assistant commissioner of Lucknow and Awadh. He started publishing *Lucknow Times, Samachar Hindustani* and *Bharat Patrika* from Lucknow. He established the Canning College at Lucknow. He was honoured with the title of 'Raja' by the Viceroy, Lord Mayo in 1871.

He established the Awadh British Indian Association in 1871 and campaigned for the formation of a provincial government with equal number of nominated and elected legislators and lost some favour with the British government. Dakshinaranjan Mukherjee died in Lucknow on 15 July 1898.

Radhanath Sikdar

Radhanath Sikdar (1813-1870) was a Bengali Indian mathematician who, among many other things, calculated the height of Peak XV in the Himalaya and showed it to be the tallest mountain above sea level. Peak XV was later named Mount Everest.

Alone among the great Derozians he took to science as his life's mainstay. When in 1831 George Everest was searching for a brilliant young mathematician with particular proficiency in Spherical Trigonometry, the maths teacher Dr. John Tytler superlatively recommended the name of his pupil Radhanath, then only 19. Radhanath joined the Great Trigonometric Survey in 1931 December as a "computor".

Soon he was sent to Sironj near Dehra Dun where he excelled in geodetic surveying. Apart from mastering the usual processes, he invented quite a few of his own. Everest was extremely pleased with his performance, so much so that when Sikdar wanted to leave GTS and be a Deputy Collector, Everest intervened, proclaiming that no government officer can change over to another department without the approval of his boss. Everest retired in 1843 and Col. Waugh became the Director. After 20 years in the

North, he was transferred to Calcutta in 1851. Here apart from his duties of the GTS, he also served as the Superintendent of the Meteorological department.

Here he introduced quite a few innovations that were to remain standard procedure for many decades to come.The most notable was the conversion to 32 degrees Fahrenheit the barometric readings taken at different temperatures.

At the order of Col. Waugh he started measuring the snow capped mountains near Darjeeling. Compiling data about Peak XV from six different observations, he eventually came to the conclusion the Peak XV was the tallest in the world. He gave a full report to Waugh who was cautious enough not to announce this discovery before checking with other data.

When after some years, he was convinced, only then did he publicly announce the same. The norm, strictly followed by Everest himself, was that while naming a peak, the local name should be preferred. But in this case, Waugh made an exception. He paid a tribute to his ex-boss Everest by giving the peak his name. Sikdar was conveniently forgotten. Nevertheless, in recognition of Sikdar's mathematical genius the German Philosophical Institute's Bavaria branch of Natural Science made him a Corresponding Member in 1864, a very rare honour those days. Sikdar had retired from service in 1862.

Sikdar worked for the Surveyor General of India, a division of the British Raj in India at that time. He joined the Great Trigonometric Survey in 1832 and was educated at Phiringi Kamal Bose's School and Hindu College (now called Presidency College) in Calcutta, India. In 1854, he started the journal *Masik Patrika*, for the education and empowerment of women. He died on 17 May 1870 at Gondalpara, Chandannagar in his villa by the side of the Ganga

Some Indians, including the former Prime Minister Atal Bihari Vajpayee, are of the opinion that Mount Everest should be renamed after Sikdar.

The Department of Posts, India, launched a postal stamp on June 27, 2004, commemorating the establishment of the Great Trigonometric Survey in Chennai, India on April 10, 1802. The stamps feature Radhanath Sikdar and Nain Singh, two significant contributors to society. The Great Arc refers to the systematic exploration and recording of the entire topography of the Indian subcontinent which was spear-headed by the Great Trigonometric Survey. References: Jogesh Chandra Bagal, Unabingsha Shatabdir Bangla, 1941 Sivanath Shastri, Ramatanu Lahiri o Tatkalin BangaSamaj, 1904 Ajana Chaudhury, R R Kelkar and A. K. Sen Sarma, 'Technology: Through the haze of time & neglect', The Statesman, Kolkata, 1 March 2009

The Work of Debendranath Tagore and Ishwar Chandra Vidyasagar

The Brahmo Samaj founded by Raja Rammohan Roy had existed without much significance but was revived by Debendranath Tagore. He was a product of the best of traditional Indian learning and the new western education. He founded the Tatvabodhini Sabha in 1839, which propagated the ideas of Raja Rammohan Roy. In time it came to include followers of Raja Rammohan Roy and Derozians. It also included many independent thinkers like Ishwar Chandra Vidyasagar and Akhay Kumar Dutt.

Ishwar Chandra Vidyasagar was a great social reformer of the period and the probable successor to Raja Rammohan Roy. He also believed in the blending of western and eastern cultures. He contributed significantly to the development of Sanskrit and Bengali literature. He fought vehemently for widow rights and pushed hard for widow remarriage, which resulted in a law that made it legal. He protested against child marriage and worked for women's rights.

He worked hard at promoting education for women, which was an uphill task. People believed that educated girls could lose their husbands, or that girls who had received western education would turn their husbands into slaves. In spite of pressure from society and threats on his life Ishwar Chandra Vidyasagar continued his struggle against the social evils that plagued Indian society.

After the revolt of 1857, the work of social reform still continued and was taken up by people like Ramakishna, Vivekananda (a disciple of Ramakrishna who founded the Ramakrishna mission), Swami Dayanad (founded the Arya Samaj), Sayyid Ahmad Khan and Muhammed Iqbal amongst several others.

The reformers were all great figures and are still remembered and revered today. Most of them gave up their own comfortable lives and struggled to reform Indian society. Their efforts helped greatly in reforming Indian society and in the enactment of laws that began to prevent many social evils like sati etc.

Some of their efforts continue even today, for instance the Brahmo Samaj and Arya Samaj are still active organizations today and continue the work started by Raja Rammohan Roy and Swami Dayanand. These reformers gave the Indian people a different viewpoint to everything they had earlier believed in, and reformed India into the tolerant and modern country that it is today.

5

Rammohan Roy and the Advent of Constitutional Liberalism in India

This paper seeks to situate the dramatic emergence of modern Indian liberal thought during the 1810s and 1820s in a wider Asian, European and American context, further developing the notion of a global or trans-national sphere of intellectual history. From the perspective of British and British imperial history, the paper contributes to the story of how provincial and overseas interests came together to construct an ideological challenge to the "despotism" of the Court of Directors of the East India Company. British radicals and the still small group of English-educated Indian public men gathered in Bombay and Calcutta viewed the Company as the epitome of metropolitan Toryism and a classic form of the "old corruption". The concern of the paper is not to insert the Indian political ideas of this period into broad, predetermined teleological categories such as "old patriotism", colonial modernity, nationalist modernity, multiple modernity and so on as historians of India have been inclined to do. Rather, it is to consider the political ideas in their own terms and in their own period, neither lauding a culturally authentic Indian renaissance nor simply treating the debates of these years as derivative ofWestern intelletual prowess.

Some contemporary theorists view liberalism as a general doctrine of absences: liberty from political, religious or intellectual oppression, but with little positive commitment to civic virtue. The early Indian and expatriate British liberals discussed here emerged out of a specific intellectual context. They feared the tyrannical features of the French Revolution as much as those of the returning monarchical despotisms of 1815. Yet, though cautious, their liberalism was constructive. They were advocates of "mixed" constitutional government, republican in spirit, but leaving space for popular monarchies. They assigned a critical role to a free press and local forms of representation. They wished to build "a public" in India. But they were often conservative or, rather, Whiggish in their attitude to property, believing that large landed proprietors stabilized society, unlike their more radical successors of a few years later.

I begin with a description of a striking event that took place in Calcutta in August 1822 on the banks of the River Hughly and later in the Calcutta Town Hall. This was a celebration of the second anniversary of the proclamation of constitutional government in Portugal. It was recorded by two Calcutta newspapers, the *Bengal Hurkaru* (the word means "messenger"), a free-trading liberal newspaper, and the *Calcutta Journal*. The *Journal* was India's first daily newspaper, a radical publication edited by the later parliamentary reformer James Silk Buckingham, who was soon to be arrested and transported back to Britain by the Company's government. According to the *Journal* the huge crowd at the river included "the children of Lusitania" along with "those of Britain and India", government officials, ecclesiastics of the Roman church and other creeds wearing, unusually, the cockade symbol of liberty. Along with them stood "the enlightened Brahmin whose name is never mentioned without praise". This was Rammohan Roy, the main focus of the essay, and someone who is rightly regarded as India's first consciouslymodern political thinker. The *Calcutta Journal* demanded rhetorically, "who shall henceforth dare to say that Public Opinion is not favourable to the spread of liberal sentiments in India?"

The other main liberal publication, the *Hurkaru*, carried a long report on the subsequent dinner. "European Portuguese from Lisbon and the Brazils" hosted the dinner. But many local Portuguese and Eurasian Portuguese from Calcutta and the Bengal countryside attended as their guests. According to Messrs Pires and de Silva, Portugal had finally been delivered from the "thraldom of priest craft and the fetters of despotism". The Spanish nation had been the first to raise the standard of liberty in 1812, but soon, it was said, "the cause of liberty will be as famous and triumphant as in the days of Cato and Brutus". The speeches at the dinner illustrated the range of international constitutional liberalism at this particular moment. The breadth of Iberian liberal connections across the world was also highlighted by a solemn act of remembrance of a Portuguese patriot in Goa who had been assassinated on the orders of the reactionary Portuguese monarchy, then installed in Rio de Janeiro. India indeed had direct experience of European revolutions. A series of liberal coups and monarchical counter-coups was taking place in what are now the major holiday venues of western India. Liberals in Goa, mainly creoles, who claimed descent from the earliest settlers (*luso descendentes*) had recently issued an official newspaper invoking Rousseau and stating that the "general wish" of the Portuguese people was invested in the Cortes which had ordained political change for the colony.

Speakers at the Calcutta dinner took up related struggles for liberty. There were toasts to "the Marquess of Hastings [the outgoing Governor General] and the Liberty of the Indian press" and "les lib′erales of France". Later speeches lauded Jeremy Bentham, the Carbonari and the reformof the British parliament. Mr. Patrick, an Irishman, raised his glass to Colonel James Young, the radical head of the agency house Alexander and Co., who was soon to return to Britain. A friend of Rammohan, Young later worked closely with Jeremy Bentham and Daniel O'Connell for the reform of Parliament and the Company's monopoly. Finally, "Ypsilanti and the Greeks" were remembered. Alexander Ypsilanti, a former Tsarist officer, had just invaded OttomanMoldavia. TheGreek merchants of the Indian cities awaited the liberation of their country. Greece was also on the mind of Young Bengal. In the Hindu College, Calcutta, the young Eurasian poet and democrat Henry Derozio wrote on the heroic struggles of the Greeks through the ages and the equal greatness of ancient India. The distant connection between Greece and India was soon to be demonstrated anew in the career of Leicester Stanhope, a follower of Bentham, who agitated for the freedom of the Indian press and went on to found patriotic newspapers across Greece.

This surge of support for awide range of constitutional liberal reforms in India, Britain, Iberia, Greece and Latin America explains why Bishop Reginald Heber described the small Bengali intelligentsia as "advancedWhigs" when he came to India a few years later. Overwhelmed by the return of reactionary governments throughout the world after 1815, liberals and radicals depicted despotisms, from the Bourbons to the Ottomans and the Tsars, as an international unholy alliance against the people. The directors of the East India Company were a willing component of this junta according to British and other European liberals and free-traders in the East. They deplored the Company's monopoly, high taxation and constant frontier wars. Any successful rebellion against autocracy across the world was therefore a cause for rejoicing in Calcutta. The Portuguese celebration was not unique. Rammohan Roy himself hosted several celebrations in Calcutta Town Hall for the Spanish, Portuguese and Latin American revolutions between 1820 and 1823. At a less heady time, on the fall of Neapolitan republic in 1821, Rammohan was so distressed that he was unable to visit his British radical friend, Buckingham.

India's dawning interest in European concepts of freedom and constitutional government was reciprocated. When Spanish reformers reissued the original 1812 Cadiz constitution, it was dedicated as follows: "Al liberalismo del noble, sabio, y virtuoso Brahma Ram-Mohan Roy". The Swiss political economist J. de Sismondi, writing later in the Paris *Revue encyclop'edique*, remarked that reports of Rammohan's presence at events such as this clearly disproved the stereotype, purveyed by British colonialists, that India was doomed to social stagnation by caste prejudices against socialmixing. What we see in this liberal constitutionalist moment, then, was the emergence of a small international public sphere—including Indians—that was unified not so much by coherent intellectual influence, but by political affect. This global imagining of constitutional liberty was made possible by the great expansion of the press and the idea of association at world level since the 1780s. Political theorists now fashioned their arguments against the background of displays of ritual emotion that purported to represent the people.

This essay seeks to provide a trans-national context for the political ideas of Rammohan and other early Indian liberals. Roy became an iconic figure to Indians and Britons very early on. Born into a Brahmin Mughal service family, he moved through an early phase of personal religious enquiry and become closely associated with a number of British scholar officials and Unitarian ministers in Bengal. He learnt several European languages and, by 1815, had become spokesman for a religious tendency in Hinduism that rejected;

"idol worship" and asserted that true Hinduism was monotheistic and little concerned with issues of caste. He founded the Atmiya Sabha (Friendly Society) and later the Brahmo Samaj (Society for the Supreme Being). His opposition to the burning of widows on their husbands' funeral pyres, *sati*, a relatively uncommon but ideologically charged practice, earned him the enmity of the neo-orthodox in Bengal. His insistence that modern Hinduism was a corrupt form of a pure and monotheistic ancient religion caused his mother to disown him and his relations to try to disinherit him. But the crusade against corrupt practices, especially widow-burning, led him to publish numerous pamphlets in English, Bengali and Sanskrit and to found the subcontinent's earliest Indian-run newspapers.

In turn, what Rammohan and his British liberal friends took to be a reactionary and "Tory" turn in Indian government after the departure of Lord Hastings in 1818 drew him into sustained political comment on the policies of the East India Company and the British government, including its foreign policy in relation to Iberia, France and Greece. Indo-Islamic India had long had its moralists and its public critiques of authority, but the international range of Rammohan's imagined political community made him, in effect, India's first indigenous "public man". He argued for restricted European colonization of India and for free trade to end the East India Company's monopoly. He went to Europe in 1832, visiting England at the time of the Reform bills and France after the revolution of 1830. He died in Bristol in 1833 when he was contemplating taking ship for the United States, at the behest of his Bostonian Unitarian friends.

This essay broadly accepts Bruce Robertson's argument that the core of Rammohan's political philosophy was the ideal of the virtuous householder striving for spiritual liberation (*mukti*) in this world according to the tradition of Vedanta. Rammohan's version of enlightenment embraced Hindu, Muslim and Western notions of virtue. Yet though he undoubtedly contributed to their development, he was really neither a prophet of contemporary Indian secularism nor a modern cosmopolitan. In his English and Bengali writings he emerges very much as an exponent of a specific form of constitutional liberalism that flourished in the 1810s and 1820s.

Rammohan's reading of European debates about constitutional government informed his construction of India's past and its future. In 1822, at the height of the liberal euphoria over the Spanish and Portuguese revolutions, he published "Modern Encroachments on the Ancient Rights of Females According to the Hindu Law of Inheritance". This tract aimed to show that it was the corrupt and defective understanding of Bengal's Dayabhaga laws of inheritance that resulted in the practice of widow-burning, the abolition of which had become his major public project. Fully Benthamite in the sense that it argued that bad laws make a bad society, Rammohan's interpretation was much more historicist and concerned with education than were the later utilitarians' harder positions. He wished to explain that India had once had a constitution and it was the decline of this constitution and its checks and balances that had sunk India into backwardness. Yet, equally, he implied that if the Indianmind had oncemanaged to conceive the notion of constitutional balance and the separation of powers, it would one day do so again.

The narrative went like this. Deep in the Indian past, the "second tribe", the Rajput or warrior caste, had established despotic rule as a reaction to internal warfare. "Arbitrary and despotic practices" of all sorts, including the oppression of women, had resulted. In time the other castes, under a great leader, Parasurama, had revolted and defeated "the royalists and put cruelly to death almost all the males of that tribe". Thereafter, Rammohan said, a kind of division of powers existed. The Brahmins had "legislative authority", while the "second tribe should exercise the executive authority". After this, India enjoyed peace and harmony for many centuries. Then, unfortunately, "an absolute form of government gradually came again to prevail". Brahmins abandoned their legislative role and began to take offices "in the political department", becoming dependent on the Rajput and later Maratha rulers. This despotism allowed the Muslims to invade India from the twelfth century, "destroying temples, universities and all other sacred and literary establishments". The British might well establish "quiet and happiness". But the auguries were not good. In many respects, the East India Company had perpetuated despotism, allowing the consolidation of executive and judicial powers in the office of the revenue collector and his corrupt post-Mughal deputies. Rammohan's picture of the evolution of the Indian constitution represented a melding of *itihasa*, divine legend, with a particular, "Hindu", view of medieval history. This was novel, though it built on an Indian tradition of interpreting and historicizing family and clan histories (*vamshavalis*) as much as on the work of European orientalists. At the broadest level, liberal historicizing, whether about Anglo-Saxon England, ancient Athens, Rome or India, represented an appeal to history and civilization that circumvented the legitimacy of present despotisms. This was of the utmost importance in a racially charged colonial situation where

Indians in general and Bengalis in particular were denounced as backward. In referring to "royalists", the return of despotism and popular rebellion, Rammohan was locating Indian history within the wider realm of international constitutional liberalism. Yet Parasurama, the leader of the legendary rebellion of the Shastras, is a complex figure for Hindus. He was amatricide and murdered his Rajput enemies' families. Violent rebellion necessarily involves impious acts and problems of ends and means. At first sight, Parasurama is an analogue of Oliver Cromwell. The Lord Protector was himself in a limbo status in British historiography at this time, represented as a regicide, but also as a just rebel. Yet Rammohan's imaginary history is in reality closer to the one being invoked by his Portuguese and Spanish friends in the same year when the tract on women's rights was published. Like Indians, Iberians had to reach far into the classical past to find a constitution that pre-dated centuries of royal autocracy, fixing on classical figures such as Brutus and Cato as their constitutional heroes. Brutus, like Parasurama the matricide, was a morally dubious as well as a heroic figure. One critical aspect of Rammohan's vision of an Indian constitution, however, was that it depended on Indian agency. Earlier British constructs of a "Hindu constitution" gave a much more static picture of Indian history: it was the British who would re-establish ancient India's "constitution".

How did India's ancient constitution relate to its present travails? To begin with, Rammohan's own vision of political progress was international. Reform and nation-building in India depended on the success of constitutional revolutions throughout the world. Following setbacks in Iberia and Latin America, he was delighted by the overthrow of the Bourbons in France and visited Louis-Philippe several times during his final European trip of 1832 and 1833. When first denied entry to France by the London consulate, he raged against artificial barriers placed between nations and proposed an Anglo-French congress. Above all, Rammohan argued tirelessly for the reform of Parliament. He watched the passage of the Reform Bill with trepidation, stating in 1832 that if it failed in Parliament he would sever all ties with Britain. Nevertheless, he appears to have hoped that a liberal rule in Westminster would reduce the power of the Company to that of a territorial government. Parliament would oversee Indian legislation more closely and divide judicial from executive powers across the subcontinent. Separate cadres of Indian judges and local executive officers would strengthen and eventually replace the European civil service, which would itself increasingly work in Indian languages.

This concern with the separation of powers and local agency marked Rammohan out more as a disciple of Montesquieu than of Bentham. It is at this point in his argument, however, that we see his ideal constitution becoming actualized in contemporary political prescription. Parliament would, at least for the time being, assume the role of the Brahmin legislators and the Company that of the Rajput protectors. Rammohan was advocating a "mixed constitution", as described by Hume, in which learned and aristocratic governance would be complemented by a limited popular check. Thus at this stage Rammohan did not advocate the establishment of a representative government or council in India itself, as did a few British radicals, notably Robert Rickards, and the younger generation of Bengalis educated at the Hindu College. Rammohan was as sceptical as Bentham of the concept of natural rights, including a natural right to self-rule. Instead, he hoped that the Imperial Parliament would act as the legislative guardian of India and other dependencies. He also supported the idea, promoted by some British politicians of both parties, including Bentham, that representatives of India and the colonies should sit in the reformed Parliament, turning it into something more like the French Assembly or the forum demanded by American colonists before 1776. This system would replace the corrupt East India and West India interests which had marred the unreformed Parliament. Yet Rammohan also feared a "colonial form of government" in which a British minister might become overwhelmingly powerful in Indian affairs. Someone who knew him well later remarked that he distrusted the "subservience" of Parliament to ministers. Here Rammohan perhaps had in mind what he knew of the causes of the American Revolution. Better would be "a limited government presenting a variety of checks on any abuse of its powers".

Rammohan tended to use the word "separation" to envision the eventual end of direct British rule in India, as did the liberal Governor General, Lord Hastings. He apparently believed that this would only happen some long time in the future. Yet resident British radicals as well as some Indians were already using the word "independence". This was as early as 1832. The *Colombo Journal* wrote deprecating this talk. The *Bengal Hurkaru* responded that though distant in time, the education and improvement of Indians would ensure that "some moment will occur favourable to independence".

A mutually damaging independence was more likely to happen if the Company continued to grind the Indian peasant into the soil. Meanwhile, an Indian author argued that uncontrolled "colonisation" might have the same effect as it had in Ireland. Clearly, what David Armitage has called the "contagion of sovereignty" had rapidly spread to India in the minds of a few intellectuals at least. The presence of American merchants and Calcutta's connection with American Unitarians is important here. The Iberian and Latin American examples were perhaps even more instructive. At this time what some appear to have envisioned was a free "creole" empire of India, ruled by a small number of resident British expatriates along with mixed-race people and educated indigenes. This imaginary construction of India was similar to contemporary Brazil. Others, however, pondered an independent princely union of India under the crown or an indigenous ascendancy of propertied and liberal aristocrats based on the Bengal *zamindar*s (landholders).

Since Rammohan advocated neither direct local political representation nor the early separation of India, it is difficult to see him as the first nationalist, as some historians did in the early twentieth century. Yet he can perhaps be described as a colonial patriot, someone who conceived of India as a cultural and geographical unity. He increasingly came to refer to India, rather than Hindustan, as "a nation" and argued that from the cultural and moral perspective Indians, or "Asiatics" more generally, were the equals of Europeans. At other times, he used the word Hinduism (*Hindur* in Bengali), both positively and negatively, and he was one of the first Indians to do this. Contemporaries were aware of this. Disappointed Unitarians believed that he had opted for "Hindu Unitarianism" rather than Christian Unitarianism in 1818 because of his "patriotism". Since he held that all religions have an equal claim to authority, custom and a sense of solidarity would define a "national cult" and consequently a nation. To that extent, he was once again closer to Edmund Burke than to later British liberals such as J. S.Mill, who left little room for a sense of nationality, as Uday Mehta has noted. Later the Calcutta Tory newspaper *John Bull* ridiculed Rammohan's embassy to England on behalf of the Mughal emperor as unnatural since the emperor was a Muslim. Rammohan's veiled threats that Muslim India would revolt if maltreated were suggested, the paper went on, by "a species of patriotism which likely enough owes its birth to the 'March of Intellect School.'" Tories often branded their ideological opponents with Condorcet's phrase, which they tried to associate with radical innovation and atheism.

At the broadest level, Rammohan was attempting to build an Indian "public" or civil society from the ground up, so that within a generation Indians would begin to share in power and legislative authority. Where possible, like his European liberal peers, he sought to reduce and tame the despotic power of the Company, even if this meant an accession of authority to the distant sovereignty of the Westminster parliament. This stands out even more sharply in two cases where Rammohan was more radical: juries and the press. For him, the element of popular balance in his mixed constitution depended on the proper working of these institutions and, once again, their antecedents in the Indian past had to be envisioned.

The issue of juries emerged in the 1820s as a domestic British imperial problem, that of the press as an international liberal cause. To constitutionalist thinkers in Britain from Blackstone to J. S. Mill the jury was at the heart of the constitution, more important in some senses than parliamentary representation itself. The 1825 Juries Act gave jurymen the power to judge points of law as well as of fact. But contemporary British ideologies of cultural difference clashed with the need for the sense of the community. At this time Indians were still debarred from selection for grand juries on the grounds that, being non-Christians, they were incapable of taking a meaningful oath. Nor, it was said, would they send their own people for punishment, particularly if they were Brahmins. More open critics, such as James Mill, argued that Indians were morally depraved as a race by long eras of despotism. But this struck at the heart of the evangelical case that the "Hindu mind" was capable of moral reform and regeneration and would later be converted to Christianity. There was also a practical problem since Indian merchants, who underpinned much of the credit of Asian trade, were excluded from being jurors on critical cases involving commercial interests.

Being born in India, even Eurasian Christians were barred from service with the result that itinerant sailors, petty European merchants and hangers-on of the East India Company were compelled into jury service. Eurasians and British liberals opposed to the Company fully supported a change. Several developments across the British Empire in the 1820s brought the issue to a head. Indians, Chinese and Malays had recently been given jury rights in Stamford Raffles's model settlement of Singapore. The same had been the case in the crown colony of Ceylon where native Christians, Buddhists and a few Hindus now sat on grand juries. More striking, freed slaves and local Africans could be jurymen in Sierra Leone. Rammohan and his group, along with his learned Madras and Bombay contemporaries, argued strongly for a change in the Indian regulations to permit their countrymen to serve. The argument was, first, that respectable Indians were morally fully capable of taking oaths and that Hindu religion abominated lying. Second, an ancient system of jury, the *panchayat* (literally, a body of five men) had always existed in India. Finally, by taking part in judgment, Hindus and Muslims would be contributing their essential local knowledge to the proceedings, while at the same time learning to participate in a growing civil society. Concurrently, Ram Raz, a judge in the princely state of Mysore, was among the first Indians to designate the judicial tribunal the foundation of Indian political philosophy. In a letter of 1828 he traced an analogy of the *panchayat* to the ancient Hindu law books, where it was called the *sabha*. Ram Raz went on to argue that the judgment of the sabha was absolute and the king merely executed its will. The sabha could be a multi-caste body and operated both in civil and criminal cases. The system had not died out in antiquity, but persisted into the present. Ram Raz stated that he had been a "native judge" in the princely state of Mysore:

I am personally acquainted with several instances in which the faujdar [the military governor] of Bangalore, an officer who as his name implies, must originally have belonged to the army... summoned an assembly called the panchayet, composed of all classes of people indiscriminately to attend at his kacchari [court] for the purposes of deciding civil causes.

It is significant that since the British defeat of Mysore's ruler in 1799 there had been continuous debate about the "ancient Hindu constitution of Mysore". Various corporate bodies within the state, including the royal house, Maratha Brahmin administrators and the Lingayat merchants, had played a part in practically defining its future workings and the limitation of British power within it. Ram Raz began the process of theorizing and historicizing Mysore's institutions. Here and in his work on Hindu architecture he vigorously assaulted British misrepresentations of Indian civilization, especially by the unnamed James Mill. It was Ram Raz's term panchayat that was taken up by writers in north India to describe local judicial agency. This was one of the first all-India symbols of cultural autonomy and later entered the nationalist canon in the works of Gandhi. *Panchayati Raj*—local government by *panchayat*—became an important institution of Nehru's India.

Parliament eventually conceded Indian participation in grand juries in principle by the East India Juries Act of 1828. But a long battle with the directors over the interpretation of the act ensued. The jury issue was one of the first of a series of conflicts between Indian liberals and the ruling power about Indian representation that continued until 1947. In every one of these disputes, Indian spokesmen tried to play on cleavages within British opinion that arose from domestic political argument.

The third British context for the emergence of Indian liberalism in addition to the constitution and the jury was the issue of press freedom. Free communication was an essential dimension of the liberal theory of civil society, as important as free trade and, like free trade, regarded as a moral as well as an economic imperative. Ferguson, Stewart and Bentham were all cited in India as champions of the rôle of the press as a foundation of free societies. In some respects, indeed, the Indian debate on the press went beyond the standard British Whig and liberal arguments precisely because the subcontinent remained an autocracy. The development of newspapers would in the eyes of Rammohan and his British conferrers actually create a civil society and open up government to scrutiny.

The key figure here was James Silk Buckingham. He appears as co-proprietor with Rammohan of the *Calcutta Journal*, a short-lived radical journal which both printed translations of articles in Rammohan's indigenous newspapers and supplied material to them. Buckingham was a classic figure of the reforming era. Born in Falmouth, Cornwall, he belonged to the mercantile, Nonconformist and sea faring world that so consistently supported parliamentary reform. As a seaman on the Atlantic run, he had strong American connections and sympathies and later travelled widely in the USA. In the east, however, he encountered the full force of British despotism as he sawit, in the East India Company and its Levantine agencies. Deported from and returning to India, he took up a series of radical issues in the *Calcutta Journal*. These included parliamentary reform, temperance, anti-slavery (he claimed that the Company was running a clandestine slave trade) and improvement of the conditions of British and Indian seamen, the so-called "lascars".

Buckingham was transported from India by Lord Amherst in 1823 after he had offended its officials once too often. His deputy editor, Sandford Arnot, later followed him under restraint. The Indian government had brought in full press censorship and several Indian-language newspapers closed down rather than pay compulsory sureties. The measure was not repealed until Charles Metcalfe became Governor General in 1835. In the meantime, Buckingham mounted a ferocious campaign against the directors of the East India Company in Britain, suing them for lost income and arbitrary arrest. He agitated in the Company's Court of Proprietors, a body that had long been a popular forum. He toured the major provincial commercial cities involved in the reform movement, such as Glasgow, Liverpool and Manchester. The liberal establishment led by Hume, Grey and Russell took up the cause and sponsored a bill in Parliament against the Company on his behalf. All the while, he edited in England the *Oriental Herald*, which carried on the work of the *Calcutta Journal* of supporting Indian reform and sponsoring the name of Rammohan Roy.

The first generation of Indian newspaper editors and public men adapted many of their ideas from Buckingham's publications.

In defence of liberty of the press, for instance, a correspondent of the *Calcutta Journal* (or possibly an editor under a pseudonym) deployed the classic liberal argument, attributed in this case to Blackstone:

Any laws, that is restraints imposed upon the actions of men, not absolutely required for the benefit of society are tyrannical.... Civil liberty, therefore, is the right of doing all things not prohibited by just and necessary laws. From this it appears that any unnecessary restraints on civil liberty or civil rights are unjustifiable.

This is the doctrine of liberalism as a negative value as described by Raymond Geuss. At the same time, however, the early liberals, British and Indian, also had the more positive goal of diffusing reason and information through society and improving the workings of government by creating a reading public. According to the Indians, the press, like the jury and the constitution itself, had indigenous antecedents. These were the news writers (*akhbar naviss*) of Mughal India who informed officials of infractions of justice and upheld the rule of law. Rammohan's Bengali newspaper, the *Sambad Kaumudy* (Moon of Intelligence), functioned as just such a newssheet (*akhbarat*), bringing details of events such as the fate of the liberal constitutions of Europe but at the same time pointing to acts of official oppression across north India.

The issue of press freedom came to a head initially when John Adam, the Marquess of Hastings's successor as Governor General, imposed press censorship in response to Buckingham's publications. The *Calcutta Journal* had drawn attention to the fact that the Revd James Bryce, a Church of Scotland minister and editor of the "Tory" newspaper *John Bull, was* a placeman of the Company. He had become secretary to the Calcutta stationery department. The radicals indicted the Company for corrupting public opinion by using patronage to support a journal that promulgated the "Tory" line and persistently derogated from the "rights of freeborn Englishmen" in India. The rhetoric of press freedom struck an international tone. Censorship under the Bourbon autocracy in France was "less severe than what is considered law in India" and summary banishment had been "deprecated recently even in the despotic capital of Turkey".

It is difficult to believe, however, that Buckingham's and Arnot's close connection with Rammohan and the increasingly assertive Indian public men of Calcutta was not another cause for the disproportionate official response to this "insult" to government. The "delicacy" of the British position in India in regard to indigenous opinion had often been mentioned as a reason for a strong executive. Shortly before the *John Bull* issue there had been two examples of this assertiveness. *John Bull* had complained that Rammohan's Persian newspaper, the *Mirat al-Akhbar*, had used the word *tursa* (Christian) to describe Europeans in India. Though he denied in the pages of the *Calcutta Journal* that the word was derogatory, it nevertheless conveyed a sense of religious error and low status to its readers. The honour of the "ruling race" was at issue here.

Both the *Akhbar* and the *Journal* had taken up the issue of the contemporary famine in the west and south of Ireland, an event that followed shortly after serious agrarian disturbances in Munster. Subscriptions for the Irish poor collected by Calcutta's European inhabitants had allegedly raised little money. "Native inhabitants" demonstrated their superior charity by subscribing much more. To drive home the point about the responsibility and generosity of the Indian public, the *Mirat al-Akhbar* published an article on "Ireland: The Causes of its Distress and Discontents". Ireland, the article said, had been fighting off the unjust rule of the kings of England for a thousand years. Its peasants were impoverished, yet non-resident Anglo-Irish landlords remitted huge sums of cash regularly to England. Rammohan had carefully followed the rise of O'Connell's movement.

It is again difficult to believe that this articulate concern with Ireland was not, and was not perceived to be, a veiled attack on the Company's rule in India. One of Rammohan's arguments for the colonization of India by select bodies of Europeans was precisely that an analogous flow of money back to Britain from India would be inhibited if more respectable Europeans actually lived in the country. Here, indeed, we may see one of the earliest expressions of an argument which was to become central to the ideology of Indian nationalism: the idea of the "drain of wealth" from India, later elaborated by the Bombay nationalist leader and liberal MP Dadhabhai Naoroji.

Indians and British liberals put up fierce opposition to arbitrary deportation of editors and formal press censorship. Government recourse to trial for libel was adequate to protect public order in India, they asserted. British governments of the period frequently resorted to libel trials in the King's Bench court to punish radical sedition or insults to the crown. Rammohan's argument worked at two levels. First, at a practical level, he argued that a free press was essential in the discovery of arbitrary acts by figures in authority; it had in effect, a representative aspect. Again, an Indian public could only come into existence through the expansion of public knowledge and the press was an organ of education. At a second level, Rammohan and his followers argued that the notion that press freedom would lead to Indian unrest was a fiction. India's polite and commercial society had already demonstrated its implicit loyalty to the British connection through massive investments of wealth in property and businesses around Calcutta and in East India Company and British bonds and financial instruments. This was a significant reflection on the fact that British imperialism in India was built almost entirely in Indian, not British, capital. It also represented an Indian version of the early liberal theory that the national debt, rather than being a sign of the corruption of power, as in France, was in fact a sign of trust between state and civil society.

Conclusion

Rammohan Roy has conventionally been termed "the father of modern India". But that paternity is clearly a complex phenomenon. Most of his contemporaries regarded him as a pseudo-Christian or even an out caste. Many younger people, grouped around Derozio, regarded him as too conservative on the matter of civic "rights" and representation. Even some of his British contemporaries endorsed Indian local self-government more vigorously than did he. The Brahmo Samaj which he founded became in time a somewhat inverted, caste-like religion of the Bengali intelligentsia. Yet he was both an original thinker and an inspiration to later generations. He produced the first identifiable "canon" of modern Indian political thought. He was the first Indian to represent the growth of freedom in India as an essential part of a wider trans-national quest of humanity for self-realization. The Brahmo Samaj, moreover, had a much wider influence on both Indian liberalism and conservatism than its limited number of supporters would suggest. The dominant strand of Indian political ideology in the nineteenth and twentieth centuries was neither Gandhian "neighbourliness" nor neo-Hindu revival, but liberal, secular, republican progressivism, represented by figures such as Dadabhai Naoroji, Jawaharlal Nehru and today's Indian democratic left. Rammohan Roy's arguments were constantly reappropriated and reconstituted by thinkers and politicians of this temper.

This essay, however, has been concerned not so much an individual or a "tradition", but with a distinct "moment" in the history of Indian ideas. What is so striking about the press and political publications in Calcutta, and to a lesser extent Bombay and Madras, in the first three decades of the nineteenth century is how many of the key themes of modern Indian thought—national and international, radical and, indeed, neo-conservative—were already in circulation in articulate form. Before 1830 British and Indian radical journals were discussing India's "independence" or "separation", the evils or advantages of "colonisation", the "drain of wealth" from India, and the need for balance between central power and local agency in a future constitution. Early Indian liberals—though not Rammohan and his immediate circle—had already developed an anti-landlord rhetoric as vigorous as William Cobbett's. They also debated the need for "local self-government", though at this time through the jury and the *panchayat* system. Landlord associations had been founded to argue for the "rights" of property owners, while a neo-conservative ideology depicting India as a Hindu space in need of a protective national political economy had emerged simultaneously with this radical critique, and certainly before the appropriation in Bengal of the ideas of the German economic thinker Friedrich List. Every one of these themes was to disappear and resurface regularly in debates through to the later twentieth century.

Of course, modern political ideas of this sort emerged dramatically across the whole world in the aftermath of the American and European revolutions. And there was no simple teleology that linked this efflorescence of radicalism to the advent of democratic politics either in the West or in India. As late as 1907 the liberal Calcutta journal the *Modern Review* lamented that British publications were incapable of imagining Indian independence at the beginning of the twentieth century, whereas they had readily done so nearly a century before.

Again, it was perhaps only a few hundred Indians who in 1825 fully understood the context of these slogans and doctrines. Some of them, like Rammohan, were alienated from their families and castes. Nevertheless, thousands of other Indians responded to the power of these ideas in less articulate ways and they became ever more influential as the century progressed. Thus the fecundity of the production of political theory in India at this time needs some explanation. The diffusion of radical themes from Europe to India was undoubtedly important. All of Rammohan's major political arguments related directly to British and European debates on equivalent issues. This was the period before the Reform Act of 1832 when domestic British politics was violently contentious and radicals were acutely aware of the European and American dimensions of constitutional liberalism. Reformers regarded the ascendant press not merely as a medium of communication, but as an embodiment of the process by which diffusion of useful and moral sentiments would ultimately create a liberated, trans-national civil society.

British radical doctrines concerning education, civic responsibility and constitutional empowerment, however, found appropriate "ecological niches" in India at this time because of the particular conditions that prevailed in the subcontinent. Indian spokesmen displayed great virtuosity in reconstructing and relocating these arguments within their own traditions that they were beginning to historicize. Events in Goa and the French settlements dramatized the European movement for constitutional government. The radical attack on the Company drew Indians' attention to the contradictions and injustices of "distant sovereignty", thus creating a pervasive crisis of legitimacy for the Company's rule. The prospect of a political appeal to the "freedom-loving British Nation" beyond the purview of the Company was novel and alluring. The supreme courts of the presidencies, and beyond them, the Privy Council, seemed to offer a more immediate check on local executive power, dramatizing a doctrine of division of powers distantly glimpsed in the writings of Montesquieu and his followers. Indians had been flooding to the supreme courts since the 1770s and had become habituated to the language of legal conflicts about rights, property and the powers of the state. Out of this emerged India's constitutional liberal "moment" of the 1810s and 1820s.

6

Ramakrishna and Vivekananda

Sri Ramakrishna Paramahamsa (February 18, 1836-August 16, 1886), born Gadadhar Chattopadhyay was a famous mystic of 19th-century India. His religious school of thought led to the formation of the Ramakrishna Mission by his chief disciple Swami Vivekananda-both were influential figures in the Bengali Renaissance as well as the Hindu renaissance during the 19th and 20th centuries. Many of his disciples and devotees believe he was an *avatar* or incarnation of God.

Ramakrishna was born in a poor Brahmin Vaishnava family in rural Bengal. He became a priest of the Dakshineswar Kali Temple, dedicated to the goddess Kali, which had the influence of the main strands of Bengali *bhakti* tradition. His first spiritual teacher was an ascetic woman skilled in Tantra and Vaishnava *bhakti.* Later an *Advaita Vedantin* ascetic taught him non-dual meditation, and according to Ramakrishna, he experienced *nirvikalpa samadhi* under his guidance. Ramakrishna also experimented with other religions, notably Islam and Christianity, and said that they all lead to the same God. Though conventionally uneducated, he attracted attention of the Bengali intelectuals and middle class.

Biography

Birth and Childhood: Ramakrishna was born in 1836, in the village of Kamarpukur, in the Hooghly district of West Bengal, into a very poor but pious, orthodox Brahman family. Located far from the railroad, Kamarpukur was untouched by the glamour of the city and contained rice fields, tall palms, royal banyans, a few lakes, and two cremation grounds. His parents were Khudiram

Chattopadhyay and Chandramani Devî. According to traditional accounts, Ramakrishna's parents experienced supernatural incidents, visions before his birth. His father Khudiram had a dream in Gaya in which Lord Gadadhara (a form of god Vishnu), said that he would be born as his son. Chandramani Devi is said to have had a vision of light entering her womb from Shiva's temple.

Ramakrishna was a popular figure in the village, with a natural gift for fine arts. Though he attended a village school with some regularity for 12 years, he later rejected the traditional schooling saying that he was not interested in a "bread-winning education". Kamarpukur, being a transit-point in well-established pilgrimage routes to Puri, brought him into contact with renunciates and holy men. He became well-versed in the *Puranas*, the *Ramayana*, the *Mahabharata*, and the *Bhagavata Purana*, hearing them from wandering monks and the *Kathaks*—a class of men in ancient India who preached and sang the *PuraGas*. He could read and write in Bengali.

Ramakrishna describes his first spiritual ecstasy at the age of six: while walking along the paddy fields, a flock of white cranes flying against a backdrop of dark thunder clouds caught his vision. He reportedly became so absorbed by this scene that he lost outward consciousness and experienced indescribable joy in that state. Ramakrishna reportedly had experiences of similar nature a few other times in his childhood—while worshipping the goddess *Vishalakshi*, and portraying god Shiva in a drama during *Shivaratri* festival. From his tenth or eleventh year on, the trances became common, and by the final years of his life, Ramakrishna's *samadhi* periods occurred almost daily.

Ramakrishna's father died in 1843, after which time family responsibilities fell on his elder brother Ramkumar. This loss drew him closer to his mother, and he spent his time in household activities and daily worship of the household deities and became more involved in contemplative activities such as reading the sacred epics.

When Ramakrishna was in his teens, the family's financial position worsened. Ramkumar started a Sanskrit school in Calcutta and also served as a priest. Ramakrishna moved to Calcutta in 1852 with Ramkumar to assist in the priestly work.

Priest at Dakshineswar Kali Temple

In 1855 Ramkumar was appointed as the priest of Dakshineswar Kali Temple, built by Rani Rashmoni—a rich woman of Calcutta who belonged to the *kaivarta* community. Ramakrishna, along with his nephew Hriday, became assistants to Ramkumar, with Ramakrishna given the task of decorating the deity. When Ramkumar died in 1856, Ramakrishna took his place as the priest of the Kali temple. The name Ramakrishna is said to have been given to him by Mathur Babu, the son-in-law of Rani Rashmoni.

After Ramkumar's death Ramakrishna became more contemplative. He began to look upon the image of the goddess Kali as his mother and the mother of the universe. He became seized by a desire to have a *darshana* (vision) of Kali—a direct realization of her reality—and believed the stone image to be living and breathing and taking food out of his hand. At times he would weep bitterly and cry out loudly while worshipping, and would not be comforted, because he could not see his mother Kali as perfectly as he wished. People became divided in their opinions—some held Ramakrishna to be mad, and some took him to be a great lover of God. Ramakrishna was said to become deeply offended when others would not show the same level of devotion for the goddess Kali as he did. He would become angry when others would tell him that he was not really experiencing the presence of Kali. Yet Through his faith, and his spiritual devotion, others would soon begin to believe in not only what Ramakrishna was seeing, but in his teachings as well. One day, brought to the point of suicide by this longing, he had the experience of goddess Kali as the universal Mother, which he described as "... houses, doors, temples and everything else vanished altogether; as if there was nothing anywhere! And what I saw was an infinite shoreless sea of light; a sea that was consciousness. However, far and in whatever direction I looked, I saw shining waves, one after another, coming towards me."

Marriage

Rumors spread to Kamarpukur that Ramakrishna had become unstable as a result of his spiritual exercises at Dakshineswar. Ramakrishna's mother and his elder brother Rameswar decided to get Ramakrishna married, thinking that marriage would be a good steadying influence upon him—by forcing him to accept responsibility and to keep his attention on normal affairs rather than being obsessed with his spiritual practices and visions. Far from objecting to the marriage, Ramakrishna mentioned that they could find the bride at the house of Ramchandra Mukherjee in Jayrambati, three miles to the northwest of Kamarpukur. The five-year-old bride, Saradamani Mukhopadhyaya was found and the marriage was duly solemnised in 1859. Ramakrishna was 23 at this point, but the age difference was typical for 19th century rural Bengal. They later spent three months together in Kamarpukur. Sarada Devi was fourteen while Ramakrishna was thirty-two. Ramakrishna became a very influential figure in Sarada's life, and she became a strong follower of his teachings. Their marriage is now seen in India, to be one of the most spiritual and perfect unions between a man and a woman.. After the marriage, Sarada stayed at Jayrambati and joined Ramakrishna in Dakshineswar at the age of 18.

Sarada Devi

Sarada Devi (1853—1920), born Saradamani Mukhopadhyaya, was the wife and spiritual counterpart of Ramakrishna Paramahamsa, a nineteenth century mystic of Bengal. Sarada Devi is also reverentially addressed as the Holy Mother (*Sri Maa*) by the followers of the Ramakrishna monastic order. Sarada Devi played an important role in the growth of the Ramakrishna Movement.

Sarada Devi was born in Jayrambati. At the age of five she was betrothed to Ramakrishna, whom she joined at Dakshineswar when she was in her late teens. According to her traditional biographers, both lived lives of unbroken continence, showing the ideals of a householder and of the monastic ways of life. After Ramakrishna's death, Sarada Devi stayed most of the time either at Jayrambati or at the Udbodhan office, Calcutta. The disciples of Ramakrishna regarded her as their own mother, and after their guru's passing looked to her for advice and encouragement. The followers of the Ramakrishna movement regard Sarada Devi as an incarnation of the Divine Mother.

Biography

Birth and Parentage

At Dakshineswar, Sarada Devi stayed in a tiny room in the

nahabat (musical tower). Sarada Devi stayed at Dakshineswar until 1885, except for short periods when she visited her village Jayrambati. By this time Ramakrishna had already embraced the monastic life of a sannyasin; as a result, the marriage was never consummated. As a priest, Ramakrishna performed the ritual ceremony—the *Shodashi Puja* where Sarada Devi was made to sit in the seat of goddess Kali, and worshipped as the Divine mother. According to Saradananda a direct disciple of Ramakrishna, Ramakrishna married in order to show the world an ideal of a sexless marriage. Ramakrishna regarded Sarada as the incarnation of Divine Mother, addressing her as *Sree Maa* (Holy Mother) and it was by this name that she was known to Ramakrishna's disciples.

Sarada Devi's day began at 3 am. After finishing her ablutions in the Ganges, she would practice *japa* and meditation until daybreak. Ramakrishna taught her the sacred *mantras,* and instructed her how to initiate people and guide them in spiritual life. Sarada Devi is regarded as Ramakrishna's first disciple. Except for her hours of meditation, most of her time was spent in cooking for Ramakrishna and the growing number of his devotees. While Sarada Devi remained completely in the background, her unassuming but warm personality attracted some female devotees to become her lifelong companions.

During Ramakrishna's last days, during which he suffered from throat cancer, Sarada Devi played an important role in nursing him and preparing suitable food for him and his disciples. It is reported that after Ramakrishna's passing away in August 1886, when Sarada Devi tried to remove her bracelets as the customs dictated for a widow, she had a vision of Ramakrishna in which he said, "I have not passed away, I have gone from one room to another." According to her, whenever she thought of dressing like a widow, she had a vision of Ramakrishna asking her not to do so. After Ramakrishna's death, Sarada Devi continued to play an important role in the nascent religious movement. She remained the spiritual guide of the movement for the next thirty four years.

Pilgrimage

After Ramakrishna's death, Sarada Devi began her pilgrimage through North India, accompanied by a party of women disciples including Lakshmi Didi, Gopal Ma, and Ramakrishna's householder and monastic disciples. The party visited the Vishwanath Temple of god Shiva at Banaras and the city of Ayodhya, which is associated with life of god Rama. Later, she visited Vrindavan which is associated with god Krishna. According to traditional accounts, at Vrindavan, she experienced *nirvikalpa sumadhi* and began her role as *guru*. She initiated several of the Ramakrishna's disciples including Mahendranath Gupta, Yogen with a *mantra*. According to her traditional biographers and disciples, to call her "Mother" was no mere expression of respect and all those who met her became aware of a maternal quality in her.

At Calcutta

After the pilgrimage, Sarada Devi stayed alone in Kamarpukur, Ramakrishna's native village. There, she endured poverty, verging on starvation for a year. In 1888, when the news reached the lay and monastic disciples of Ramakrishna that she needed their care and attention, they invited her to Calcutta and arranged for her stay. Swami Saradananda built a permanent house for Sarada Devi in Calcutta. The house was named the Udbodhan House, after the Bengali monthly magazine conducted by the Ramakrishna Math. It is also called *Mayerbati* ("Holy Mother's House"), where she spent the longest period of her life outside Jayrambati.

Sarada Devi came to Calcutta because she had many hardships in Kamarpukur. She had no financial resources and about no one could take care of her. She tried to hide her situation, but it leaked out. When the devotees at Calcutta heard this, they persuaded Sarada Devi to come to Calcutta.

At Udbodhan House, Sarada Devi was accompanied by other women disciples of Ramakrishna, Gopal Ma, Yogin Ma, Lakshmi Didi and Gauri Ma being the best known. An increasing number of people began to flock for guidance, instructions and spiritual initiation. Other Western women followers of Ramakrishna Order including Sister Nivedita and Sister Devamata formed close relationship with her. According to her biographers, her innate motherliness put visitors at ease. Swami Nikhilananda, her direct disciple writes, "Though she had no children of the flesh, she had many of the spirit." She regarded all her disciples as her own children.

Sarada Devi received the highest reverence from the Ramakrishna Order and its devotees. Ramakrishna had bade her continue his mission after his passing away and wanted his disciples not to make any distinction between himself and her. According to her devotees and traditional biographers, the hospitality of Sarada Devi was unique and was characterized by motherly care and solicitude. Traditional accounts recount the mystical experiences of her devotees. Some dreamt of her as a goddess in human form though they had never seen her picture before. Others reportedly received their initiation from her in their dream. One such example is of Girish Chandra Ghosh, the father of Bengali drama, who reportedly saw Sarada Devi in a dream when he was nineteen years old and received a *mantra*, and when he met her many years later, to his astonishment it was the same person in the dream.

Last Days

Sarada Devi spent her final years moving back and forth between Jayrambati and Calcutta. In January 1919, Sarada Devi went to Jayrambati and stayed there for over a year. During the last three months of her stay, her health seriously declined. Her strength was greatly impaired and she was brought back to Calcutta on February 27, 1920. For the next five months she continued to suffer. Before her death, she gave the last advice to the grief stricken devotees, "But I tell you one thing—if you want peace of mind, do not find fault with others. Rather see your own faults. Learn to make the whole world your own. No one is a stranger my child: this whole world is your own!". This is considered as her last message to the world. She died at 1.30 am on July 20, 1920. Her body was cremated at the Belur Math.

Teachings and Quotes

Sarada Devi did not write any books and her utterances and reminiscences have been recorded by her disciples including Swami Nikhilananda, Swami Tapasyananda. Though uneducated Sarada Devi's spiritual insight and utterances are highly regarded by scholars like Gayatri Chakravorty Spivak, who writes, "We have bits and pieces of her exquisite remarks as testimony."

- Practise meditation, and by and by your mind will be so calm and fixed that you will find it hard to keep away from meditation.
- The mind is everything. It is in the mind alone that one feels pure and impure. A man, first of all, must make his

own mind guilty and then alone can he see another man's guilt.

- "I tell you one thing. If you want peace of mind, do not find fault with others. Rather see your own faults. Learn to make the whole world your own. No one is a stranger, my child; the whole world is your own."
- One must have devotion towards one's own *guru*. Whatever may be the nature of the *guru*, the disciple gets salvation by dint of his unflinching devotion towards his *guru*.

Impact and Legacy

Sarada Devi played an important role as the advisory head of an nascent organization that became a monastic order devoted to social work—the Ramakrishna Mission. Gayatri Spivak writes that Sarada Devi "performed her role with tact and wisdom, always remaining in the background." She also initiated several prominent monks into the Ramakrishna Order. Swami Nikhilananda, who was a freedom fighter and a follower of Mahatma Gandhi, accepted Sarada Devi as his *guru* and joined the Ramakrishna Order. He eventually founded the Ramakrishna-Vivekananda Centre in New York. Though uneducated herself, Sarada Devi advocated education for women. She entrusted Devamata with the implementation of her dream—a girl's school on the Ganges, where Eastern and Western pupils could study together. In 1954, Sri Sarada Math and Ramakrishna Sarada Mission, a monastic order for women was founded in the honour of Sarada Devi.

Religious Practices and Teachers

After his marriage Ramakrishna returned to Calcutta and resumed the charges of the temple again, but instead of toning down, his spiritual fervour and devotion only increased. To cultivate humility and eliminate the distinction between his own high Brahmin caste and pariahs belonging of low caste he would clean their quarters with his own hands and long hair.

He would take gold and silver coins, and mixing them with rubbish, repeat "money is rubbish, money is rubbish". He later said that "I lost all perception of difference between the two in my mind, and threw them both into the Ganges. No wonder people took me for mad." According to Swami Vivekananda, his hatred for money became so instinctive that his body would shrink back convulsively if it were touched with a coin, even when asleep.

Many of his religious views were based on traditional Hindu thought and practice. Ramakrishna's personal and religious views focused on living a traditional life, with Hindu gods at the centre. It was very much a philosophy of godly worship and dependence. He believed that everything in life–caste, wealth, family, and personal achievement–was already determined by the gods. Though in regards to other religions, Ramakrishna did not hold traditional biased views. He believed that every religion was welcome, and that worshipping a god in any way was better than not worshipping one at all. He became very known for his views on religious tolerance and was seen as a saintly figure to many because of them. His views of tolerance were also passed on through the Ramakrishna Mission and his followers.

Bhairavi Brahmani and Tantra

In 1861, Bhairavi Brahmani, an orange-robed, middle-aged female ascetic, appeared at Dakshineshwar. She carried with her the *Raghuvir Shila*, a stone icon representing Ram and all Vaishnava deities. She was thoroughly conversant with the texts of Gaudiya Vaishnavism and practiced Tantra. According to the Bhairavi, Ramakrishna was experiencing phenomena that accompany *mahabhava*—the supreme attitude of loving devotion towards the divine –and quoting from the *bhakti shastras*, she said that other religious figures like Radha and Chaitanya had similar experiences.

The Bhairavi initiated Ramakrishna into Tantra. Tantrism focuses on the worship of *shakti* and the object of Tantric training is to transcend the barriers between the holy and unholy as a means of achieving liberation and to see all aspects of the natural world as manifestations of the divine *shakti*. Under her guidance, he went through a full course of sixty four major tantric sadhanas which were completed in 1863. He began with mantra rituals such as japa and purascarana and many other rituals designed to purify the mind and establish self-control. He later proceeded towards tantric sadhanas, which generally include a set of heterodox practices called *vamachara* (left-hand path), which utilize as a means of liberation, activities like eating of parched grain, fish and meat along with drinking of wine and sexual intercourse. According to

Ramakrishna and his biographers, Ramakrishna did not directly participate in the last two of those activities, all that he needed was a suggestion of them to produce the desired result. Ramakrishna acknowledged the left-hand tantric path, though it had "undesirable features", as one of the "valid roads to God-realization", he consistently cautioned his devotees and disciples against associating with it.

Ramakrishna took the attitude of a son towards the Bhairavi. The Bhairavi on the other hand looked upon Ramakrishna as an *avatara,* or incarnation of the divine, and was the first person to openly declare that Ramakrishna was an *avatara*. The Bhairavi also taught Ramakrishna the *kumari-puja,* a form of ritual in which the Virgin Goddess is worshipped symbolically in the form of a young girl. Under the tutelage of the Bhairavi, Ramakrishna also became an adept at Kundalini Yoga. The Bhairavi, with the yogic techniques and the tantra played an important part in the initial spiritual development of Ramakrishna.

Vaishnava Bhakti

The Vaishnava Bhakti traditions speak of five different moods, referred to as *bhavas*—different attitudes that a devotee can take up to express his love for God. They are: *úanta,* the serene attitude; *dasya,* the attitude of a servant; *sakhya,* the attitude of a friend; *vatsalya,* the attitude of a mother toward her child; and *madhura,* the attitude of a woman towards her lover.

At some point in the period between his vision of Kali and his marriage, Ramakrishna practiced *dasya bhava*. He started worshipping Rama in the attitude of Hanuman, the monkey-god, who is considered to be the ideal devotee and servant of Rama. According to Ramakrishna, towards the end of this *sadhana,* he had a vision of Sita, the consort of Rama, merging into his body.

In 1864, Ramakrishna practiced *vatsalya bhava* under a Vaishnava guru Jatadhari. During this period, he worshipped a metal image of Ramlala (Rama as a child) in the attitude of a mother. According to Ramakrishna, he could feel the presence of child Rama as a living God in the metal image.

Ramakrishna later engaged in the practice of *madhura bhava*—the attitude of the Gopis and Radha towards Krishna. During the practise of this *bhava,* Ramakrishna dressed himself in women's attire for several days and regarded himself as one of the Gopis of Vrindavan. According to the Ramakrishna, *madhura bhava* is practised to root out the idea of sex, which is seen as an impediment in spiritual life. According to Ramakrishna, towards the end of this *sadhana*, he attained *savikalpa samadhi*—vision and union with Krishna.

Ramakrishna visited Nadia, the home of Chaitanya and Nityananda, the 15th-century founders of Bengali Gaudiya Vaishnava bhakti. According to Ramakrishna, he had an intense vision of two young boys merging into his body. Earlier, after his vision of Kali, he is said to have cultivated the *Santa bhava*—the passive "peaceful" attitude — towards Kali.

Views on Ramakrishna

Many authors have expressed their views on Ramakrishna (1836-1886), a famous 19th-century Indian mystic whose teachings are the foundation of the Ramakrishna religious movement and the Ramakrishna Mission.

Religious Views

Christianity: Ramakrishna's first encounter with Christianity was in 1874, when he heard the Bible being read at his devotee Malik's house. He later practiced Christianity, and according to Ramakrishna, he later had a vision of Jesus Christ. Ramakrishna regarded Jesus as "the great Yogi". Ramakrishna's teachings and personality have been studied from the point of Christianity by several scholars including Romain Rolland, Paul Hourihan.

Romain Rolland called Ramakrishna as the "younger brother of Christ". Another book, *Ramakrishna & Christ, the Supermystics: New Interpretations* compares the lives and spiritual beliefs of Ramakrishna with that of Jesus Christ.

Francis X Clooney, a Roman Catholic priest and member of the Society of Jesus, writes that Ramakrishna's vision of Christ, "shows Christians like myself a way to respond to the mystery, beauty and holiness of non-Christian religious experiences". Religious scholar D.S. Sharma and Romain Rolland notes similarities between Ramakrishna's mystic experiences and other religious personalities—St. Paul, Henry Suso—a German mystic of the 14th century, Richard Rolle of Hampole, and St.Theresa of Avila.

Islam

Ramakrishna also practiced Islam as a part of his *sadhana* (spiritual disciplines). According to Ramakrishna, his practice of Islam culminated in the vision of Mohammed. Ramakrishna's teachings and experiences have been studied from the perspective of Islam, and compared with teachings of the Sufi saints by scholars like A. J. A. Tyeb.

Tyeb notes that Ramakrishna's *sadhana* of meditating alone at night in the forest for several days is similar to the 19th century mystic, Sayed Sah Murshid Ali Quaderi. Tyeb writes that Ramakrishna's prayer to goddess *Kali* is similar to that of Rabia, who is described as 'a woman who lost herself in union with the Divine'. Tyeb also writes that Al Muhasibi, a 9th century Sufi of Baghdad, spoke of meditation in the same way as Ramakrishna did.

Bhawuk in his journal, *Culture's influence on creativity: the case of Indian spirituality* wrote that Ramakrishna's contribution to humanity is particularly significant for the world after the bombing of the twin towers of the World Trade Centre on September 11, 2001. Bhawuk writes that, Islam is not to be blamed for the incident of September 11, and no religion should be blamed for any act of terrorism, because the life of Ramakrishna proclaims that all religions lead to the same God.

Psychoanalysis and Sexuality

Ramakrishna's personality and actions have been a popular topic of psychologcal analysis by scholars and writers, especially in the Western world. Besides his mystical experiences, much attention has been paid to his attitudes towards sexuality and the role of sex in his philosophical and religious views. Some of these studies have been extremely controversial.

Swami Vivekananda

Swami Vivekananda, who would in time become Ramakrishna's most ardent and prominent disciple, initially viewed Ramakrishna's ecstasy as pathological, questioned his qualification of Kali as the "mother of universe", and did not accept him as an *avatara*. Vivekananda regarded the *Advaitist Vedantism* of identity with the Absolute as blasphemy and madness. After a period of revolt, Ramakrishna was accepted as a *guru*.

Referring to the practice of *Madhura Bhava,* by his guru, years later in 1896 in one of his speeches *My Master,* Vivekananda said,

One of the Sadhanas was to root out the sex idea. Soul has no sex, it is neither male nor female. It is only in the body that sex exists, and the man who desires to reach the spirit cannot at the same time hold to sex distinctions. Having been born in a masculine body, this man wanted to bring the feminine idea into everything. He began to think that he was a woman, he dressed like a woman, spoke like a woman, gave up the occupations of men, and lived in the household among the women of a good family, until, after years of this discipline, his mind became changed, and he entirely forgot the idea of sex; thus the whole view of life became changed to him.

Referring to the teaching of *Kama-Kanchana,* Vivekananda said,

Man is a soul, and soul is sexless, neither man nor woman. The idea of sex and the idea of money were the two things, he thought, that prevented him from seeing the Mother. This whole universe is the manifestation of the Mother, and She lives in every woman's body. "Every woman represents the Mother; how can I think of woman in mere sex relation?" That was the idea: Every woman was his Mother, he must bring himself to the state when he would see nothing but Mother in every woman. And he carried it out in his life.

Romain Rolland

In his book *The Life of Ramakrishna* (1929), Romain Rolland, argues that Ramakrishna's experiences were not pathological. Rolland also argues the inapplicability of psychoanalysis on Ramakrishna, Swami Vivekananda and other mystics. Rolland had correspondence with Freud. In his letter of December 5, 1927, Rolland indicated that he was researching a book on the Hindu saints Ramakrishna and Vivekananda. The references to Freud and psychoanalysis in these books are considered as direct response to *Civilization and Its Discontents.*

Leo Schneiderman

Leo Schneiderman in his work, *Ramakrishna: Personality and Social Factors in the Growth of a Religious Movement* (1969) argues that Ramakrishna's "bizarre" behaviour (*samadhi*) must be judged within its proper cultural context. According to Schneiderman, since Ramakrishna was a Brahmin priest who combined the performance of traditional religious functions with demonstrations of divine possession, especially in *samadhi,* he could appeal to a wide clientele and he was both an exemplar of Redfield's "great tradition" of Hinduism, and of village shamanism, sublimated to a very high plane. Schneiderman argues that Ramakrishna's trances and other dramatic manifestations, including perhaps, even his psychotic behaviour, were not truly aberrations from the standpoint of the non-Sanskritic popular culture.

Walter G. Neevel

In the 1976 essay, "The Transformation of Sri Ramakrishna", Walter G. Neevel argues that Ramakrishna's life went through three "transformations". The first—the transformation of the "madman" of the early years to the benign, saintly figure of the later years—appears to have been brought about more by shifting public gaze than some personal spiritual progression. According to Neevel, the second and third transformations, are seen to reflect not historically verifiable ideas or events in the life of the saint, but myth-making and misrepresentation, often performed by his most intimate followers and disciples. Neevel argues that, the saint is incorrectly depicted as an advaitin of the Sankarite school.

Amiya P. Sen argues that Neevel's essay overlooks certain problems. Neevel does not situate the ascriptions of Ramakrishna as an advaitin or vedantin in the historical context of Indian philosophy which had the influence of Western-educated intelligentsia like Ram Mohan Roy. Amiya Sen writes that contrary to what Neevel suggests, "the maddened state of Ramakrishna" during his early practice is described by the *Vivekachudamani,* an advaitic text as one of the spiritually exalted states. Sen further argues that "Vivekananda derived the social service gospel under direct inspiration from Ramakrishna rests very substantially on the liminal quality of the Master's message". Neevel attributes Ramakrishna's ability to lapse into trance was largely due to his esthetic and emotional sensitivity.

Narasingha Sil

In 1991, historian Narasingha Sil wrote *Ramakrishna Paramahamsa: A Psychological Profile,* an account of Ramakrishna that argues that Ramakrishna's mystical experiences were pathological and originated from alleged childhood sexual trauma. Narasingha Sil links Ramakrishna's teaching of *Kamini-Kanchana* to traditional rural Bengali misogyny. Sil also says that Ramakrishna made his wife into a deity in order to avoid thinking of her as sexual.

Other scholars, most notably psychologist Sudhir Kakar, argued that Sil's study was simplistic and misleading. Sil's theory has also been deemed as reductive by William B. Parsons, who has called for an increased empathetic dialogue between the classical/adaptive/transformative schools and the mystical traditions for an enhanced understanding of Ramakrishna's life and experiences. Bengali Scholar William Radice wrote that, "Sil has debunked the saint so thoroughly and gleefully that it is hard to see how he will recover, once Sil's book becomes widely known."

Dr.Jeanne Openshaw

Dr.Jeanne Openshaw, a senior lecturer in Religious Studies, and who specializes in the area of Bengali Vaishnavism and Culture, argues that the behaviour or religious practices of Ramakrishna are not necessarily abnormal. Openshaw argues that from the context of devotional Bengali *Vaishnavism*, where femininity represents the highest attainable condition, the cultivation of femininity by men in various ways is not necessarily abnormal, nor can it necessarily be taken as a sign of homosexuality. Openshaw writes that in rural Bengal, male celibacy, and conservation of semen are considered important. Openshaw argues that Ramakrishna's attempt to see all women as mothers rather than as sexual partners, cannot be seen in terms of homoerotic tendencies.

Sudhir Kakar

In 1991, Sudhir Kakar wrote *"The Analyst and the Mystic"* Gerald James Larson wrote, "Indeed, Sudhir Kakar...indicates that there would be little doubt that from a psychoanalytic point of view Ramakrishna could be diagnosed as a secondary transsexual." Kakar sought a meta-psychological, non-pathological explanation that connects Ramakrishna's mystical realization with creativity. Kakar also argued that culturally relative concepts of eroticism and gender have contributed to the Western difficulty in comprehending Ramakrishna. In 2003, Sudhir Kakar wrote a novel, *Ecstasy*, in which an aspiring *sadhu* in 20th century India endures sexual molestation as a child, and has a feminine appearance and ambiguous sexuality. According to the author, the characters were modelled on Ramakrishna and Vivekananda.

Somnath Bhattacharya

Somnath Bhattacharya further elaborates on the views related to transvestite and transsexuality traits of Ramakrishna. Bhattacharya argues that dressing up in feminine attire as part of a legitimate and culturally accepted *sadhana* for a short period of time does not amount to transvestism, since Ramakrishna also dressed like a *Shakta* and a *Vaishnava* during his Shakti and Vaishnava sadhana days, and like a Muslim during his Islam sadhana, which was in male attire. Bhattacharrya argues that Ramakrishna's dressing habits were in line with this religious practice. Bhattacharrya also argues that Ramakrishna cannot be described as a secondary transsexual. He quotes Ramakrishna's words. "Formerly I too used to see many visions, but now in my ecstatic state I don't see so many. I am gradually getting over my feminine nature; I feel nowadays more like a man. Therefore I control my emotions; I don't manifest it outwardly so much. ..." Bhattacharya also notes that the American Psychiatric Association defines transsexuality as a strong and persistent cross-gender identification, and not merely a desire for any perceived cultural advantages of being the other sex; it is a disorder always involving distress to the person, with a feeling of estrangement from the body and a felt need to alter the appearance of the body.

Jeffrey Kripal

In 1995, religious scholar J. Kripal wrote a highly controversial book *Kali's Child: The Mystical and the Erotic in the Life and Teachings of Ramakrishna*, a psychoanalytic study of Ramakrishna. A review by W. Parsons described *Kali's Child* as a book "which performs a classic Freudian interpretation by seeing symptoms of repressed homoeroticism in the visions and acts of Ramakrishna, but then, in exemplifying the interdisciplinary approach of this dialogue, legitimates Ramakrishna's religious visions by situating psychoanalytic discourse in a wider Tantric world view."

The book caused intense controversy among both Western and Indian audiences which (as of 2004) was still unresolved. In 1998 Kripal published a second edition of *Kali's Child*, for which he claimed to have corrected the translation errors pointed out by the critics in the first edition.

In 1999, B. Hatcher reported that, although some scholars of religion and South Asian culture had misgivings, their overall evaluation of *Kali's Child* was positive, and at times highly laudatory.

However many reviewes were extremely negative. In India the book became known mainly through a scathing review by religious scholar Narasingha Sil in *The Statesman*, Calcutta's major English-language daily, which resulted in a great deal of angry correspondence.

The deductions of *Kali's Child* and Kripal's credentials as a psychoanalyst were questioned by several Ramakrishna followers, such as Swami Tyagananda, and Swami Atmajnanananda, and by several scholars. Alan Roland claimed that Freudian approaches are not applicable to study Asian cultures. In 2001, Huston Smith derided Kripal's work as "colonialism updated". Somnath Bhattacharya claimed that Kripal is not qualified in psychoanalysis, and that *Kali's Child* conntains many grave errors and distortions. In 2004, John Hawley revised his earlier positive evaluation of *Kali's Child*, and wrote that Ramakrishna's torment should not devolve to a bodily level, and that people with different sexual orientations should not indiscriminately impose their thoughts on religious communities. In 2007, Gayatri Spivak still claimed that Kripal has misinterpreted "Ramakrishna's life as a *bhakta*, as tantric practice" and claimed the book was full of cultural and linguistic mis-translations, so its general premise could not be taken seriously.

Kripal responded to the criticisms in journal articles and postings on his website, but stopped participating in the discussion in late 2002.

J.S. Hawley

John Stratton Hawley, Professor of Religion at Barnard College, in his paper *The Damage of Separation: Krishna's Loves and Kali's Child* examines the following:

- Is it right to think of the religious and erotic realms as overlapping, particularly when a homosexual dimension is involved.
- Second, if Hindus and Hinduism are the subject, should non-Hindus refrain from speaking?

In this study, J.S.Hawley, revisits the Kali's Child debate highlighting one of its central terms — the *vyakulata* feeling of Ramakrishna. J.S.Hawley argues that "neither the gopis' torment nor Ramakrishna's must be allowed to devolve to a bodily level." Hawley further argues that "communities of people who respond to different sexual orientations should not indiscriminately impose their thoughts on religious communities....Eros is dangerous"

Alan Roland

Attempts by modern authors to psychoanalyze Ramakrishna are questioned by practicing psychoanalyst Alan Roland, who has written extensively about applying Western psychoanalysis to Eastern cultures, and charges that psychoanalysis has been misapplied to Ramakrishna. Roland decries the facile decoding of Hindu symbols, such as Kali's sword and Krishna's flute, into Western sexual metaphors—thereby reducing Ramakrishna's spiritual aspiration to the basest psychopathology. The conflation of Ramakrishna's spiritual ecstasy, or samadhi, with unconscious dissociated states due to repressed homoerotic feelings is not based on common psychoanalytic definitions of these two different motivations, according to Roland. He also writes that it is highly questionable whether Ramakrishna's spiritual aspirations and experiences involve regression—responding to modern attempts to reduce Ramakrishna's spiritual states to a subconscious response to an imagined childhood trauma.

Kelley Ann Raab

While most of the studies have been conducted from either a primarily psychoanalytic perspective or from the perspective of a devotee, Kelley Ann Raab's work — *Is There Anything Transcendent about Transcendence? A Philosophical and Psychological Study of Sri Ramakrishna*, focuses upon Ramakrishna from both a philosophical perspective and a psychoanalytic perspective. The study argues that neither a purely psychological explanation nor a solely philosophical account of his visions is adequate to understand his madness or his godliness, but that together psychology and philosophy can deepen our understanding of Ramakrishna and find a common meeting ground. Raab argues that,

- By philosophical analysis of Ramakrishna's devotional mysticism and tantric underpinnings, his visions and behaviour were in keeping with his culture and tradition.

- By psychological analysis of Ramakrishna's behaviour, he broke through dualistic thought patterns defining gender, humanity, and God by dressing as and imitating a woman.

Gayatri Chakravorty Spivak

Professor Gayatri Chakravorty Spivak, taking the example of a "dvaita" gaze of a "boy looking up obliquely at the clay and wattle frame of the image of Durga" writes that when we read the photo through Sigmund Freud's psychoanalysis it would be wrongly diagnosed as "double anxiety of castration and decapitation." Spivak writes that Freud's analysis is not culturally receptive and writes that Freud's psychoanalysis is an "occupational hazard". She writes that Ramakrishna was a "Bengali *bhakta* visionary" and that as a *bhakta,* he turned chiefly towards Kali.

Tantra Sadhana

Different views on Ramakrishna's tantric *sadhana* have been expressed. The Tantra *sadhana* consisted of the "right-handed path" consisting of Kularnava, Mahanirvana and Kamalakala Vilasa involving celibate vegetarian lifestyle, japa, breath control, concentration, meditation and a set of heterodox practices but not limited to the Vamachara—termed as "left-handed path", which involves drinking wine, eating rotten flesh, sexual intercourse. Depending on an aspirant's disposition, Tantra prescribes a particular method for spiritual practice. In general, the Tantras classify people into three major groups *pasu* (animal), *vira* (hero), *divya* (godlike). According to Saradananda, Ramakrishna was in the *vira* stage during the practice of vamachara. Elizabeth U. Harding writes that the Tantra practices are aimed at rousing the *Kundalini* and peircing the six *chakras*. Elizabeth argues that Tantra is one of the paths for God-realization and cannot be branded as sensualism.

Christopher Isherwood writes that the object of the tantrik disciplines is "to see, behind all phenomena, the presence of God and to overcome the obstacles to this insight — attraction and aversion". Further Isherwood argues that words which normally carry sensual associations suggested higher meanings to Ramakrishna in his exalted state. For example, the word *yoni,* which normally means the female sex-organ, would mean for him the divine source of creation. According to Isherwood, for Ramakrishna the most unconditionally obscene words were sacred to him as the vocabulary of the scriptures during the tantra *sadhana*. Religious scholars note that the word *linga* represented *purusha*, and *yoni* represented *prakriti*.

Neevel argues that some of Ramakrishna's followers tend to be apologetic about his taking up tantric practices because of the eroticism that has discredited tantric schools in general and those of Bengal in particular. Neevel argues that the influence of tantra on this spiritual development is underestimated.. Ramchandra Datta one of the early biographers of Ramakrishna is reported to have said, "We have heard many tales of the Brahmani but we hesitate to divulge them to the public."

In *Kali's Child*, Jeffery Kripal argues that "Ramakrishna's world, then, was a Tantric world". Kripal further argues that Ramakrishna's Tantric practices were "omnipresent, defining virtually every point along Ramakrishna's spiritual development." Amiya P.Sen writes that "it is really difficult to separate the Tantrik Ramakrishna from the Vedantic", since Vedanta and Tantra "may appear to be differ in some respects", but they also "share some important postulates between them".

Totapuri and Vedanta

In 1865, Ramakrishna was initiated into *sannyasa* by Tota Puri, an itinerant monk who trained Ramakrishna in *Advaita Vedanta*, the Hindu philosophy which emphasizes non-dualism.

Totapuri first guided Ramakrishna through the rites of *sannyasa*—renunciation of all ties to the world. Then he instructed him in the teaching of *advaita*—that "Brahman alone is real, and the world is illusory; I have no separate existence; I am that Brahman alone." Under the guidance of Totapuri, Ramakrishna reportedly experienced *nirvikalpa samadhi*, which is considered to be the highest state in spiritual realisation.

Totapuri stayed with Ramakrishna for nearly eleven months and instructed him further in the teachings of *advaita*. After the departure of Totapuri, Ramakrishna reportedly remained for six months in a state of absolute contemplation. Ramakrishna said that this period of *nirvikalpa samadhi* came to an end when he received a command from the Mother Kali to "remain in *Bhavamukha*; for the enlightenment of the people". *Bhavamukha* being a state of existence intermediate between *samadhi* and normal consciousness.

Islam and Christianity

In 1866, Govinda Roy, a Hindu guru who practiced Sufism, initiated Ramakrishna into Islam. Ramakrishna said that he "devoutly repeated the name of Allah, wore a cloth like the Arab Moslems, said their prayer five times daily, and felt disinclined even to see images of the Hindu gods and goddesses, much less worship them—for the Hindu way of thinking had disappeared altogether from my mind." According to Ramakrishna, after three days of practice he had a vision of a "radiant personage with grave countenance and white beard resembling the Prophet and merging with his body".

At the end of 1873 he started the practice of Christianity, when his devotee Shambu Charan Mallik read the Bible to him. Ramakrishna said that for several days he was filled with Christian thoughts and no longer thought of going to the Kali temple. According to Ramakrishna, one day when he saw the picture of Madonna and Child Jesus, he felt that the figures became alive and had a vision in which Jesus merged with his body. In his own room amongst other divine pictures was one of Christ, and he burnt incense before it morning and evening. There was also a picture showing Jesus Christ saving St. Peter from drowning in the water.

Arrival of Followers

In 1875, Ramakrishna met the influential Brahmo Samaj leader Keshab Chandra Sen. Keshab had accepted Christianity, and had separated from the Adi Brahmo Samaj. Formerly, Keshab had rejected idolatry, but under the influence of Ramakrishna he accepted Hindu polytheism and established the "New Dispensation" (*Nava Vidhan*) religious movement, based on Ramakrishna's principles—"Worship of God as Mother", "All religions as true" and "Assimilation of Hindu polytheism into Brahmoism". Keshab also publicized Ramakrishna's teachings in the journals of *New Dispensation* over a period of several years, which was instrumental in bringing Ramakrishna to the attention of a wider audience, especially the Bhadralok (English-educated classes of Bengal) and the Europeans residing in India.

Following Keshab, other Brahmos such as Vijaykrishna Goswami started to admire Ramakrishna, propagate his ideals and reorient their socio-religious outlook. Many prominent people of Calcutta—Pratap Chandra Mazumdar, Shivanath Shastri and

Trailokyanath Sanyal—began visiting him during this time (1871–1885). Mozoomdar wrote the first English biography of Ramakrishna, entitled *The Hindu Saint* in the *Theistic Quarterly Review* (1879), which played a vital role in introducing Ramakrishna to Westerners like the German indologist Max Müller. Newspapers reported that Ramakrishna was spreading "Love" and "Devotion" among the educated classes of Calcutta and that he had succeeded in reforming the character of some youths whose morals had been corrupt.

Ramakrishna also had interactions with Debendranath Tagore, the father of Rabindranath Tagore, and Ishwar Chandra Vidyasagar, a renowned social worker. He had also met Swami Dayananda. Ramakrishna is considered as one of the main contributors to the Bengali Renaissance. However, some Brahmos like Upadhyay Brahmabandhab disapproved of his avatarahood and ascetic renunciation and considered Ramakrishna's samadhi as a nervous malady.

Among the Europeans who were influenced by Ramakrishna was Principal Dr. W.W. Hastie of the Scottish Church College, Calcutta. In the course of explaining the word *trance* in the poem *The Excursion* by William Wordsworth, Hastie told his students that if they wanted to know its "real meaning", they should go to "Ramakrishna of Dakshineswar." This prompted some of his students, including Narendranath Dutta (later Swami Vivekananda), to visit Ramakrishna.

Devotees and Disciples

Disciples of Ramakrishna

Ramakrishna Paramahamsa had sixteen disciples who became monks of the Ramakrishna Order; they are often considered his apostles. In the Ramakrishna-Vivekananda movement, the apostles have played an important role. Apart from Swami Vivekananda the direct disciples or apostles of Ramakrishna were as follows.

Monastic Disciples

Swami Brahmananda

Swami Brahmananda (1863–1922), whose original name was Rakhal Chandra Ghosh, was son of a zemindar in the Basirhat area. While studying at the Metropolitan Institution at Kolkata, he met Narendranath Dutta in a gymnasium. He was influenced by Narendranath to join the Brahmo Samaj. In 1880, his brother-in-law, Manmohan Mitra, took him to Paramahamsadev. He was so impressed that he became a disciple and was subsequently known as the 'spiritual son' of Paramahamsadev. He was a wandering monk for some time. He spent most of his time at Puri and Bhubaneswar. He set up a math at Puri. When Ramakrishna Mission was formed, he was the first president.

Swami Premananda

Swami Premananda (1861–1918), whose original name was Baburam Ghosh, was born at Antpur in Hughli district. His sister was married to Balaram Bose, one of the persons in close touch with Ramkrishna Paramahamsadev. He studied under Mahendranath Gupta at the Metropolitan Institution, Kolkata. Mahendranath Gupta, was closely associated with Ramkrishna Paramahamsadev and later became famous for his Ramakrishna Kathamrita. Rakhal Chandra Ghosh (later Swami Brahmananda) took him to Paramahamsadev in 1882. Swami Vivekananda and eight other disciples met in the house where he was born and took of serving the cause of their master as sannyasis. He virtually presided over the Ramkrishna Math (monastery) at Belur from 1902-1916. He devotedly looked after the young monks and novices in his charge.

Swami Yogananda

Swami Yogananda (1861–1899), whose original name was Jogindranath Chowdhury belonged to an aristocratic family that had declined. His father was a devout Brahmin and he was devoted to religious affairs from a young age. Popular as Jogin, he came in touch with Paramahamsadev when still at school but his family did not approve of his touch with Paramahamsadev and forced him into marriage. He joined Paramahamsadev subsequently. He had a critical mind and often criticised Swami Vivekananda's actions. He remained with Saradama till his death.

Swami Niranjanananda

Swami Niranjanananda (died 1904), whose original name was Nitya Niranjan Ghosh, had clairvoyant powers. When he came in touch with Paramahamsadev at the age of eighteen, he told him, "If you let your mind dwell on ghosts, you'll become a ghost yourself. If you fix your mind on God your life will be filled with God." That brought about a change in his thinking and he joined Paramahamsadev. He was devoted to both Paramahamsadev and Saradama. He died of cholera.

Swami Saradananda

Swami Saradananda (1865–1927), whose original name was Sarat Chandra Chakravarty, first came in touch with Paramahamsadev, with his cousin Sashi Bhusan and others when he was 18 years old. He had joined Calcutta Medical College to study medicine but gave it up to serve Paramahamsadev when he was ill. When Swami Vivekananda advised him to take up work in the West, he met him in London in 1896 and then sailed for New York. There he remained head of the Vedanta Society until his return to India in 1898. Back in the country, he was engaged in different types of work and later became the first Secretary of Ramkrishna Math and Mission. He directed the magazine named Udbodhan (Awakening) founded by Swami Vivekananda. He decided to build a house at Bagbazar that would serve both as an office for Udbodhan and a residence for Saradama. He was author of *Sri Sri Ramakrishnalila Prasanga*.

Swami Shivananda

The original name of Swami Shivananda (1854–1934) was Tarak Nath Ghosal. His father, Ramkanai Ghosal, had been a legal adviser of Rani Rasmoni and had met Paramahamsadev a number of times. He was a member of the Brahmo Samaj, and met Paramahamsadev in 1880. After Paramahamsadev's death, he became a wandering monk. He spent some time preaching Vedanta in Sri Lanka. In 1902, he opened a monastery at Varanasi and initiated work for monastery at Almora. Second president of the Ramkrishna Mission from 1922 to 1934, he was also known as Mahapurush Maharaj.

Swami Ramkrishnananda

Swami Ramkrishnananda (1863–1911), whose original name was Sashi Bhusan Chakravarty was born in an orthodox Brahmin family. He was initiated early in life into a devotional life. He had joined the Brahmo Samaj and served for sometime as private tutor of Keshub Chunder Sen's children. He met Paramahamsadev in 1883 and was immediately attracted towards him. Considered a great devotee of Paramahamsadev, he collected his relics after his death and made a shrine of them. He founded the Ramkrishna Mission at Chennai in 1902 and remained in charge of it till his death.

Swami Turiyananda

Swami Turiyananda (1863–1922), whose original name was Hari Nath Chaterjee, met Paramahamsadev when he was only fourteen years old. After he became a monk, he spent the greater part of the next thirteen years wandering from place to place or meditating in seclusion. In 1899, Swami Vivekananda took him to America with him. He established the Shanti Ashrama in the San Antonio valley, Santa Clara County, California to be used a monastery of retreat. In 1902, he was returning to India but Swami Vivekananda died before he set foot in the country. A heart broken man he spent time in meditation and spiritual austerities. Later he devoted himself to training monks.

Swami Abhedananda

Swami Abhedananda (1866–1939), whose original name was Kali Prasad Chandra, was a scholar in Sanskrit and had studied western philosophy. He was initially attracted towards Christianity but turned towards Hinduism after listening to the lectures of Brahmo leaders. Having become fascinated by the Yoga Sutras of Patanjali, he was eager to find someone who could teach him to follow the methods of meditation they prescribe. On the advice of a friend, he went to Dakshineswar and learnt the practice of yoga from Paramahamsadev. In 1896, Swami Vivekananda wanted him in England. He went and from there on to New York after a year and took charge of the Vedanta Society there. He stayed in America until 1921 teaching and lecturing. On return to Kolkata, he founded his own Sri Ramakrishna Vedanta Society in 1923 and Sri Ramakrishna Vedanta Ashram at Darjeeling in 1924. He was author of several books: *Gospel of Ramakrishna, Reincarnation, How to be a Yogi, India and her People, Atmabikash, Vedantabani, Hindu Dharme Narir Sthan*. He edited a monthly magazine *Viswabani* for nine years.

Swami Adbhutananda

Swami Adbhutananda (died 1920) was a very simple person and was absolutely devoted to his master. His earlier name

Rakhturam was shortened to Latu. He was born of humble parents in a village in the district of Chhapra in Bihar.

"Latu is the greatest miracle of Sri Ramakrishna," Swamiji once said, "Having absolutely no education, he has attained to the highest wisdom simply at the touch of the Master." He was the first among the disciples to come to Paramahamsadev.

Swami Advaitananda

Swami Advaitananda (1828–1909), whose original name was Gopal Ghosh came to Ramakrishna for solace when his wife died and decided to stay as a devotee. He was oldest amongst the disciples of Ramakrishna.

Swami Trigunatitananda

Swami Trigunatitananda (1865–1914), whose original name was Sarada Prasanna Mitra, belonged to a rich land-owning family and studied under Mahendranath Gupta at the Metropolitan Institution, Kolkata.

He started visiting Paramahamsadev at an early age and took to major relief work when he became a monk. After Swami Turiyananda returned from California in 1902, he was asked to go to the San Francisco centre. The first Hindu temple in the West was built under his supervision at San Francisco in 1906. A bomb thrown by a mentally unbalanced former student of his killed him.

Swami Akhandananda

Swami Akhandananda (1864–1937), whose original name was Gangadhar Ghatak, had met Paramahamsadev at Bosepara when he was just 13 years old. Later he introduced him to Swami Vivekananda. He was President of the Ramkrishna Mission from 1934 to 1937.

Swami Subodhananda

Swami Subodhananda (1867–1932), whose original name was Subodh Chandra Ghosh, was also known as Khoka Maharaj. He belonged to the family of Shankar Ghosh, who owned the famous Kali Temple at Thanthania, in Kolkata and had tremendous power of meditation even in his younger days and that improved since he met Paramahamsadev in 1884.

Swami Vijnanananda

Swami Vijnanananda (1869–1938), whose original name was Hari Prasanna Chaterjee, was an engineer and had met Paramahamsadev early in life but family commitments kept him away. In 1896, he became a monk. Swami Vivekananda entrusted him with the task of building the Math campus as also preparing suitable plans for a memorial temple for Paramahamsadev. He prepared it in consultation with a noted European architect of Kolkata and Swamiji approved of the same. However, due to the sudden demise of Swamiji and lack of funds, the project had to wait for a long time to be taken up. It was completed and dedicated by Swami Vijnananda himself on the 14th of January 1938. He was President of the Ramkrishna Mission in 1937-38. He established Ramakrishna Sevasram at Allahabad.

Swami Nirmalananda

Swami Nirmalananda, whose original name was Tulsi Charan Dutta, was born in an affluent family of Baghbazar of North Kolkata in 1863. Because of the premature death of his mother, he had to shift to Varanasi with his family. In the primary school, Swami Vijnanananda (Hari Prasanna) was his classmate.

Tulsi was a brilliant student. He later completed his graduation from the Calcutta University and received a gold medal in recognition of his talent. He came into contact with Sri Ramakrishna many times and in his own words, he was privileged to receive 'Spiritual guidance or Initiation' from Sri Ramakrishna.

Swami Nirmalananda after two year preaching work in U.S.A. was made the President of Ramakrishna Math in Bangalore. The Administrators of the Headquarters at Belur Math presided over by Swami Brahmananda the President appointed him.

Swami Nirmalananda is acknowledged to have played a great role in the spread of the Ramakrishna Movement in South India, specially in Karnataka and Kerala. He also did a lot of preaching work in Burma, Bombay and North India. He founded eighteen monasteries, most of them in Kerala. He had at least thirty four monastic disciples as well many other initiated disciples.

Later there were differences in the approach to Mission's Work between Swami Nirmalananda and some of the administrators in Belur Math which resulted in a law suit being filed by Belur Math in Bangalore court asking the court to state that the Ramakrishna Math in Bangalore is indeed a branch centre of the Belur Math. After five years the court ruled that Ramakrishna Math, Bangalore is indeed a branch of Belur Math but it also gave the option to Swami Nirmalananda to continue as President of the Bangalore monastery. Swami Nirmalananda however left the place and later retired to the monastery at Ottapalam in Kerala and died there in 1938, remaining a member of the Ramakrshna Order till his death. His obituary appears in the official General Report of the Ramakrsihna Mission published in 1939.

The Ramakrishna Mission, from 1985 onwards, in some of their printed books have started removing his name from the list of disciples of Sri Ramakrishna (mainly Gospel of Sri Ramakrishna by 'M', Mahendranath Gupta, Translated into English by Swami Nikhilananda) though another source book 'Life of Sri Ramakrishna with a Foreword by Mahatma Gandhi continue to mention his name as a disciple of Sri Ramakrishnadoes. Another book not considered to be a source book on Sri Ramakrishna and his disciples, The History of Ramakrishna Math and Ramakrishna Mission by Swami Gambhirananda, states rather dogmatically that Swami Nirmalananda was not a disciple of Sri Ramakrishna but of Swami Vivekananda.

Last Days

In the beginning of 1885 Ramakrishna suffered from clergyman's throat, which gradually developed into throat cancer. He was moved to Shyampukur near Calcutta, where some of the best physicians of the time, including Dr. Mahendralal Sarkar, were engaged. When his condition aggravated he was relocated to a large garden house at Cossipore on December 11, 1885.

During his last days, he was looked after by his monastic disciples and Sarada Devi. Ramakrishna was advised by the doctors to keep the strictest silence, but ignoring their advice, he incessantly conversed with visitors. According to traditional accounts, before his death, Ramakrishna transferred his spiritual powers to Vivekananda and reassured Vivekananda of his avataric status. Ramakrishna asked Vivekananda to look after the welfare of the disciples, saying, "keep my boys together" and asked him to "teach them". Ramakrishna also asked other monastic disciples to look upon Vivekananda as their leader. Ramakrishna's condition gradually worsened and he expired in the early morning hours of August 16, 1886 at the Cossipore garden house. According to his disciples, this was *mahasamadhi*. After the death of their master, the monastic disciples lead by Vivekananda formed a fellowship at a half-ruined house at Baranagar near the river Ganga, with the financial assistance of the householder disciples. This became the first Math or monastery of the disciples who constituted the first Ramakrishna Order.

Biographical Sources

According to Malcolm Mclean, the principal source for Ramakrishna's teaching is Mahendranath Gupta's *sri-sri-ramakrisna-kathamrita*. Kripal calls it "the central text of the tradition". The text was published in five volumes from 1902 to 1932. Based on Gupta's diary notes, each of the five volumes purports to document Ramakrishna's life from 1882–1886.

The main translation of the *Kathamrita* is *The Gospel of Sri Ramakrishna* by Swami Nikhilananda. Nikhilananda's translation rearranged the scenes in the five volumes of the *Kathamrita* into a linear sequence. Malcolm Mclean and Jeffrey Kripal argue that the translation is unreliable. Philosopher Lex Hixon writes that the *Gospel* is "spiritually authentic" and "powerful rendering of the *Kathamrita*"

Teachings

God-Realisation

Ramakrishna emphasised that God-realisation is the supreme goal of all living beings. Ramakrishna's mystical experiences through different religions led him to teach that various religions are different means to reach absolute knowledge and bliss—and that the different religions cannot express the totality of absolute truth, but can express aspects of it.

Kama-Kanchana

Ramakrishna taught that that the primal bondage in human life is *Kama-Kanchana* (lust and gold). When speaking to men, Ramakrishna warned them against *kamini-kanchana*, or "women and gold",

"Through the discipline of constant practice one is able to give up attachment to 'woman and gold'. That is what the Gita says.

By practice one acquires uncommon power of mind. Then one doesn't find it difficult to subdue the sense-organs and to bring anger, lust, and the like under control. Such a man behaves like a tortoise, which, once it has tucked in its limbs, never puts them out. You cannot make the tortoise put its limbs out again, though you chop it to pieces with an axe."

"The renunciation of 'woman and gold' is the true renunciation."

When speaking to women, he warned them against *purusha-kanchana,* or "man and gold." Gauri-Ma, one of Ramakrishna's prominent women disciples, said that:

[Ramakrishna] has uttered this note of warning, against gold and sensuality, against a life of enjoyment, but surely not against women. Just as he advised the ascetic-minded men to guard themselves against women's charms, so also did he caution pious women against men's company. The Master's whole life abounds with proofs to show that he had not the slightest contempt or aversion for women; rather he had intense sympathy and profound regard for them.

Avidyamaya *and* Vidyamaya

Devotees believe that Ramakrishna's realisation of *nirvikalpa samadhi* also led him to an understanding of the two sides of *maya,* or illusion, to which he referred as *Avidyamaya and vidyamaya.* He explained that *avidyamaya* represents dark forces of creation (e.g. sensual desire, evil passions, greed, lust and cruelty), which keep people on lower planes of consciousness. These forces are responsible for human entrapment in the cycle of birth and death, and they must be fought and vanquished. *Vidyamaya,* on the other hand, represents higher forces of creation (e.g. spiritual virtues, enlightening qualities, kindness, purity, love, and devotion), which elevate human beings to the higher planes of consciousness.

Harmony of Religions

Ramakrishna recognised differences among religions but realised that in spite of these differences, all religions lead to the same ultimate goal, and hence they are all valid and true. Amiya P. Sen writes that the deep foundations in *bhakti* or devotion and faith in God makes Ramakrishna's teachings look universalistic and not his culturally determied forms. The distinguished British historian Arnold J. Toynbee has written: "... Mahatma Gandhi's principle of non-violence and Sri Ramakrishna's testimony to the harmony of religions: here we have the attitude and the spirit that can make it possible for the human race to grow together into a single family–and in the Atomic Age, this is the only alternative to destroying ourselves."

Rergarding Harmony of Religions, Ramakrishna said, "I have practised all religions—Hinduism, Islam, Christianity—and I have also followed the paths of the different Hindu sects. I have found that it is the same God toward whom all are directing their steps, though along different paths. You must try all beliefs and traverse all the different ways once. Wherever I look, I see men quarrelling in the name of religion—Hindus, Mohammedans, Brahmos, Vaishnavas, and the rest. But they never reflect that He who is called Krishna is also called Siva, and bears the name of the Primal Energy, Jesus, and Allah as well—the same Rama with a thousand names..."

Bhawuk in his journal, *Culture's influence on creativity: the case of Indian spirituality* wrote that Ramakrishna's contribution to humanity is particularly significant for the world after the bombing of the twin towers of the World Trade Centre on September 11, 2001. Bhawuk writes that, Islam is not to be blamed for the incident of September 11, and no religion should be blamed for any act of terrorism, because the life of Ramakrishna proclaims that all religions lead to the same God.

Jiva is Shiva *and other Teachings*

Ramakrishna's proclamation of *jatra jiv tatra Shiv* (wherever there is a living being, there is Shiva) stemmed from his Advaitic perception of Reality. This taught his disciples, "Jive daya noy, Shiv gyane jiv seba" (not kindness to living beings, but serving the living being as Shiva Himself). According to scholars, Vivekananda derived his inspiration from this message and took initiative in social activities like famine relief, manitenance of orphanages, opening of training centres, educational institutions, dispensaries and the like—"Where should you go to seek for God? Are not all the poor, the miserable, the weak, good? Why not worship them first?...Let these people be your God..." Ramakrishna did not directly participate in social service, but entrusted the task to his chief disciple Vivekananda.

Ramakrishna, though not formally trained as a philosopher, had an intuitive grasp of complex philosophical concepts. According to him *brahmanda*, the visible universe and many other universes, are mere bubbles emerging out of *Brahman*, the supreme ocean of intelligence.

Like Adi Sankara had done more than a thousand years earlier, Ramakrishna Paramahamsa revitalised Hinduism which had been fraught with excessive ritualism and superstition in the Nineteenth century and helped it become better-equipped to respond to challenges from Islam, Christianity and the dawn of the modern era. However, unlike Adi Sankara, Ramakrishna developed ideas about the post-*samadhi* descent of consciousness into the phenomenal world, which he went on to term "*vignana*". While he asserted the supreme validity of Advaita Vedanta, he also stated that "I accept both the *Nitya* and the *Leela*, both the Absolute and the Relative."

Parables

Parables formed a very important part of Ramakrishna's teachings. Like Christ, Ramakrishna conveyed his spiritual and moral messages through tales and parables.

The Parable of the Greatest Devotee, is one of his famous parables—

"Once upon a time conceit entered into the heart of Narada and he thought there was no greater devotee than himself. Reading his heart, the Lord said, "Narada, go to such and such a place, a great devotee of mine is living there. Cultivate his acquaintance; for he is truly devoted to me." Narada went there and found an farmer who rose early in the morning, pronounced the name of Hari (God) only once, and taking his plough, went out and tilled the ground all day long. At night, he went to bed after pronouncing the name of Hari once more. Narada said to himself "How can this rustic be a lover of God? I see him busily engaged in worldly duties and he has no signs of a pious man about him." Then Narada went back to the Lord, and spoke what he thought of his new acquaintance. There upon the Lord said, "Narada, take this cup of oil and go round this city and come back with it. But take care that you do not spill even a single drop of it." Narada did as he was told, and on his return the Lord asked him, "Well, Narada, how many times did you remember me in the course of your walk round the city?" "Not once, my Lord," said Narada, "and how could I, when I had to watch this cup brimming over with oil?" The Lord then said, "This one cup of oil did so divert your attention that even you did forget me altogether. But look at that rustic, who, though carrying the heavy burden of a family, still remembers me twice every day."

The Parable of the Pandit who could not swim is another famous parable of Ramakrishna—

"Once several men were crossing the Ganges in a boat. One of them, a pandit, was making a great display of his erudition, saying that he has studied various books—the Vedas, the Vedanta, the six systems of philosophy. He asked a fellow passenger, 'Do you know the Vedanta?' 'No, revered sir.' 'The Samkhya and the Patanjala?' 'No, revered sir.' 'Have you read no philosophy whatsoever?' 'No, revered sir.' The pandit was talking in this vain way and the passenger sitting in silence, when a great storm arose and the boat was about to sink. The passenger said to the pandit, 'Sir, can you swim?' 'No', replied the pundit. The passenger said, 'I don't know the Samkhya or the Patanjala, but I can swim.'

Language

Ramakrishna used rustic colloquial Bengali in his conversations. According to contemporary reports, Ramakrishna's linguistic style was unique, even to those who spoke Bengali. It contained obscure local words and idioms from village Bengali, interspersed with philosophical Sanskrit terms and references to the Vedas, Puranas, Tantras. For that reason, according to philosopher Lex Hixon, his speeches cannot be literally translated into English or any other language. Scholar Amiya P. Sen argued that certain terms that Ramakrishna may have used only in a metaphysical sense are being improperly invested with new, contemporaneous meanings.

Ramakrishna was skilled with words and had an extraordinary style of preaching and instructing, conveying to even the most skeptical visitors to the temple. His speeches reportedly revealed a sense of joy and fun, but he was not at a loss when debating with intellectual philosophers. Philosopher Arindam Chakrabarti contrasted Ramakrishna's talkativeness with Buddha's legendary reticence, and compared his teaching style to that of Socrates.

Ramakrishna's explicitly sexual language shocked 19th-century Westerners, even scholars Max Müller who were otherwise his admirers. Müller wrote that his language was at times "abominably filthy". He admitted however that such direct speech was natural to contemporary hindus, "where certain classes of men walk stark naked", and should not be considered intentional filthiness or obscenity. Citing examples of classical poems like *Bhartrihari,* the Bible, Homer, and Shakespeare, Müller felt that few of the sayings would have to be bowdlerized..

Impact on Hinduism

His career was an important part of the renaissance that Bengal, and later India, experienced in the 19th century. Hinduism faced a huge intellectual challenge in the 19th century, from Westerners and Indians alike. The Hindu practice of *murti* came under intense pressure specially in Bengal, then the centre of British India, and was declared intellectually unsustainable by some intellectuals. Response to this was varied, ranging from the Young Bengal movement that denounced Hinduism and embraced Christianity or atheism, to the Brahmo movement that retained primacy of Hinduism but gave up idol worship, and to the staunch Hindu nationalism of Bankim Chandra Chattopadhyay. Ramakrishna's influence was crucial in this period for a Hindu revival of a more traditional kind, and can be compared to that of Chaitanya's contribution centuries earlier, when Hinduism in Bengal was under similar pressure from the growing power of Islam.

Among his contributions is a strong affirmation of the presence of the divine in an idol. To the many that revered him, this reinforced centuries-old traditions that were in the spotlight at the time. Ramakrishna also advocated an inclusive version of the religion, declaring *Joto mot toto path* (meaning *As many faiths, so many paths*). He was given a name that is from the Vaishnavite tradition (Rama and Krishna are both incarnations of Vishnu), but was a devotee of Kali, the mother goddess, and known to have followed various other religious paths including Tantrism, Christianity, and Islam.

Contributions to Humanity

Many great thinkers of the world have acknowledged Ramakrishna's contribution to humanity. Max Müller, who was inspired by Ramakrishna, said:

Sri Ramakrishna was a living illustration of the truth that Vedanta, when properly realised, can become a practical rule of life... the Vedanta philosophy is the very marrow running through all the bones of Ramakrishna's doctrine.

Leo Tolstoy saw similarities between his and Ramakrishna's thoughts. He described him as a "remarkable sage". Romain Rolland considered Ramakrishna to be the "consummation of two thousand years of the spiritual life of three hundred million people." He said:

Allowing for differences of country and of time, Ramakrishna is the younger brother of Christ.

Mohandas Gandhi wrote:

Ramakrishna's life enables us to see God face to face. He was a living embodiment of godliness.

Sri Aurobindo considered Ramakrishna to be an incarnation, or avatar, of God on par with Gautama Buddha. He wrote:

When scepticism had reached its height, the time had come for spirituality to assert itself and establish the reality of the world as a manifestation of the spirit, the secret of the confusion created by the senses, the magnificent possibilities of man and the ineffable beatitude of God. This is the work whose consummation Sri Ramakrishna came to begin and all the development of the previous two thousand years and more since Buddha appeared has been a preparation for the harmonisation of spiritual teaching and experience by the Avatar of Dakshineshwar.

Christopher Isherwood also considered Ramakrishna to be an incarnation of God.

Jawaharlal Nehru described Ramakrishna as "one of the great *rishis* of India, who had come to draw our attention to the higher things of life and of the spirit." Subhas Chandra Bose was also influenced by Ramakrishna. He said:

The effectiveness of Ramakrishna's appeal lay in the fact that he had practised what he preached and that... he had reached the acme of spiritual progress.

Philosopher Arindam Chakrabarti called Ramakrishna "The practically illiterate, faith-bound, emotional, otherworldly esoteric Ramakrishna who prayed to the Goddess: "May my rationalizing intellect be struck by thunder!" And yet in his ...views about the nature of ultimate reality, the relation between the self and the body, ways of knowing truth, moral and social duties of human beings and metatheoretical explanations of why mystics disagree...Ramakrishna was no less a philosopher than Buddha or Socrates.

On Indian Nationalism

Ramakrishna's impact on the growing Indian nationalism was, if more indirect, nevertheless quite notable. A large number of intellectuals of that age had regular communication with him and respected him, though not all of them necessarily agreed with him on religious matters. Numerous members of the Brahmo Samaj respected him. Though some of them embraced his form of Hinduism, the fact that many others did not shows that they detected in him a possibility for a strong national identity in the face of a colonial adversary that was intellectually undermining the Indian civilisation. As Amaury de Riencourt states,"The greatest leaders of the early twentieth century, whatever their walk of life— Rabindranath Tagore, the prince of poets; Aurobindo Ghosh, the greatest mystic-philosopher; Mahatma Gandhi, who eventually shook the Anglo-Indian Empire to destruction — all acknowledged their over-riding debt to both the Swan and the Eagle, to Ramakrishna who stirred the heart of India, and to Vivekananda who awakened its soul." This is particularly evident in Ramakrishna's development of the Mother-symbolism and its eventual role in defining the incipient Indian nationalism.

Vivekananda, Ramakrishna Math and the Ramakrishna Mission

Vivekananda, Ramakrishna's most illustrious disciple, is considered by some to be one of his most important legacies. Vivekananda spread the message of Ramakrishna across the world. He also helped introduce Hinduism to the west. He founded two organisations based on the teachings of Ramakrishna. One was Ramakrishna Mission, which is designed to spread the word of Ramakrishna. Vivekananda also designed its emblem. Ramakrishna Math was created as a monastic order based on Ramakrishna's teachings.

The temples of Ramakrishna are called the *Universal Temples*. The first *Universal temple* was built at Belur, which is the headquatress of the Ramakrishna Mission. Daily arathi, pooja and devotional singing are conducted everyday.

Views and Studies

Religious School of Thought

Several scholars have tried to associate Ramakrishna with a particular religious school of thought—*Bhakti*, Tantra and Vedanta.

In his influential 1896 essay "A real mahatma: Sri Ramakrishna Paramahansa Dev" and his 1899 book *Ramakrishna: His Life and Sayings*, the German philologist and Orientalist Max Müller portrayed Ramakrishna as "a wonderful mixture of God and man" and as "...a Bhakta, a worshipper or lover of the deity, much more than a Gnanin or a knower."

In London and New York in 1896, Swami Vivekananda delivered his famous address on Ramakrishna entitled "My Master." He said of his master: "this great intellect never learnt even to write his own name, but the most brilliant graduates of our university found in him an intellectual giant." Vivekananda criticized his followers for "brazenly" projecting Ramakrishna as an *avatara* and miracle-worker. Narasingha Sil has argued that Vivekananda revised and mythologized Ramakrishna's image after Ramakrishna's death. Amiya Sen writes that that Vivekananda's "social service gospel" stemmed from direct inspiration from Ramakrishna and rests substantially on the "liminal quality" of the Master's message.

Indologist Heinrich Zimmer was the first Western scholar to interpret Ramakrishna's worship of the Divine Mother as containing specifically Tantric elements. Neeval also argued that tantra played a main role in Ramakrishna's spiritual development.

Philosopher Lex Hixon writes Ramakrishna was an *Advaita Vedantin*. Postcolonial literary theorist Gayatri Chakravorty Spivak wrote that Ramakrishna was a "Bengali *bhakta* visionary" and that as a *bhakta*, "he turned chiefly towards Kali." Amiya P.Sen writes that "it is really difficult to separate the Tantrik Ramakrishna from the Vedantic", since Vedanta and Tantra "may appear to be differ in some respects", but they also "share some important postulates between them".

Psychoanalysis and Sexuality

The dialogue between psychoanalysis and Ramakrishna began in 1927 when Sigmund Freud's friend Romain Rolland wrote to him that he should consider spiritual experiences, or "the oceanic feeling," in his psychological works. Romain Rolland described the mystical states achieved by Ramakrishna and other mystics as an "'oceanic' sentiment," one which Rolland had also experienced. Rolland believed that the universal human religious emotion resembled this "oceanic sense." In his 1929 book *La vie de Ramakrishna*, Rolland distinguished between the feelings of unity and eternity which Ramakrishna experienced in his mystical states and Ramakrishna's interpretation of those feelings as the goddess Kali.

Christopher Isherwood who wrote the book *Ramakrishna and his Disciples* (1965) said in a late interview,"Ramakrishna was completely simple and guileless. He told people whatever came into his mind, like a child. If he had ever been troubled by homosexual desires, if that had ever been a problem he'd have told everybody about them.(...) His thoughts transcended physical love-making. He saw even the mating of two dogs on the street as an expression of the eternal male-female principle in the universe. I think that is always a sign of great spiritual enlightenment."

In 1995, Kripal argued that the Ramakrishna Movement has manipulated Ramakrishna's biographical documents, that the Movement has published them in incomplete and bowdlerized editions, that the Movement has suppressed Ram Chandra Datta's *Srisriramakrsna Paramahamsadever Jivanavrttanta*. These views were disputed by Swami Atmajnanananda, who wrote that *Jivanavrttanta* has been reprinted nine times as of 1995 and the translations of *Kathamrita* considered "western decorum" into consideration and are not "bowdlerized". In the 1997 book review of Kripal's book, Malcolm McLean of Otago University supported Kripal's view and argued that the movement presents "a particular kind of explanation of Ramakrishna, that he was some kind of neo-Vedantist who taught that all religions are the same". In 1998, Kripal wrote that he had "overplayed" the suppression of *Jivanavrttanta* and "the Ramakrishna Order reprinted Datta's text the very same summer Kali's Child appeared, rendering my original claims of a conscious concealment untenable."

Some scholars of Indian religion, including Narasingha Sil, Jeffrey Kripal, and Sudhir Kakar, analyze Ramakrishna's mysticism and religious practices using psychoanalysis, arguing that his mystical visions, refusal to comply with ritual copulation in Tantra, *Madhura Bhava*, criticism of *Kamini-Kanchana* (women and gold) reflects homosexuality. Jeffrey Kripal's controversial *Kali's Child: The Mystical and the Erotic in the Life and Teachings of Ramakrishna* (1995) argued that Ramakrishna rejected Advaita Vedanta in favour of Shakti Tantra. In this psychoanalytic study of Ramakrishna's life, Kripal argued that Ramakrishna's mystical experiences were symptoms of repressed homoeroticism. Other scholars and psychoanalysts including Romain Rolland, Alan Roland, Kelly Aan Raab, Somnath Bhattacharya,, J.S. Hawley and Gayatri Chakravorty Spivak argue that psychoanalysis is unreliable and Ramakrishna's religious practices were in line with Bengali tradition.

In his 1991 book *The Analyst and the Mystic,* Indian psychoanalyst Sudhir Kakar saw in Ramakrishna's visions a spontaneous capacity for creative experiencing. Kakar also argued that culturally relative concepts of eroticism and gender have contributed to the Western difficulty in comprehending Ramakrishna. Kakar saw Ramakrishna's seemingly bizarre acts as part of a *bhakti* path to God.

Postcolonial Studies

Postcolonial studies try to locate Ramakrishna in the historical background of Calcutta during the mid-19th Century.

In 1999, postcolonial historian Sumit Sarkar argued that he found in the *Kathamrita* traces of a binary opposition between unlearned oral wisdom and learned literate knowledge. He argues that all of our information about Ramakrishna, a rustic near-illiterate Brahmin, comes from urban *bhadralok* devotees, "...whose texts simultaneously illuminate and transform."

Other postcolonial studies have been done by Partha Chaterjee, Amiya P. Sen.

Swami Vivekananda

Swami Vivekananda (January 12, 1863–July 4, 1902), born Narendranath Dutta is the chief disciple of the 19th century mystic Sri Ramakrishna Paramahamsa and the founder of Ramakrishna Mission. He is considered a key figure in the introduction of Vedanta and Yoga in Europe and America and is also credited with raising interfaith awareness, bringing Hinduism to the status of a world religion during the end of the 19th century. Vivekananda is considered to be a major force in the revival of Hinduism in modern India. He is best known for his inspiring speech beginning with "sisters and brothers of America", through which he introduced Hinduism at the Parliament of the World's Religions at Chicago in 1893.

Swami Vivekananda was born in an aristocratic Bengali Kayastha family of Calcutta in 1863. His parents influenced the Swami's thinking – the father by his rational mind and the mother by her religious temperament. From his childhood, he showed inclination towards spirituality and God realization. While searching for a man who could directly demonstrate the reality of God, he came to Ramakrishna and became his disciple. As a guru, Ramakrishna taught him *Advaita Vedanta* and that all religions are true, and service to man was the most effective worship of God. After the death of his Guru, Vivekananda became a wandering monk, touring the Indian subcontinent and getting a first-hand account of India's condition. He later sailed to Chicago and represented India as a delegate in the 1893 Parliament of World Religions. An eloquent speaker, Vivekananda was invited to several forums in United States and spoke at universities and clubs. He conducted several public and private lectures, disseminating Vedanta, Yoga and Hinduism in America, England and a few other countries in Europe. He also established Vedanta societies in America and England. He later sailed back to India and in 1897 founded the Ramakrishna Math and Ramakrishna Mission, a philanthropic and spiritual organization.

In a short span of 39 years he awakened and inspired great many souls that followed his precepts. His most famous statement was "Arise, Awake and stop not till the goal is achieved." Today many people of different nationalities, religions, races, colours, sects and creeds follow the teachings of Vedanta he introduced in late 19th and early 20th centuries. He is most popular among young adults. Present day youth and many aspiring souls seek inspiration from his teachings and messages even to date. While still alive, Swami Vivekananda proclaimed that though he would leave his body like discarding his clothes but would continue to work towards the upliftment of all humanity. After departing from his mortal coils, Swami Vivekananda is believed to have interacted with great souls to fulfil his work. He gave a new direction to religion by transcending ritual concepts of religions and promoted formless and nameless meditative practices like

Raja Yoga and Spirituality. Swami Vivekananda is regarded as one of India's foremost nation-builders. His teachings influenced the thinking of other national and international leaders and philosophers, like Mahatma Gandhi, Martin Luther King, Jawaharlal Nehru, Subhas Chandra Bose, Aurobindo Ghosh, Sarvepalli Radhakrishnan.

Biography

Birth and Childhood: Swami Vivekananda was born in Shimla Pally, Calcutta at 6:33 a.m on Monday, 12 January 1863, during the eve of Makra Sankranti festival and was given the name Narendranath Dutta. His father Vishwanath Dutta was an attorney of Calcutta High Court. He was considered generous, and had a liberal and progressive outlook in social and religious matters. His mother Bhuvaneshwari Devi was pious and had practiced austerities and prayed to *Vireshwar Shiva* of Varanasi to give her a son. She reportedly had a dream in which Shiva rose from his meditation and said that he would be born as her son.

Narendranath's thinking and personality were influenced by his parents—the father by his rational mind and the mother by her religious temperament. From his mother he learnt the power of self-control. One of the sayings of his mother Narendra quoted often in his later years was, "Remain pure all your life; guard your own honour and never transgress the honour of others. Be very tranquil, but when necessary, harden your heart." He was reportedly adept in meditation and could reportedly enter the state of *samadhi*. He reportedly would see a light while falling asleep and he reportedly had a vision of Buddha during his meditation. During his childhood, he had a great fascination for wandering ascetics and monks.

Narendranath had varied interests and a wide range of scholarship in philosophy, history, the social sciences, arts, literature, and other subjects. He evinced much interest in scriptural texts, *Vedas*, the *Upanishads*, *Bhagavad Gita*, *Ramayana*, *Mahabharata* and the *Puranas*. He was also well versed in classical music, both vocal and instrumental and is said to have undergone training under two Ustads, Beni Gupta and Ahamad Khan. Since boyhood, he took an active interest in physical exercise, sports, and other organizational activities. Even when he was young, he questioned the validity of superstitious customs and discrimination based on caste and refused to accept anything without rational proof and pragmatic test.

College and Brahmo Samaj

Narendranath started his education at home, later he joined the Metropolitan Institution of Ishwar Chandra Vidyasagar in 1871 and in 1879 he passed the entrance examination for Presidency College, Calcutta, entering it for a brief period and subsequently shifting to General Assembly's Institution. During the course, he studied western logic, western philosophy and history of European nations. In 1881 he passed the Fine Arts examination and in 1884 he passed the Bachelor of Arts.

Narendranath is said to have studied the writings of David Hume, Immanuel Kant, Johann Gottlieb Fichte, Baruch Spinoza, Georg W. F. Hegel, Arthur Schopenhauer, Auguste Comte, Herbert Spencer, John Stuart Mill, and Charles Darwin. Narendra became fascinated with the Evolutionism of Herbert Spencer, and translated Spencer's book on *Education* into Bengali for Gurudas Chattopadhyay, his publisher. Narendra also had correspondence with Herbert Spencer for some time. Alongside his study of Western philosophers, he was thoroughly acquainted with Indian Sanskrit scriptures and many Bengali works. According to his professors, student Narendranath was a prodigy. Dr. William Hastie, the principal of Scottish Church College, where he studied during 1881-84, wrote, "Narendra is really a genius. I have travelled far and wide but I have never come across a lad of his talents and possibilities, even in German universities, among philosophical students." He was regarded as a *srutidhara*—a man with prodigious memory. After a discussion with Narendranath, Dr. Mahendralal Sarkar reportedly said, "I could never have thought that such a young boy had read so much!"

Narendranath became the member of a Freemason's lodge and the breakaway faction from the Brahmo Samaj led by Keshab Chunder Sen another Freemason. His initial beliefs were shaped by Brahmo concepts, which include belief in a formless God and deprecation of the worship of idols. Not satisfied with his knowledge of Philosophy, he wondered if God and religion could be made a part of one's growing experiences and deeply internalized. Narendra went about asking prominent residents of contemporary Calcutta whether they had come "face to face with

God". but could not get answers which satisfied him. His first introduction to Ramakrishna occurred in a literature class in General Assembly Institute, when he heard Principal Reverend W. Hastie lecturing on William Wordsworth's poem *The Excursion* and the poet's nature-mysticism. In the course of explaining the word *trance* in the poem, Hastie told his students that if they wanted to know the real meaning of it, they should go to Ramakrishna of Dakshineswar. This prompted some of his students, including Narendranath to visit Ramakrishna.

With Ramakrishna

His meeting with Ramakrishna Paramahamsa in November 1881 proved to be a turning point in his life. About this meeting, Narendranath said, "He [Ramakrishna] looked just like an ordinary man, with nothing remarkable about him. He used the most simple language and I thought 'Can this man be a great teacher?'– I crept near to him and asked him the question which I had been asking others all my life: 'Do you believe in God, Sir?' 'Yes,' he replied. 'Can you prove it, Sir?' 'Yes.' 'How?' 'Because I see Him just as I see you here, only in a much intenser sense.' That impressed me at once. [...] I began to go to that man, day after day, and I actually saw that religion could be given. One touch, one glance, can change a whole life."

Even though Narendra did not accept Ramakrishna as his guru initially and revolted against his ideas, he was attracted by his personality and visited him frequently. He initially looked upon on Ramakrishna's ecstasies and visions as, "mere figments of imagination", "mere hallucinations". As a member of Brahmo samaj, he revolted against idol worship and polytheism, and Ramakrishna's worship of Kali. He even rejected the *Advaitist Vedantism* of identity with absolute as blasphemy and madness, and often made fun of the concept

Though Narendra could not accept Ramakrishna and his visions, he could not neglect him either. It had always been in Narendra's nature to test something thoroughly before he would accept it. He tested Ramakrishna, who never asked Narendra to abandon reason, and faced all of Narendra's arguments and examinations with patience—"Try to see the truth from all angles" was his reply. During the course of five years of his training under Ramakrishna, Narendra was transformed from a restless, puzzled, impatient youth to a mature man who was ready to renounce everything for the sake of God-realization. In time, Narendra accepted Ramakrishna as guru, and when he accepted, his acceptance was whole-hearted and with complete surrendering as disciple.

In 1885 Ramakrishna suffered from throat cancer and he was shifted to Calcutta and later to Cossipore. Vivekananda and his brother disciples took care of Ramakrishna during his final days. Vivekananda's spiritual education under Ramakrishna continued there. At Cossipore, Vivekananda reportedly experienced *Nirvikalpa Samadhi*. During the last days of Ramakrishna, Vivekananda and some of the other disciples received the ochre monastic robes from Ramakrishna, which formed the first monastic order of Ramakrishna. Vivekananda was taught that service to men was the most effective worship of God. It is reported that when Vivekananda doubted Ramakrishna's claim of *avatara*, Ramakrishna reportedly said, "He who was Rama, He who was Krishna, He himself is now Ramakrishna in this body." During his final days, Ramakrishna asked Vivekananda to take care of other monastic disciples and in turn asked them to look upon Vivekananda as their leader. Ramakrishna's condition worsened gradually and he expired in the early morning hours of August 16, 1886 at the Cossipore garden house. According to his disciples, this was *Mahasamadhi*.

Baranagar Monastery

After the death of their master, the monastic disciples led by Vivekananda formed a fellowship at a half-ruined house at Baranagar near the river Ganga, with the financial assistance of the householder disciples. This became the first *Matha* or monastery of the disciples who constituted the first Ramakrishna Order.

The dilapidated house at Baranagore was chosen because of its low rent and proximity to the Cossipore burning-ghat, where Ramakrishna was cremated. Narendra and other members of the Math often spent their time in meditation, discussing about different philosophies and teachings of spiritual teachers including Ramakrishna, Shankaracharya, Ramanuja, and Jesus Christ. Narendra reminisced about the early days in the monastery as follows, "We underwent a lot of religious practice at Baranagore Math. We used to get up at 3:00 am and become absorbed in *japa* and meditation. What a strong spirit of dispassion we had in those days! We had no thought even as to whether the world existed or not" In the early part of 1887, Narendra and eight other disciples took formal monastic vows. Narendra took the name of Swami Vividishananda.

Parivrajaka — Wandering Monk

In 1888, Vivekananda left the monastery as a *Parivrajaka*—the Hindu religious life of a wandering monk, "without fixed abode, without ties, independent and strangers wherever they go." His sole possessions were a *kamandalu* (water pot), staff, and his two favourite books—*Bhagavad Gita* and *The Imitation of Christ*. Narendranath travelled the length and breadth of India for five years, visiting important centres of learning, acquainting himself with the diverse religious traditions and different patterns of social life. He developed a sympathy for the suffering and poverty of the masses and resolved to uplift the nation. Living mainly on Bhiksha or alms, Narendranath travelled mostly on foot and railway tickets bought by his admirers whom he met during the travels. During these travels he gained acquaintance and stayed with scholars, Dewans, Rajas and people from all walks of life—Hindus, Muslims, Christians, *Pariahs* (low caste workers), Government officials.

Northern India

In 1888, he started his journey from Varanasi. At Varanasi, he met pandit and Bengali writer, Bhudev Mukhopadhyay and Trailanga Swami, a famous saint who lived in a Shiva temple. Here, he also met Babu Pramadadas Mitra, the noted Sanskrit scholar, to whom the Swami wrote a number of letters asking his advice on the interpretation of the Hindu scriptures.

After Varanasi he visited Ayodhya, Lucknow, Agra, Vrindaban, Hathras and Rishikesh. At Hathras he met Sharat Chandra Gupta, the station master who later became one of his earliest disciples as *Sadananda*. Between 1888-1890, he visited Vaidyanath, Allahabad. From Allahabad, he visited Ghazipur where he met Pavhari Baba, a *Advaita Vedanta* ascetic who spent most of his time in meditation. Between 1888-1890, he returned to Baranagore *Math* few times, because of ill health and to arrange for the financial funds when Balram Bose and Suresh Chandra Mitra, the disciples of Ramakrishna who supported the *Math* had expired.

The Himalayas

In July 1890, accompanied by his brother monk, Swami Akhandananda, he continued his journey as a wandering monk and returned to the *Math* only after his visit to the West. He visited, Nainital, Almora, Srinagar, Dehra Dun, Rishikesh, Hardwar and the Himalayas. During this travel, he reportedly had a vision of macrocosm and microcosm, which seems to be reflected in the *Jnana Yoga* lectures he gave later in the West, "*The Cosmos—The Macrocosm* and *The Microcosm*". During these travels, he met his brother monks —Swami Brahmananda, Saradananda, Turiyananda, Akhandananda, Advaitananda. They stayed at Meerut for few days where they passed their time in meditation, prayer and study of scriptures. In the end of January 1891, the Swami left his brother monks and journeyed to Delhi alone.

Rajputana

At Delhi, after visiting historical places he journeyed towards Alwar, in the historic land of Rajputana. Later he journeyed to Jaipur, where he studied Panini's *Ashtadhyayi* from a Sanskrit scholar.

He next journeyed to Ajmer, where he visited the palace of Akbar and the famous Dargah and left for Mount Abu. At Mount Abu, he met Maharaja Ajit Singh of Khetri, who became his ardent devotee and supporter. He was invited to Khetri, where he delivered discourses to the Raja. At Khetri, he also became acquainted with Pandit Narayandas, and studied *Mahabhashya* on Sutras of Panini. After two and half months at Khetri, towards end of October 1891, he proceeded towards Rajasthan and Maharastra.

Western India

Continuing his travels, he visited Ahmedabad, Wadhwan, Limbdi. At Ahmedabad he completed his studies of Mohammedan and Jain culture. At Limbdi, he met Thakore Sahed Jaswant Singh who had himself been to England and America. From the Thakore Saheb, the Swami got the first idea of going to the West to preach Vedanta. He later visited Junagadh, Girnar, Kutch, Porbander, Dwaraka, Palitana, Baroda. At Porbander he stayed three quarters of a year, in spite of his vow as a wandering monk, to perfect his philosophical and Sanskrit studies with learned *pandits*; he worked with a court *pandit* who translated the *Vedas*.

He later travelled to Mahabaleshwar and then to Pune. From Poona he visited Khandwa and Indore around June 1892. At Kathiawar he heard of the Parliament of the World's Religions and was urged by his followers there to attend it. He left Khandwa for Bombay and reached there on July 1892. In a Pune bound train he met Bal Gangadhar Tilak. After staying with Tilak for few days in Poona, the Swami travelled to Belgaum in October 1892. At Belgaum, he was the guest of Prof. G.S. Bhate and Sub-divisional Forest officer, Haripada Mitra. From Belgaum, he visited Panjim and Margao in Goa. He spent three days in the Rachol Seminary, the oldest convent-college of theology of Goa where rare religious literature in manuscripts and printed works in Latin are preserved. He reportedly studied important Christian theological works here. From Margao the Swami went by train to Dharwar, and from there directly to Bangalore, in Mysore State.

Southern India

At Bangalore, the Swami became acquainted with Sir K. Seshadri Iyer, the Dewan of Mysore state, and later he stayed at the palace as guest of the Maharaja of Mysore, Shri Chamarajendra Wadiyar. Regarding Swami's learning, Sir Seshadri reportedly remarked, "a magnetic personality and a divine force which were destined to leave their mark on the history of his country." The Maharaja provided the Swami a letter of introduction to the Dewan of Cochin and got him a railway ticket.

From Bangalore, he visited Trichur, Kodungalloor, Ernakulam. At Ernakulam, he met Chattampi Swamikal, contemporary of Narayana Guru in early December 1892. From Ernakulam, he journeyed to Trivandrum, Nagercoil and reached Kanyakumari on foot during the Christmas Eve of 1892. At Kanyakumari, the Swami reportedly meditated on the "last bit of Indian rock", famously known later as the Vivekananda Rock Memorial for three days. At Kanyakumari, Vivekananda had the "Vision of one India", also commonly called "The Kanyakumari resolve of 1892". He wrote,

"At Cape Camorin sitting in Mother Kumari's temple, sitting on the last bit of Indian rock-I hit upon a plan: We are so many sanyasis wandering about, and teaching the people metaphysics-it is all madness. Did not our *Gurudeva* used to say, `An empty stomach is no good for religion?' We as a nation have lost our individuality and that is the cause of all mischief in India. We have to raise the masses."

From Kanyakumari he visited Madurai, where he met Raja of Ramnad, Bhaskara Setupati, to whom he had a letter of introduction. The Raja became the Swami's disciple and urged him to go to the Parliament of Religions at Chicago. From Madurai, he visited Rameshwaram, Pondicherry and he travelled to Madras and here he met some his most devoted disciples, like Alasinga Perumal, G.G. Narasimhachari, who played important roles in collecting funds for Swami's voyage to America and later in establishing the Ramakrishna Mission in Madras. From Madras he travelled to Hyderabad. With the aid of funds collected by his Madras disciples and Rajas of Mysore, Ramnad, Khetri, Dewans, and other followers Vivekananda left for Chicago on 31 May 1893 from Bombay assuming the name *Vivekananda*—the name suggested by the Maharaja of Khetri.

First Visit to the West

His journey to America took him through China, Japan, Canada and he arrived at Chicago in July 1893. But to his disappointment he learnt that no one without credentials from a *bona fide* organization would be accepted as a delegate. He came in contact with Professor John Henry Wright of Harvard University. After inviting him to speak at Harvard and on learning of his not having credential to speak at the Parliament, Wright is quoted as having said, "To ask for your credentials is like asking the sun to state its right to shine in the heavens." Wright then addressed a letter to the Chairman in charge of delegates writing, "Here is a man who is more learned than all of our learned professors put together." On the Professor Vivekananda himself writes, "He urged upon me the necessity of going to the Parliament of Religions, which he thought would give an introduction to the nation."

Parliament of World's Religions

The Parliament of Religions opened on 11 September 1893 at the Art Institute of Chicago. On this day Vivekananda gave his first brief address. He represented India and Hinduism. Though initially nervous, he bowed to *Saraswati*, the goddess of learning and began his speech with, "Sisters and brothers of America!". To these words he got a standing ovation from a crowd of seven thousand, which lasted for two minutes. When silence was restored he began his address. He greeted the youngest of the nations in the name of "the most ancient order of monks in the world, the Vedic order of sannyasins, a religion which has taught the world both tolerance and universal acceptance." And he quoted two illustrative passages in this relation, from the *Bhagavad Gita*—"As the different streams having their sources in different places all mingle their water in the sea, so, O Lord, the different paths which men take, through different tendencies, various though they appear, crooked or straight, all lead to Thee!" and "Whosoever comes to Me, through whatsoever form, I reach him; all men are struggling through paths that in the end lead to Me." Despite being a short speech, it voiced the spirit of the Parliament and its sense of universality.

Dr. Barrows, the president of the Parliament said, "India, the Mother of religions was represented by Swami Vivekananda, the Orange-monk who exercised the most wonderful influence over his auditors." He attracted widespread attention in the press, which dubbed him as the "Cyclonic monk from India". The *New York Critique* wrote, "He is an orator by divine right, and his strong, intelligent face in its picturesque setting of yellow and orange was hardly less interesting than those earnest words, and the rich, rhythmical utterance he gave them." The *New York Herald* wrote, "Vivekananda is undoubtedly the greatest figure in the Parliament of Religions. After hearing him we feel how foolish it is to send missionaries to this learned nation." The American newspapers reported Swami Vivekananda as "the greatest figure in the parliament of religions" and "the most popular and influential man in the parliament".

He spoke several more times at the Parliament on topics related to Hinduism and Buddhism. The parliament ended on 27 September 1893. All his speeches at the Parliament had one common theme—Universality and stressed religious tolerance.

Lecturing Tours in America, England

"I do not come", said Swamiji on one occasion in America, "to convert you to a new belief. I want you to keep your own belief; I want to make the Methodist a better Methodist; the Presbyterian a better Presbyterian; the Unitarian a better Unitarian. I want to teach you to live the truth, to reveal the light within your own soul."

After the Parliament of Religions, held in Sept. 1893 at The Art Institute of Chicago, Vivekananda spent nearly two whole years lecturing in various parts of eastern and central United States, appearing chiefly in Chicago, Detroit, Boston, and New York. By the spring of 1895, he was weary and in poor health, because of his continuous exertion. After suspending his lecture tour, the Swami started giving free and private classes on Vedanta and Yoga. In June 1895, for two months he conducted private lectures to a dozen of his disciples at the Thousand Island Park. Vivekananda considered this to the happiest part of his first visit to America. He later founded the "Vedanta Society of New York".

During his first visit to America, he travelled to England twice—in 1895 and 1896. His lectures were successful there. Here he met Miss Margaret Noble an Irish lady, who later became Sister Nivedita. During his second visit in May 1896, while living at a house in Pimlico, the Swami met Max Müller a renowned Indologist at Oxford University who wrote Ramakrishna's first biography in the West. From England, he also visited other European countries. In Germany he met Paul Deussen, another famous Indologist.

He also received two academic offers, the chair of Eastern Philosophy at Harvard University and a similar position at Columbia University. He declined both, saying that, as a wandering monk, he could not settle down to work of this kind.

He attracted several sincere followers. Among his other followers were, Josephine MacLeod, Miss Muller, Miss Noble, E.T. Sturdy, Captain and Mrs. Sevier—who played an important role in the founding of Advaita Ashrama and J.J.Goodwin—who became his stenographer and recorded his teachings and lectures. The Hale family became one of his warmest hosts in America. His disciples—Madame Louise, a French woman, became Swami Abhayananda, and Mr. Leon Landsberg, became Swami Kripananda. He initiated several other followers into Brahmacharya.

Swami Vivekananda's ideas were admired by several scholars and famous thinkers—William James, Josiah Royce, C. C. Everett, Dean of the Harvard School of Divinity, Robert G. Ingersoll, Nikola Tesla, Lord Kelvin, and Professor Hermann Ludwig Ferdinand von Helmholtz. Other personalities who were attracted by his talks were Harriet Monroe and Ella Wheeler Wilcox—two famous

American poets, Professor William James of Harvard University; Dr. Lewis G. Janes, president of Brooklyn Ethical Association; Sara C. Bull wife of Ole Bull, the Norwegian violinist; Sarah Bernhardt, the French actress and Madame Emma Calve, the French opera singer.

From West, he also set his Indian work in motion. Vivekananda wrote a stream of letters to India, giving advice and sending money to his followers and brother monks. His letters from the West in these days laid down the motive of his campaign for social service. He constantly tried to inspire his close disciples in India to do something big. His letters to them contain some of his strongest words. In one such letter, he wrote to Swami Akhandananda, "Go from door to door amongst the poor and lower classes of the town of Khetri and teach them religion. Also, let them have oral lessons on geography and such other subjects. No good will come of sitting idle and having princely dishes, and saying "Ramakrishna, O Lord!"—unless you can do some good to the poor." Eventually in 1895, the periodical called *Brahmavadin* was started in Madras, with the money supplied by Vivekananda, for the purpose of teaching the Vedanta. Subsequenly, Vivekananda's translation of first six chapters of *The Imitation of Christ* was published in *Brahmavadin* (1889).

Vivekananda left for India on 16 December 1896 from England with disciples, Capitan and Mrs. Sevier, and J.J.Goodwin. On the way they visited France, Italy, seeing Leonardo Da Vinci's *The Last Supper*, and set sail for India from the Port of Naples on December 30, 1896. Later, he was followed to India by Miss Muller and Sister Nivedita. Sister Nivedita devoted the rest of her life to the education of Indian women and the cause of India's independence.

Back in India

Colombo to Almora

Vivekananda arrived in Colombo on January 15, 1897 and received a grand welcome. Here, he gave his first public speech in East, *India, the Holy Land*. From there on, his journey to Calcutta was a triumphal progress. He travelled from Colombo to Pamban, Rameshwaram, Ramnad, Madurai, Kumbakonam and Madras delivering lectures. People and Rajas gave him enthusiastic reception. In the procession at Pamban, the Raja of Ramnad personally drew the Swami's carriage. On way to Madras, at several places where the train would not stop, the people squatted on the rails and allowed the train to pass only after hearing the Swami. From Madras, he continued his journey to Calcutta and continued his lectures up to Almora. While in the West he talked of India's great spiritual heritage, on return to India the refrain of his 'Lectures from Colombo to Almora' was uplift of the masses, eradication of the caste virus, promotion of the study of science, industrialization of the country, removal of poverty, the end of the colonial rule. These lectures have been published as *Lectures from Colombo to Almora*. These lectures are considered to be of nationalistic fervor and spiritual ideology. His speeches had tremendous influence on the Indian leaders, including Mahatma Gandhi, Bipin Chandra Pal and Balgangadhar Tilak.

Founding of Ramakrishna Math and Mission

Advaita Ashrama, Mayavati, a branch of the Ramakrishna Math, founded on March 19, 1899, later published many of Swami Vivekananda's work, now publishes Prabuddha Bharata journal

On 1 May 1897 at Calcutta, Vivekananda founded the "Ramakrishna Math"—the organ for propagating religion and "Ramakrishna Mission"—the organ for social service. This was the beginning of an organized socio-religious movement to help the masses through educational, cultural, medical and relief work. The ideals of the Ramakrishna Mission are based on *Karma Yoga*.

Two monasteries were founded by him, one at Belur, near Calcutta, which became the Headquarters of Ramakrishna Math and Mission and the other at Mayavati on the Himalayas, near Almora called the *Advaita Ashrama* and later a third monastery was established at Madras. Two journals were started, *Prabuddha Bharata* in English and *Udbhodan* in Bengali. The same year, the famine relief work was started by Swami Akhandananda at Murshidabad district.

Vivekananda had inspired Sir Jamshetji Tata to set up a research and educational institution when they had travelled together from Yokohama to Chicago on the Swami's first visit to the West in 1893. About this time the Swami received a letter from Tata, requesting him to head the Research Institute of Science that Tata had set up. But Vivekananda declined the offer saying that it conflicted with his spiritual interests.

He later visited Punjab, in Pakistan with the mission of establishing harmony between the *Arya Samaj* which stood for reinterpreted Hinduism and the *Sanatanaists* who stood for orthodox Hinduism. At Rawalpindi, he suggested methods for rooting out antagonism between Arya Samajists and Muslims. His visit to Lahore is memorable for his famous speeches and his inspiring association with Tirtha Ram Goswami, then a brilliant professor of Mathematics, who later graced monasticism as Swami Rama Tirtha and preached *Vedanta* in India and America. He also visited other places, including Delhi and Khetri and returned to Calcutta in January 1896. He spent the next few months consolidating the work of the *Math* and training the disciples. During this period he composed the famous *arati* song, *Khandana Bhava Bandhana* during the event of consecration of Ramakrishna's temple at a devotees' house.

Second Visit to the West

He once again left for the West in June 1899, amid his declining health. He was accompanied by Sister Nivedita, Swami Turiyananda. He spent a short time in England, and went on to America. During this visit, he founded the Vedanta societies at San Francisco and New York. He also founded "*Shanti Ashrama*" (peace retreat) at California, with the aid of a generous 160 acre gift from an American devotee. Later he attended the Congress of Religions, in Paris in 1900. The Paris addresses are memorable for the scholarly penetration evinced by Vivekananda related to worship of *Linga* and authenticity of the *Gita*. From Paris he paid short visits to Brittany, Vienna, Constantinople, Athens and Egypt. For the greater part of this period, he was the guest of Jules Bois, the famous thinker. He left Paris in October 24, 1900 and arrived at the Belur Math in December 9, 1900.

Last Years

Vivekananda spent few of his days at Advaita Ashrama, Mayavati and later at the Belur Math. Henceforth till the end he stayed at Belur Math, guiding the work of Ramakrishna Mission and Math and the work in England and America. Thousands of visitors came to him during these years including The Maharaja of Gwalior and in December 1901, the stalwarts of Indian National Congress including Lokamanya Tilak. In December 1901, he was invited to Japan to participate in the Congress of Religions, however his failing health made it impossible. He undertook pilgrimages to Bodhgaya and Varanasi towards his final days.

His tours, hectic lecturing engagements, private discussions and correspondence had taken their toll on his health. He was suffering from Asthma, diabetes and other physical ailments. Few days prior to his demise, he was seen intently studying the almanac. Three days before his death he pointed out the spot for this cremation—the one at which a temple in his memory stands today. He had remarked to several persons that he would not live to be forty. On the day of his death, he taught *Shukla-Yajur-Veda* to some pupils in the morning at Belur Math. He had a walk with Swami Premananda, a brother-disciple, and gave him instructions concerning the future of the Ramakrishna Math. Vivekananda expired at ten minutes past nine P.M. on July 4, 1902 while he was meditating. According to his disciples, this was *Mahasamadhi*. Afterward, his disciples recorded that they had noticed "a little blood" in the Swami's nostrils, about his mouth and in his eyes. The doctors remarked that it was due to the rupture of a blood-vessel in the brain, but they could not find the real cause of the death. According to his disciples, *Brahmarandhra*— the aperture in the crown of the head must have been pierced when he attained *Mahasamadhi*. Vivekananda had fulfilled his own prophecy of not living to be forty-years old.

Teachings and Philosophy

Vivekananda believed that the essence of Hinduism was best expressed in the Vedanta philosophy, based on the interpretation of Shankaracharya.

He summarised the Vedanta's teachings as follows:

- Each soul is potentially divine.
- The goal is to manifest this Divinity within by controlling nature, external and internal.
- Do this either by work, or worship, or psychic control, or philosophy—by one, or more, or all of these—and be free.
- This is the whole of religion. Doctrines, or dogmas, or rituals, or books, or temples, or forms, are but secondary details.

According to Vivekananda, an important teaching he received from Ramakrishna was that "Jiva is Shiva" (each individual is divinity itself). This became his Mantra, and he coined the concept of *daridra narayana seva*-the service of God in and through (poor) human beings. "If there truly is the unity of Brahman underlying all phenomena, then on what basis do we regard ourselves as better or worse, or even as better-off or worse-off, than others?"- This was the question he posed to himself. Ultimately, he concluded that these distinctions fade into nothingness in the light of the oneness that the devotee experiences in Moksha. What arises then is compassion for those "individuals" who remain unaware of this oneness and a determination to help them.

Swami Vivekananda belonged to that branch of Vedanta that held that no one can be truly free until all of us are. Even the desire for personal salvation has to be given up, and only tireless work for the salvation of others is the true mark of the enlightened person. He founded the Sri Ramakrishna Math and Mission on the principle of Atmano Mokshartham Jagat-hitaya cha.

Vivekananda advised his followers to be holy, unselfish and have shraddha (faith). He encouraged the practice of Brahmacharya (Celibacy). In one of the conversations with his childhood friend Priya Nath Sinha he attributes his physical and mental strengths, eloquence to the practice of Brahmacharya.

Vivekananda did not advocate the emerging area of parapsychology, astrology (one instance can be found in his speech *Man the Maker of his Destiny, Complete-Works, Volume 8, Notes of Class Talks and Lectures*) saying that this form of curiosity doesn't help in spiritual progress but actually hinders it.

Influence

Several leaders of 20th Century India and philosophers have acknowledged Vivekananda's influence. The first governor general of independent India, Chakravarti Rajagopalachari, once observed that "Vivekananda saved Hinduism, saved India." According to Subhas Chandra Bose, Vivekananda "is the maker of modern India" and for Mohandas Gandhi, Vivekananda's influence increased his "love for his country a thousandfold." National Youth Day in India is held on his birthday, January 12, to commemorate him. This was a most fitting gesture as much of Swami Vivekananda's writings concerned the Indian youth and how they should strive to uphold their ancient values whilst fully participating in the modern world.

Swami Vivekananda is widely considered to have inspired India's freedom struggle movement. His writings inspired a whole generation of freedom fighters including Aurobindo Ghose and Bagha Jatin. Vivekananda was the brother of the extremist revolutionary, Bhupendranath Dutta. Subhash Chandra Bose one of the most prominent figures in Indian independence movement said,

I cannot write about Vivekananda without going into raptures. Few indeed could comprehend or fathom him even among those who had the privilege of becoming intimate with him. His personality was rich, profound and complex... Reckless in his sacrifice, unceasing in his activity, boundless in his love, profound and versatile in his wisdom, exuberant in his emotions, merciless in his attacks but yet simple as a child, he was a rare personality in this world of ours

Aurobindo Ghosh considered Vivekananda as his spiritual mentor.

Vivekananda was a soul of puissance if ever there was one, a very lion among men, but the definitive work he has left behind is quite incommensurate with our impression of his creative might and energy. We perceive his influence still working gigantically, we know not well how, we know not well where, in something that is not yet formed, something leonine, grand, intuitive, upheaving that has entered the soul of India and we say, "Behold, Vivekananda still lives in the soul of his Mother and in the souls of her children. —Sri Aurobindo in *Vedic Magazine*(1915)

The French Nobel Laureate, Romain Rolland writes, "His words are great music, phrases in the style of Beethoven, stirring rhythms like the march of Handel choruses. I cannot touch these sayings of his, scattered as they are through the pages of books, at thirty years' distance, without receiving a thrill through my body like an electric shock. And what shocks, what transports, must have been produced when in burning words they issued from the lips of the hero!

Vivekananda inspired Jamshedji Tata to set up Indian Institute of Science, one of India's finest Institutions. Abroad, he had some interactions with Max Müller. Nikola Tesla was one of those influenced by the Vedic philosophy teachings of the Swami Vivekananda.

Above all Swami Vivekananda helped restore a sense of pride amongst the Hindus, presenting the ancient teachings of India in its purest form to a Western audience, free from the propaganda spread by British colonial administrators, of Hinduism being a caste-ridden, misogynistic idolatrous faith. Indeed his early foray into the West would set the path for subsequent Indian religious teachers to make their own marks on the world, as well herald the entry of Hindus and their religious traditions into the Western world.

Swami Vivekananda's ideas have had a great influence on the Indian youth. In many institutes, students have come together and formed organizations meant for promoting discussion of spiritual ideas and the practice of such high principles. Many of such organizations have adopted the name Vivekananda Study Circle. One such group also exists at IIT Madras and is popularly known as (VSC). Additionally, Swami Vivekananda's ideas and teachings have carried on globally, being practiced in institutions all over the world.

Mahatma Gandhi said, "Swami Vivekananda's writings need no introduction from anybody. They make their own irresistible appeal." At the Belur Math, Gandhi was heard to say that his whole life was an effort to bring into actions the ideas of Vivekananda. Many years after Vivekananda's death, Rabindranath Tagore a Nobel Poet Laureate had said, "If you want to know India, study Vivekananda. In him everything is positive and nothing negative."

Vivekananda and Science

In his book *Raja Yoga,* Vivekananda explores traditional views on the supernatural and the belief that the practice of Raja Yoga can confer psychic powers such as 'reading another's thoughts', 'controlling all the forces of nature ', become 'almost all-knowing', 'live without breathing', 'control the bodies of others' and levitation. He also explains traditional eastern spiritual concepts like kundalini and spiritual energy centres (chakras).

However, Vivekananda takes a skeptical approach and in the same book states:

"It is not the sign of a candid and scientific mind to throw overboard anything without proper investigation. Surface scientists, unable to explain the various extraordinary mental phenomena, strive to ignore their very existence. "He further says in the introduction of the book that one should take up the practice and verify these things for oneself, and that there should not be blind belief. "What little I know I will tell you. So far as I can reason it out I will do so, but as to what I do not know I will simply tell you what the books say. It is wrong to believe blindly. You must exercise your own reason and judgment; you must practise, and see whether these things happen or not. Just as you would take up any other science, exactly in the same manner you should take up this science for study.

"Vivekananda (1895) rejected ether theory before Einstein (1905), stating that it cannot explain the space itself.

In his paper, read at the World Parliament of Religions (1893), Vivekananda also hinted about the final goal of Physics, what in these days, is attempted by theories like the String Theory.

"Science is nothing but the finding of unity. As soon as science would reach perfect unity, it would stop from further progress, because it would reach the goal. Thus Chemistry could not progress farther when it would discover one element out of which all other could be made. Physics would stop when it would be able to fulfil its services in discovering one energy of which all others are but manifestations...All science is bound to come to this conclusion in the long run. Manifestation, and not creation, is the word of science today, and the Hindu is only glad that what he has been cherishing in his bosom for ages is going to be taught in more forcible language, and with further light from the latest conclusions of science. "

The great electrical engineer, Nikola Tesla, after listening to Vivekananda's speech on Sankhya Philosophy, was much interested in its cosmogony and its rational theories of the Kalpas (cycles), Prana and Akasha. His notion based on the vedanta led him to think that matter is a manifestation of energy. After attending a lecture on vedanta by Vivekananda Tesla also concluded that, modern science can look for the solution of cosmological problems in Sankhya philosophy, and he could prove that mass can be reduced to potential energy mathematically.

Works

Vivekananda left a body of philosophical works which Vedic scholar Frank Parlato has called, "the greatest comprehensive work in philosophy ever published." His books (compiled from lectures given around the world) on the four Yogas (Raja Yoga, Karma Yoga, Bhakti Yoga, Jnana Yoga) are very influential and still seen as fundamental texts for anyone interested in the Hindu practice of Yoga. His letters are of great literary and spiritual value. He was also considered a very good singer and a poet. By He had composed many songs including his favourite *Kali the Mother*. He used humor for his teachings and was also an excellent cook. His language is very free flowing. His own Bengali writings stand testimony to the fact that he believed that words-spoken or written should be for making things easier to understand rather than show off the speaker or writer's knowledge.

Sister Nivedita

Sister Nivedita (1867-1911), born Margaret Elizabeth Noble, was an Anglo-Irish social worker, author, teacher and disciple of Swami Vivekananda. She met Vivekananda in 1895 in London and travelled to India (Kolkata) in 1898. Swami Vivekananda gave her the name Nivedita (meaning "Dedicated to God") when he initiated her into the vow of Brahmacharya on March 25 1898.

Early Life

She was born on October 28, 1867. She was born in Ireland to Mary Isabel and Samuel Richmond Noble. Her father gave the valuable lesson that service to mankind is the true service to God. His words made a profound impression on her. She was very fond of music and art. After completing her education, she took up the job of a teacher and worked for a period of ten years from 1884 to 1894. She was gifted as a teacher.

Meeting Swami Vivekananda

She started taking interest in the teachings of Lord Buddha. It is during this time that she met Swami Vivekananda, who stressed that ignorance and selfishness pave the way for our sufferings. His principles and teachings influenced her and this brought about a visible change in her. Seeing the fire and passion in her, he could foresee her future role in India. She became the first Western woman to be received into an Indian monastic order.

Her Works

In November 1898 she started a school for girls who were

deprived of even basic education. She took part in various altruistic activities. She worked to improve the lives of Indian women of all castes. Nivedita was a good friend of many intellectuals and artists in the Bengali community, including the Nobel laureate Rabindranath Tagore. She was very close to eminent scientist Jagadish Chandra Bose and his wife Abala Bose, Abanindranath Tagore, and Okakura Kakuzo.

In fact, she is one of the inspirations for development of original art and paintings in India. Artist Nandalal Bose reminded this several times. Later she would take up the cause of Indian independence. Sri Aurobindo was one of her friend as well. This deep relation with the independence movement compelled her to take the decision to break up the "official" linkage with the Ramakrishna Mission monastic order, so that British government cannot unnecessarily disturb the monastic order.

She knew and trusted Sri Anirvan [1] well, leaving many extraordinarily valuable documents with him. When Shankari Prasad Basu Mahashay came to Anirvan asking about her life, he simply handed over these papers, carefully preserved. Her identity as a western born and being a disciple of Swami Vivekananda enabled her to do several things that might have been difficult for other Indians. She promoted pan-Indian nationalist. She worked tirelessly serving the people and society at large. She died on October 13, 1911 at Darjeeling, India. A benediction written to Sister Nivedita by Swami Vivekananda is available in wikiquotes here.

Ramakrishna Math

Ramakrishna Math is a religious monastic order, considered part of the Hindu reform movement. It was set up by Swami Vivekananda to follow the teachings of Sri Ramakrishna. The *Ramakrishna Math* is headquartered at Belur Math (in West Bengal, India), and shares the location with the related organisation, the Ramakrishna Mission.

It also has a Advaita Ashrama branches at Mayavati, near Almora and in Kolkata.

Monastic Order

Ramakrishna Math consists of monks (Sannyasins and Brahmacharins) belonging to a monastic order for men. After the passing away of their Master Sri Ramakrishna in 1886 the young disciples under the leadership of Swami Vivekananda organized themselves into a new monastic order. The original monastery at Baranagar called Baranagar Math was shifted in January 1899 to a newly acquired plot of land at Belur in the district of Howrah.

Belur Math

This monastery, known as Belur Math, serves as the Mother House for all the monks of Ramakrishna Order who live in the various branch centres of Ramakrishna Math and/or the related Ramakrishna Mission in different parts of India and the world.

Twin Ideals

Here the Math started the task of training vigorously a band of monks and novices. They were inspired with the twin ideals of meaning Self-realisation and Service to the world.

The Philosophy of Vedanta

The fundamental truth as taught by all religions is that man has to transform his base human nature into the divine that is within him. In other words, he must reach the deeper strata of his being, wherein lies his unity with all mankind. And Vedanta can help us to contact and live that truth which unfolds our real nature — the divinity lying hidden in man.

Vedanta is not a particular religion but a philosophy which includes the basic truths of all religions. It teaches that man's real nature is divine; that it is the aim of man's life on earth to unfold and manifest the hidden Godhead within him; and that truth is universal...

Thus Vedanta preaches a universal message, the message of harmony. In its insistence on personal experience of the truth of God, on the divinity of man, and the universality of truth it has kept the spirit of religion alive since the age of the Vedas (ancient scriptures). Even in our time there have been Ramakrishna, Vivekananda, and men like Gandhi. The modern apostle of Vedanta, Vivekananda, describes the ideal religion of tomorrow as follows:

Vivekananda on the Ideal Religion of Tomorrow

If there is ever to be a universal religion it would be one that would occur within the confines of a palace of no location or time. This palace will be infinite and within these walls God will preach its holy sum. Its warm rays will shine down upon the followers of Krishna, Mohammed, Christ, Buddhists, and all teachers alike. These walls will ever grow to encompass the infinite space of the soothing heart. This religion will know that every virtue of man is to be held and witnessed all from the grovelling savage not far removed from the brute, to the highest man. It will be here that standing still, towered by the virtues of his head and heart will he remain making society stand in awe of him. It will be his religion where there shall be no space for persecution or intolerance within its politic. It will be a place which will recognize its divinity in every man and woman and whose whole scope and force will be centred in aiding humanity to realize its own true point.

Each Religion is a Path

This "sum total" of all religions does not mean that all people on earth have to come under the banner of one prophet or worship one aspect of God. If Christ is true, Krishna and Buddha are also true. Let there be many teachers, many scriptures; let there be churches, temples, and synagogues. Every religion is a path to reach the same goal. When the goal is reached the Christian, the Jew, the Islamist, the Hindu, and the Buddhist realize that each has worshipped the same Reality. One who has attained this knowledge is no longer a follower of a particular path or a particular religion. He has become a man of God and a blessing to mankind.

Management

The Ramakrishna Math was registered as a Trust in 1901. The management of the Math is vested in a Board of Trustees who are only monks. The Math with its branches is a distinct legal entity. It has well defined rules of procedure. It lays emphasis on religious practices and preaching of Dharma. The Math has its own separate funds and keep detailed accounts which are annually audited by qualified chartered accountants. It has 57 Branch centres in India and abroad. The Math and the Mission both have their Headquarters at Belur Math.

Bibliography

Adikaram, E. W.: *Early History of Buddhism in Ceylon,* D. S. Puswella, Migoda, 1946.

Agrawala, V. S.: *Shiva Mahadeva: The Great God,* Veda Academy, Varanasi, 1966.

Ahmad, Imtiaz: *State and Foreign Policy: India's Role in South Asia,* Vikas, New Delhi, 1993.

Ahmad, Jamil-ud-din: *Some Recent Speeches and Writings of Mr. Jinnah,* Lahore, Ashraf, 1952.

Aiyar, R. Krishnaswami: *Outlines of Vedaanta,* Chetana, Bombay, 1978.

Archer, W. G.: *The Kama Sutra,* Unwin Hyman, London, 1990.

Ashton, S.R. : *British Policy Towards the Indian States, 1905-1939,* London, Curzon, 1982.

Aurobindo, Sri: *Vyasa and Valmiki,* Acharya Press, Pondicherry, 1956.

Avalon, Arthur and Ellen: *Hymns to the Goddess,* Ganesh and Co., Madras, 1964.

Aziz, Ashraf: *Light of the Universe: Essays on Hindustani Film Music,* Three Essays Collective, New Delhi, 2003.

Bagchi, P. C.: *Studies in Dharmashastra,* University of Calcutta Press, Calcutta, 1939.

Bahadur, K.P.: *The Wisdom of Vedaanta,* Sterling Publishers Private Limited, New Delhi, 1996.

Banerjea, J. N.: *Pauranic and Vedanta Religion,* University of Calcutta, Calcutta, 1996.

Bankimchandra, C.: *Essentials of Dharma,* Sanskrit Book Depot, Calcutta 1979.

Basu, Manoranjan: *Dharmashastra: A General Study,* Shrimati Mira Basu, Calcutta, 1976.

Beaumont, Roger : *Sword of the Raj: The British Army in India, 1747-1947*, Indianapolis, Bobbs-Merrill, 1977.

Benjamin, Joseph : *Scheduled Castes in Indian Politics and Society*, New Delhi, Ess Ess Publications, 1989.

Bhattacharyya, B.: *Nispannayogavali of Mahapandita Abhyakara Gupta*, Oriental Institute, Baroda, 1949.

Borchert, Bruno: *Mysticism: Its History and Challenge*, Samuel Wiser, York Beach, 1994.

Bose, D. N.: *Dharmashastra: Their Philosophy and Occult Secrets*, Kali Press, Calcutta, 1965.

Bowle, John: *The Imperial Achievement: The Rise and Transformation of the British Empire*, Little, Brown, 1974.

Brockington, J. L.: *Righteous Rama: The Evolution of an Epic*, Oxford, London, 1984.

Bromley, D.: *Krishna Consciousness in the West*, Bucknell University Press, Lewisburg, 1989.

Brooks, E.: *The Original Analects: Sayings of Confucius and His Successors*. Columbia University Press, New York, 1988.

Bruhn, Klaus: *The Jina-Images of Deogarh*, MacMillan, Leiden, 1969.

Burke, Mary Louise: *Swami Vivekananda in America: New Discoveries*, Advaita Ashrama, Calcutta, 1966.

Chaudhary, M.: *Partition and the Curse of Rehabilitation*, Calcutta, Bengal Rehabilitation Organization, 1964.

Chaudhuri, Nirad: *Thy Hand, Great Anarch! India: 1921-1952*, London, Chatto & Windus, 1987.

Coomeraswamy, Ananda K.: *Buddha and the Gospel of Buddhism*, MacMillan, London, 1928.

Crawford, Cromwell S.: *Ram Mohan Roy: His Era and Ethics*, Acharya Press, New Delhi, 1984.

Dalton, Dennis : *Gandhi's Power : Nonviolence in Action*, New Delhi, OUP, 2001.

Danielou, Alain: *The Complete Kama Sutra*, Park Street Press, Rochester, 2000.

Dasgupta, Shahana: *Rani Lakshmibai: The Indian Heroine*, Rupa & Company, Calcutta, 2002.

Datta, V.N.: *Sati: Widow Burning in India*, Manohar, New Delhi, 1990.

David, M. D.: *John Wilson and his Institutions*, Mumbai, 1957.

De Bary: *Self and Society in Ming Thought*, Columbia University Press, New York, 1970.

De, Sushil Kumar: *Ancient Indian Erotics and Erotic Literature*, Firma K. L. Mukhopadhyay, Calcutta, 1959.

Deak, Istvan: *The Lawful Revolution: Louis Kossuth and the Hungarians 1848-1849*, Columbia University Press, 1979.

Dhar, Niranjan: *Vedanta and Bengal Renaissance*, Minerva Associates, Calcutta, 1977.

Dikshit, D.P. *Political History of the Chalukyas of Badami*. New Delhi: Abhinav, 1980.

Donat, K.: *Meditate the Tantric Yoga Way*, George Allen and Unwin, London, 1973.

Doniger, W.: *The Rig Veda: An Anthology*, Penguin, New York, 1981.

Duboi, Abbe: *Hindu Manners, Customs and Ceremonies*, Fifth Indian Impression, CUP, 1985.

Dwivedi, M.: *The Principal Upanishads*, Adyar Library, Madras, 1931.

Eaton, Richard M.: *Sufis of Bijapur, 1300-1700: Social Roles of Sufis in Medieval India*, Princeton University Press, Princeton, 1978.

Edwardes, Michael: *Battles of the Indian Mutiny*, London; B. T. Batsford Ltd., 1963.

Erickson, Erik H.: *Gandhi's Truth: On the Origins of Militant Nonviolence*, Norton, New York, 1970.

Farquhar, J.N.: *Modern Religious Movements in India*, Munshiram, New Delhi, 1967.

Fay, Peter Ward: *The Opium War, 1840-42*, University of North Carolina Press, 1975.

Fisher, Michael H.: *The Politics of British Annexation of India - 1757-1857*, Oxford, 1996.

Frauwallner, E..: *History of Indian Philosophy*, Motilal, Delhi, 1973.

Gambhirananda, S.: *Brahma Sutra Shamkar Bhasya*, Adavita Ashrama, Calcutta, 1977.

Gambhirananda, Swami: *Brahma Sutra Shamkar Bhasya*, Adavita Ashrama, Calcutta, 1977.

Gandhi, M. K.: *The Story of My Experiment With Trust*, Washington, Public Affairs Press, 1948.

Garbe, R.: *The Philosophy of Ancient India*, Chicago University Press, Chicago, 1899.

Goradia, Nayana: *Lord Curzon: The Last of the British Moghuls*, New Delhi, Oxford University Press, 1993.

Goudriaan, T.: *Ritual and Speculation in Early Tantrism*, State University of New York Press, New York, 1992.

Gough, A.E.: *The Philosophy of the Upanisads and Ancient Indian Metaphysics*, MacMillan, London, 1882.

Grant, G. P.: *Philosophy in the Mass Age*, Copp Clark, Toronto, 1959.

Grisenold, H.D.: *Insights into Modern Hinduism*, Oxford, New York, 1934.

Growse, F. S.: *The Ramayana of Tulasidasa*, Motilal Banarsidass, Delhi, 1995.

Gurumurthy, S. : *Hindu Heritage, Assimilative, Not Divisive*, Vigil, Madras 1993.

Haich, E.: *Sexual Energy and Yoga*, Aurora Press, New York, 1982.

Hasan, Murhirul: *Legacy of a Divided Nation: India's Muslims Since Independence*, New Delhi, Oxford, 1997.

Hasan, Mushirul: *India's Partition: Process, Strategy and Mobilization*, New Delhi, Oxford UP, 1993.

Heifetz, Hank: *The Origin of the Young God: Kalidasa's Kumara-sambhava*, University of California Press, Berkeley, 1985.

Heimann, Betty: *Facets of Indian Thought*, Geroge Allen & Unwin, London, 1964.

Heinsath, Charles: *Indian Nationalism and Hindu Social Reform*, Princeton University Press, Princeton, 1964.

Heschel, J.: *God in Search of Man: A Philosophy of Judaism*, Noonday Press, New York, 1997.

Hirschman, Edwin: *White Mutiny: The Ilbert Bill Crisis in India and the Genesis of the Indian National Congress*, New Delhi, Heritage, 1980.

Hixon, L.: *Mother of the Universe: Visions of the Goddess, Tantric Hymns of Enlightenment*, Quest Books, Wheaton, 1994.

Hopkins, J.: *Kalachakra Tantra Rite of Initiation*, Wisdom Publications, Boston, 1982.

Hopkirk, Peter: *The Great Game: The Struggle for Empire in Central Asia*, Kodansha, 1992.

Hume, R.E.: *The Thirteen Principle Upanishads*, Oxford University Press, London, 1971.

Hutchins, Francis: *Spontaneous Revolution: The Quit India Movement*, New Delhi, Manohar, 1971.

Irene, S.: *Vedic Heritage Teaching Program*. Arsha Vidya Gurukulam, Coimbatore, 1994.

Iyar, K.: *Vedanta: The Science of Reality*, Ganesh and Co., Mardas, 1930.

Iyengar, B.K.S.: *Light on the Yoga Sutras of Patanjali*, Aquarian Press, London 1993.

Jacob, K.: *Religion and Ethics in Advaita*, C.M.S. Press, Kottayam, 1982.

Jafar, Malik Muhammad: *Jinnah as a Parliamentarian*, Lahore, Afzar Publications, 1977.

Jain, Kailash Chand, *Lord Mahavira and His Times*, Saraswati Press, Delhi, 1974.

James, Lawrence: *The Rise and Fall of the British Empire*, St. Martin's, 1997.

James, Robert Rhodes: *The British Revolution, 1880-1939*, New York, Knopf, 1976.

Jean, M.: *Tantrik Yoga*, The Aquarian Press, Wellingborough, 1970.

John, B.: *Mantras: Sacred Words of Power*, George Allen and Unwin, London, 1977.

John, Elsner: *Pilgrimage: Past and Present in the World Religions*, Harvard University Press, Cambridge, 1995.

John, K.: *The Origin and Development of the State Cult of Confucius*, Paragon Book, New York, 1966.

Karmarkar, D.: *Sankara's Advaita*, Karnatak University, Dharwar, 1976.

Kaushik, Asha : *Globalization, Democracy and Culture : Situating Gandhian Alternatives*, Jaipur, Pointer, 2002.

Kaviraj, G.: *Aspects of Indian Thought*, University of Burdwan, Calcutta, 1966.

Kavlekar, K.K. : *Non-Brahmin Movement in Southern India, 1873-1949*, Kolhapur, Shivaji University, 19790

Keith, A.B. : *Rigveda Brahmanas*, Harvard University Press, Cambridge, 1920.

Keith, Arthur Berriedale: *The Religion and Philosophy of the Veda and Upanishads*, MacMillan, Delhi, 1925.

Kishwar, Madhu : *Religion at the Service of Nationalism, and Other Essays*, OUP, Delhi, 1998.

Klaus, K.: *A Survey of Hinduism*, State University of New York Press, Albany, 1989.

Knipe, M.: *Hinduism: Experiments in the Sacred*, Harper, San Francisco, 1991.

Knott, K.: *Hinduism, A Very Short Introduction*, Oxford University Press, New York, 1998.

Kosambi, D. D. : *The Culture and Civilisation of Ancient India in Historical Outline*, London, Routledge and Kegan Paul, 1956.

Kottackal, Jacob: *Religion and Ethics in Advaita*, C.M.S. Press, Kottayam, 1982.

Kuiper, F.B.J. : *Aryans in the Rigveda*, Rodopi, Amsterdam, 1991.

Kuppuswamy, Sastri S.: *Compromises in the History of Advaitic Thought*, Kalyani Press, Madras, 1940.

Louis, Fischer: *Essential Gandhi: An Anthology of His Writings*, Vintage, New York, 1983.

Low, D. A. and Brasted, Howard: *Freedom, Trauma, Continuities: Northern India and Independence*, New Delhi, Sage Publications, 1998.

Maheshwari, Shriram: *Rural Development in India: A Public Policy Approach*, New Delhi, Sage, 1995.

Makhan, L.: *The Ramayana of Valmiki*, Munshiram Manoharlal, New Delhi, 1978.

Mathew, Arnold: *Culture and Anarchy*, The University Press, Cambridge, 1935.

Mayer, A. : *Caste in an Indian Village: Change and Continuity 1954-1992*, Delhi, OUP, 1996.

Mazumder, Sukhendu : *Politico-Economic Ideas of Mahatma Gandhi: Their Relevance in the Present Day*, New Delhi, Concept Pub., 2004.

Mearns, David J.: *Shiva's Other Children: Religion and Social Identity amongst Overseas Indians*, Sage, Walnut Creek, 1995.

Mearns, J.: *Shiva's Other Children: Religion and Social Identity amongst Overseas Indians*, Sage, Walnut Creek, 1995.

Mehra, Parshotam: *A Dictionary of Modern Indian History, 1707-1947*, New Delhi, Oxford University Press, 1985.

Metcalf, Thomas R.: *The Aftermath of the Revolt: India, 1857-1870*, Princeton, Princeton University, 1964.

Mohan, K.: *The Mahabharata*, Munshiram Manoharlal, Delhi 1997.

Mookerjee, Ajit: *Kali The Feminine Force*, Thames and Hudson, London, 1988.

Mookerji, Satkari: *Modern Polity and Vedanta*, Sanskrit College, Calcutta, 1972.

Moon, Penderel: *The British Conquest and Dominion of India*, London, Duckworth, 1989.

Morris-Jones, W.H.: *The Government and Politics of India*, London, Hutchinson, 1971.

Nanda, B. R. : *Gandhi and His Critics*, Oxford University Press, Delhi, 1993.

Neale, Walter C.: *Economic Change in Rural India: Land Tenure and Reform in the United Provinces, 1800-1955*, New Haven, 1962.

Nevile, P.: *Lahore: A Sentimental Journey*, New Delhi, Penguin, 1993.

Oddie, G.A. : *Hindu and Christian in South-East India*, London, Curzon Press, 1991.

Pathak, Dr S.P.: *Jhansi during the British Rule*, Ramanand Vidya Bhawan, Delhi, 1987.

Preston, Diana: *The Boxer Rebellion*, Berkley Books, 2000.

Raimundo Panikkar: *The Vedic Experience: Mantramanjari*, Longman Todd, London, 1977.

Raja, C. Kunhan : *The Taittiriya Sarvanukramani of Yaska*, Madras, 1931.

Ramamurti, A.: *Advaitic Mysticism of Sankara*, Visvabharati, Santiniketan, 1974.

Ranajit Guha: *A Construction of Humanism in Colonial India*, CASA, Amsterdam, 1993.

Renou, Louis: *The Nature of Dharmashastra*, Walker and Co., New York, 1997.

Robson, Brian: *Sir Hugh Rose and the Central India Campaign*, Sutton Publishing Ltd for the Army Records Society, UK, 2000.

Satyapal Verma: *Role of Reason in Sankara Vedanta*, Parimal Publication, Delhi, 1992.

Savarkar, Vinayak Damodar : *The Indian War of Independence* 1857 Rajdhani Granthagar, Delhi, 1988.

Scheftelowitz, Isidor : *Die Kasmirische Rezension von Katyayanas Sarvanukramani,* Zeitschrift fur Indologie und Iranistik, 1922.

Shukla, D. N.: *Vastu-Shastra,* Motilal Banarsidass, Delhi, 1966.

Singh, Birendra Kumar: *Early Chalukyas of Vatapi, circa A.D. 500 to 757,* Delhi, Eastern Book Linkers, 1991.

Smith, Col. J. T. : *Silver and the India Exchanges*, Effingham Wilson, London, 1876.

Strauss, L.: *Political Philosophy,* The Bobbs Merrill Co., New York, 1975.

Swami Vishnu Tirtha: *Devatma Shakti,* Swami Shivom Tirth, Rishikesh, 1962.

Talageri, Shrikant : *Aryan Invasion Theory and Indian Nationalism,* Voice of India, Delhi, 1993.

Tejomayananda, Swami: *Hindu Culture: An Introduction,* Chinmaya Publications, Piercy, 1993.

Thapar, Romila : *Ashoka and the Decline of the Mauryas,* London, Oxford University Press, 1961.

Thompson, Edward: *The Making of the Indian Princes,* Oxford University Press, London, 1943.

Trautmann, Thomas R.: *Kautilya and the Arthasastra: A Statistical Study,* Leiden, Brill, 1971.

Trimingham, J.: *Sufi Orders in Islam,* Oxford University Press, New York, 1998.

Utpat, V.N.: *Riddles of Buddha and Ambedkar,* Itihas Patrika Prakashan, Thane 1988.

Vable, D.: *The Arya Samaj. Hindu without Hinduism.* Vikas Publ., Delhi, 1983.

Vedalankar, Pandit Nardev : *Basic Teachings of Hinduism,* Veda Niketan, Durban, 1978.

Visvantha, K.: *Essentials of Hinduism,* Narosa Pub. House, New Delhi, 1989.

Wendy Doniger: *Siva: The Erotic Ascetic,* Oxford University Press, Delhi, 1998.

Zaidi, A. Moin: *Evolution of Muslim Political Thought in India,* New Delhi: S. Chand, 1975.

Index

□□□